Return to the Desert

A Journey from Mount Hermon to Mount Sinai

DAVID PRAILL

To Meg Painter

Best Wishes

David Praill

Fount
An Imprint of HarperCollinsPublishers

Fount Paperbacks is an Imprint of
HarperCollins*Religious*
Part of HarperCollins*Publishers*
77-85 Fulham Palace Road, London W6 8JB

First published in Great Britain
in 1995 by Fount Paperbacks

1 3 5 7 9 10 8 6 4 2

A catalogue record for this book is
available from the British Library

000 627830-2

Printed and bound in Great Britain by
HarperCollinsManufacturing Glasgow

To Sarah,
Polly and Phoebe

Acknowledgements

The author and publisher acknowledge with thanks permission to reproduce copyright material. Where available, copyright information is listed below:

Excerpt from the unpublished sections of the doctoral thesis of Yizhar Hirschfeld. Reproduced by permission of Yizhar Hirschfeld.
Excerpt from *Memories, Dreams, Reflections* by C. G. Jung. Reproduced by permission of Pantheon Books, New York.
Excerpt from *The Hero Within* by Carol S. Pearson. Reproduced by permission of HarperCollins*Publishers*, Inc., New York.
Excerpt from *A Far Off Place* by Laurens van der Post (Chatto & Windus). Reproduced by permission of Chatto & Windus.
Excerpt from *Souls on Fire* by Elie Wiesel, © 1993, 1972 by Elie Wiesel. Reproduced by permission of Georges Borchardt, Inc. for the author.

Every effort has been made to trace copyright owners, and the publishers apologize to anyone whose rights have inadvertently not been acknowledged. This will be corrected in any reprint.

Contents

CHAPTER ONE

The Birth of an Idea

*Above all, do not lose your desire to walk: every day I walk myself into
a state of well-being and walk away from every illness; I have walked
myself into my best thoughts, and I know of no thought so burdensome
that one cannot walk away from it . . . but by sitting still, and the
more one sits still, the closer one comes to feeling ill . . .. Thus if one
just keeps on walking, everything will be alright.*

SØREN KIERKEGAARD, LETTER OF 1847 TO JETTE;
QUOTED BY BRUCE CHATWIN, *SONGLINES*

*Amma Syncletia said, 'If you find yourself in a monastery do not go to
another place, for that will harm you a great deal. Just as the bird
who abandons the eggs she was sitting on prevents them from
hatching, so the monk or the nun grows cold and their faith dies,
when they go from one place to another.'*

FROM BENEDICTA WARD: *SAYINGS*

IT MIGHT BE SAID that I stumbled into working for a hospice. An advert in the *Guardian* together with a sense of belonging on my first exploratory visit. After surveying my curriculum vitae, the chairman of the interview panel asked why it was that I wanted the job when my first love appeared to be the desert. It was one of those rare occasions when I knew that my future depended on what I might say. Words, which in the city often seem so easy to come by and yet so difficult to trust, were suddenly hard to find. How was I to put into a few sentences in the strangely unreal atmosphere of a job interview that which I did not fully understand myself, with which I had been struggling ever since I had decided to apply. I falteringly suggested that it had something to do with the similarly perceived barrenness of the desert and terminal illness: both of which were seen on closer examination, though harsh, to be full of life. It was perhaps connected to the similarly humbling effect of a direct encounter with either. It was also somehow linked to self knowledge and integrity. In neither a desert nor a terminal illness is it possible to hide from yourself though in both there are mirages in which you might try to hide.

I realized that despite the unfinished nature of my thoughts I had struck a chord. Showing my ability to do the job was far easier than explaining my motivation. Little did I think that two years on from that interview I would have the opportunity of bringing these two worlds closer together: a fund raising walk for the hospice through the desert.

I first visited the Sinai Desert in 1981 when I spent ten days, with 30 others from 16 countries, exploring and sleeping under the stars. I had never experienced anything like it before. As we travelled south from Jerusalem through pre-dawn hours in the open-sided 'Leviathan' (as the custom built Mercedes was known) I was overwhelmed by a surging of emotions from deep within. I was in love with the desert before I knew her. It was like an arranged marriage that worked, organized by some unseen hand. If the desert had not existed I would have had to invent it, so aching was my spirit for such an undisturbed space and adventure. Nothing else mattered; it was as though I had not lived until that day.

Never before had I been so intensely aware of each passing moment. The cares of the city were shed layer by layer with the passing of each kilometre. Perhaps it was a passion such as this that led St Jerome to exclaim, 'Then the desert held me; would that it had never let me go!'

It was reassuring to discover later that I was not alone with such emotions. Michael Asher, who with Mariantonietta Peru was the first to complete a west-east crossing of the Sahara begins one of his books in the following way:

> This book is the result of a love affair. Like many Englishmen, I was captivated by the desert from the moment I first saw it, and even now my image of its grandeur and beauty is undiminished . . . I felt drawn to this wasteland, in no way that I could articulate, but through a growing sense of excitement within.
>
> MICHAEL ASHER: *FORTY DAYS ROAD*

I was in good company at least.

Carl Jung first visited North Africa in 1920 and he was equally overwhelmed. It was not until some years later, when staying in tropical Africa, that he was able to draw some tentative conclusions about the powerful nature of that experience. He suggested that the seemingly alien Arab surroundings awaken an archetypal memory of an apparently forgotten prehistoric past. The remembering of a potentiality of life that had been largely overgrown by civilization. Is this what happened to me: the unsought rediscovery of a long dormant heritage?

My wife, Sarah, has never been able fully to understand my seduction by the desert. Its awesomeness certainly left its mark on her; but her soul feeds off the buzz and culture of the city. The desert and the city, male and female: in our case at least. Our life together has been a constant battle to reconcile these opposing forces. Over the years our quite different characters have developed a shared spiritual twilight zone within which our differing energies are able to fire one another. The negative side of this creative fusion is the recurring temptation to forget that we are born of different worlds where the same words can have different meanings, where priorities are often diametrically opposed, where values vary and body language ceases to be understood. Sarah earths my esoteric encounters with wilderness and I like to think that I keep her from the worst of the arrogance of modern western culture. Sarah still gets nervous when I tell the story of Fr Johannes from the monastery of St Macarios in Wadi Natrun, a large desert valley north-west of Cairo that boasts a number of ancient monasteries. Over supper in Birmingham I asked him how he became a monk, and he began by saying that he had once been engaged to be married. Then, during a Sunday liturgy, he was convinced that God was calling him through the words of the gospel reading: 'If any will come after me let him deny himself and take up his cross and follow me'. In response he placed his engagement ring in the collection plate, had a word in the ear of the priest and left for the desert. He did assure me that his fiancée was half expecting this to take place.

Fr Johannes was not the first to be drawn thus to the desert. In 313 the wealthy and youthful Amoun went through with the wedding cere-mony before persuading his bride that they should not consummate their marriage but devote themselves to a life of chastity. She consented upon the condition that they should share the house as brother and sister, which they did for 18 years. By then she had come to realize the excellence of the solitary way, so Amoun left her in the house and built himself two domed cells in the desert mountains of Nitria returning to visit his wife but twice a year. He lived thus for a further 22 years and upon his death St Anthony was said to have seen Amoun's soul being transported to heaven.

St Nilus of Sinai left it even later than Abba Amoun before responding to the call of the desert. He described it thus:

A powerful longing towards Sinai seized me, and neither with my bodily eyes nor with those of the spirit could I find joy in anything, so strongly was I attracted to that place of solitude. Indeed, when love of a thing lays hold of the heart, it distracts the heart from even the dearest persons, and leads it so powerfully away that

neither sorrow nor grief nor disgrace form any obstacle. Since the
desire for solitude drove me irresistibly, I took my two children
with me and went to their mother, gave one to her and kept the
other with me, and told her of my decision. . . . It was only with
a heavy heart and with tears that she agreed.

Perhaps Sarah got off lightly with nothing more than a six-week absence
for this walk.

When in August 1981 I arrived at Tel Aviv's Ben Gurion Airport for the
first time, as a back packing student, I was overwhelmed by a sense of
having come home. Prior to applying for a scholarship to study in
Jerusalem I hardly knew where Israel was. I had never been further
south than Italy's Lake Trasimeno. I was no closet Zionist and I did not
at that time realize that I had Jewish ancestors lurking a couple of rungs
up the family tree. At the time my reaction disturbed me; but I have
since come to realize that it was far from unusual: thousands speak of a
similar sense of inexplicable belonging. A year later I felt compelled to
warn Sarah – who had rashly agreed to marry me rather than ruin a
beautiful moment – that we would live in Israel one day. I had no idea
how or when, I just knew we would. In this instance my hunch proved
correct.

Sarah's first visit to Jerusalem, and thus to the desert that laps so
provocatively its eastern fringes, was on our honeymoon. This doubled
up as an interview for a position on the staff of St George's College
where I had previously studied. To begin with we spent ten days on our
own in a dilapidated convent run by Italian Franciscan Sisters on the
Mount of Beatitudes, overlooking the Sea of Galilee. Having travelled
by the Egged bus from Jerusalem we arrived at the end of the drive that
leads to the convent. This would have been but a five minute walk were
it not for the suitcases. A tour bus carrying an American group kindly
stopped and we climbed in through the rear door.

'My you're English. I just adore your accent. Where are you going?'
This in a high-pitched southern drawl.

'We're on our honeymoon' Sarah was quick and eager to say.

'Well, isn't that romantic; and what a coincidence, this is kind of our honeymoon as well isn't it honey?' He proceeded to come to life as her elbow made contact with his ribs.

'This is my third husband.' I was hardly surprised.

'Is this your first or second?' she asked Sarah.

The convent is situated next to an octagonal church that few realize was built in 1937 on the orders of Mussolini. The date can be found in the floor by the entrance, 'XV Italica Gens', 15 of the Italian people, that is of the fascist regime. The octagonal design is meant to remind us of the eight beatitudes in St Matthew's Gospel, and symbols of the seven virtues — justice, charity, prudence, faith, fortitude, hope and temperance — are to be found in the pavement around the altar. (Exactly the kind of topics you want to dwell on on your honeymoon!) It has been described as one of the best places from which to contemplate the spiritual dimension of the lake. That was not, however, our motivation for being there, and it was wasted on us — though the beauty and night-time cicadas were not. I had not the intentions of Amoun! The sisters were extremely friendly but obviously not used to honeymooners. Only once before could they remember any staying with them. As fate would have it, that couple, who were Palestinian Christians, would one day be our neighbours in Jerusalem.

The interview went well. We returned to Jerusalem in January 1985, and stayed for five years during which time Sarah studied graphic art and design at the Bezalel (lit., 'In the shadow of God') School of Art which is attached to the Hebrew University. She got on to the course despite (or perhaps because) she declared in one of her interviews that she could not stand the blue used by El Al. She did not appreciate that this was also the national colour of the state of Israel.

Polly, our eldest daughter, was born in Jerusalem which by definition makes her a 'Sabra'. This is the name given to a native born Israeli. It is Hebrew for the prickly pear, a fruit with long needles on the outside but soft and succulent within. I will never forget the LaMaze birth classes we attended at the new Misgav Ladah maternity hospital in West

Jerusalem. They were led by Shoshana, a dynamic and imposing mother of 13 whose husband spent much of the time working overseas. So would I with that number of children. There was a fascinating cross-section of Israeli society present including hangover hippies with goatskin flasks of water and camel hair jackets, and the similarly dressed but to all intents and purposes completely different Israeli-American settlers (a term used to describe those Israeli's living on territory captured by Israel during the Six Day War of 1967), who seemed frighteningly casual in their attitude to the Uzi submachine-gun that followed them everywhere. There was a Hasidic couple of whom the husband had to avert his eyes or even leave the room when photographs showing female flesh were displayed. He would not even look upon his wife naked and had to don gardening gloves when present at the birth! They appeared to be reconciled to their chosen path but it was alien and difficult to relate to. In stark contrast a Scottish gentleman boasted of how, upon making Aliyah (that is, emigration to Israel) he advertised in the *Jerusalem Post* for a wife. There were 13 replies each of whom, it was claimed, was interviewed between the sheets, and his present wife was judged to be by far the best! She positively beamed with pride as he told the tale.

As director of studies of St George's College most of my time was spent organizing and helping execute study tours for highly-motivated adult students who came to Jerusalem from all over the world to explore the roots of their faith traditions. It was exciting but it could get exhausting always having 40 people in tow for whom it was a once in a lifetime experience. Whenever possible I would escape for a day's walking on my own. And thus it was that the dream of one day walking the length of the country began. I had no plans as to how or when it might happen, and as with many such ideas it was neatly tucked away and forgotten. It unexpectedly resurfaced during one of my weekly meetings with the hospice chairman. A sponsored walk from Dan to Beersheva was the original suggestion but the unfamiliarity of these names provoked the appealing alternative of Mt Hermon to Mt Sinai. Thus this 400-mile journey, which would take me through the world's lowest places where 80% of my time would be spent in the desert, was conceived.

Hospices originally provided care and sustenance for pilgrims making what was likely to be a fairly perilous journey to the holy places of their faith. Today, hospices continue to provide such support for those embarked on the often frightening and uncharted journey through terminal illness to death. Thus the idea of simultaneously making this pilgrimage and raising funds for today's hospices seemed appropriate.

It is still thought by some that a hospice is simply a place where you go to die. Not so long ago a small financial gift was delivered to our door and the donor refused to come in, fearful of something. Friends find it hard to believe when I say that it is the most cheerful place that I have ever worked. The modern hospice movement grew out of a general dissatisfaction with the care of dying people in Britain after the Second World War (see David Field, *The Future for Palliative Care*) and the emphasis has always been on enabling people to live life as fully as possible. To be left alone at home is far more likely to hasten your demise when you are seriously ill than to be cared for, spoilt even, in a fully equipped day care centre. There can be no denying the terminal nature of the illnesses we treat but only the most rash of people would spell out exactly what that means timewise.

Take Sheila for example. She arrived with a prognosis of but a few months remaining and yet for almost two years she reigned supreme as an example of how much life there was still to be lived despite the ravages of cancer. She was one of those rare people who succeeded in climbing above her own suffering. Others would turn to her for advice as on the occasion when a young mother asked, 'How will I explain it to my children when the chemo-therapy begins to make my hair fall out?' Without hesitating and with no undue show of emotion Sheila replied, 'Buy a wig now, before the treatment starts. Let your children get used to it and then you can deal with the traumas of hair loss without the added pain of their confusion as well.' No one else could have said that. To begin with she had been depressed and she could not even be bothered to knit because she was so convinced that she wouldn't finish anything. Eighteen months later she presented me with two tiny cardigans for Phoebe, our second daughter. Administrators don't always have the opportunity to get close to the patients but Sheila was an exception as I had to interview her for a newsletter. She regained her dignity and a sense of purpose during her time with us. Sheila was particularly enthusiastic about the walk and I knew that memories of her would help sustain me when the going got rough.

I received mixed reactions when I told friends, family and colleagues about my plans. Some were clearly envious and would have given anything to participate. Most, though, thought me slightly crazy which was perhaps understandable. At each step of our planning I was amazed by the support we received. Some provided equipment while others gave prizes in order to encourage the collecting of sponsors' monies. All our publicity materials were designed and printed free of charge. Perhaps most important of all were those who went out and filled in sponsorship forms. It was as though there was a hidden reservoir of generosity just waiting for an opportunity to express itself.

There was a great deal of work involved in organizing the journey. Accommodation had to be sought in unusual places and equipment brought together. *Which?* magazine led us to our lightweight walking boots; a cycle shop to rehydration salts as used by marathon runners; and self-inflating mats were recommended for desert nights. Maps had to be found and then translated from Hebrew into English; and tape recorders, cameras and binoculars were gathered. Many books gave useful hints about socks and where to put talcum powder in order to reduce rubbing but nowhere could I find any advice about underwear. This is where the real rubbing took place while training.

Originally our route zig-zagged through every interesting site in the country but for practical reasons it had to be reduced to the shortest possible distance between the two mountains. Beginning on the ski slopes of Mt Hermon, on the north-east corner of the Golan Heights where Syria, Lebanon and Israel meet, we planned to descend via the

Hula Valley to the Sea of Galilee. Also known as Lake Kinnereth meaning harp (alluding to its shape) it is, at 200 m. below sea level, the lowest freshwater lake in the world. All being well we would then continue south through the Jordan Valley and the Wilderness of Judea to Jericho and the Dead Sea which, at 400 m. below sea level, is the lowest point on the surface of the earth. Following this we will tackle the longest and potentially toughest stretch of the walk between the Dead Sea and Eilat which takes us through the Aravah – a wind tunnel of a valley between the hills of the Negev Desert to the west and the mountains of Edom (encompassing the ancient rose-red city of Petra) to the east. From Eilat we will follow the Gulf of Aqaba for 30 miles before heading west, with the assistance of camels, to St Catherine's Monastery and finally, at 2,276 m. the summit of Mt Sinai. It all seemed quite manageable on paper!

Concern was expressed about the safety of the venture. We planned to set out for our first day's walking from Kibbutz Snir at the foot of Mt Hermon and not long before our departure the members of the kibbutz (*kibbutzniks*) were having to spend time in air raid shelters because of the occasional firing of Ketusha rockets into Israel by the Hizbollah of Southern Lebanon. I was not unduly worried because I knew how quickly situations can change in the region. However, we did decide to write to the Foreign and Commonwealth Office Consular Department for advice. Their only slight worry was the section through the West Bank because of its close proximity to Jordan. A lorry had exploded at a roadside café earlier in the year and it may be that we wouldn't even be allowed to walk this section. But how could we avoid Jericho, with all the talk of limited Palestinian autonomy being established there and in Gaza? The Israeli Embassy did not share the British concerns.

My fitness was more of a worry during the planning stage than any possible dangers we might encounter *en route*. Sarah was convinced that I was going to be the first long-distance walker to be airlifted out on day one. Her confidence in me was inspirational. But she was rightly concerned about my fitness. Three months before setting out it had all seemed easy. Plenty of time to tone up the muscles, walk in the boots, get psyched-up or whatever it is that you are meant to do by way of mental preparation. I even went to see Roger Uttley (sportsmaster at Harrow School and until recently coach for the England Rugby squad) for advice. An attack of what was either gout or arthritis in the big toe of my left foot wasn't the best of premonitions. Barely able to walk, I felt mildly stupid meeting my editor for the first time to discuss this book.

The fear of failing was something I could not face up to. It was as though I had invested too much in the venture. It wasn't the possible shame that bothered me; my fear lay deeper. It had something to do with failing myself as though this were a test I had set and which I needed to pass in order to prove something to myself. I was relieved to be pronounced completely healthy after a thorough going over at the Harrow Health Centre. But healthy is not the same as fit. Fifteen miles through London might not be a problem, but how do I compare that with 20 miles through the desert, day in and day out. On top of which there is the very real danger of dehydration to be taken into account.

A man stranded in the open desert on a summer day without water or shelter will feel no discomfort at all in the early morning, the temperature being a comfortable 20°C. By mid- to late morning, having lost perhaps 2 litres without knowing it, and with the air temperature having risen to 35°C he will feel rather warm and thirsty. By midday, with the air temperature at 40°C and our man having lost 4 or 5 litres, he will feel very thirsty indeed, and drowsy with heat. By mid-afternoon, with the temperature of the air approaching 45°C and his loss of body water by perspiration exceeding 7 litres, the man will be fatigued and perhaps delirious. After sundown he will experience relief from heat, but then shiver through the cold of the night. When dawn arrives, he may at first welcome the warmth of the rising sun, only to die the painful death of dehydration and heat prostration sometime during his second day in the desert. This is undoubtedly an upsetting description, but unfortunately a realistic one.

DANIEL HILLEL: *NEGEV*

The American Episcopalian bishop, Jim Pike, died in this manner not far from Bethlehem. His wife made an incredible escape. I once visited his grave in an overgrown plot overlooking the Mediterranean Sea just south of Jaffa. Among the last words spoken to his wife Diane he said, 'If I die here I am at peace, and I have no regrets'. She has bravely told the story in her own words:

> As I left [him], I saw Jim turn over on his left side to get into a better position for sleep. I had gone only a short way when I heard him cry out, 'Diane!' It frightened me. 'What is it?' I called back. 'Tell them to bring lots of water; and yell "Help me!" all the way along.'
> 'Oh, my God,' I said, catching my breath. 'I thought you had fallen. Yes, of course I'll yell "Help me!" Of course I'll tell them to bring water.'
> I looked at my watch. It was 6.10 p.m. There had been something almost frantic about Jim's crying out like that and about the echo of his cry against the canyon wall. It jarred me: resounding with a kind of emptiness. That was the last time I heard his voice.

DIANE PIKE: *SEARCH*

I first realized that the project was going to materialize when others expressed a serious interest in participating. I first met George in Wales, overlooking the Barmouth Estuary from the George III Hotel in Penmaenpool, just outside Dolgellau, next to the old wooden toll bridge and bird sanctuary. He rang me out of the blue one day and expressed an interest in doing something for the hospice. Little did he realize where it would lead. He is a disgustingly fit 55-year-old, who seems able to devour a 12-mile jog in less time than it takes me to read one chapter of an average novel. However hard I tried I could not convince George to take on the whole venture; he was determined to return when we reached Eilat. I even suggested that he had a secret camel phobia but he claimed more valid reasons. I attempted to kid myself that I was going to cope with the heat better than him for there was no way that I could compete over fitness.

George was concerned to make it clear from the outset that he is agnostic going on atheist. It worried him that religious expectations might make the journey uncomfortable. We went out for lunch together and attempted to give the whole issue a thorough airing. When I lived in Jerusalem I didn't like people knowing that I was an Anglican priest until they had had the opportunity to know me as a person. It created an enormous agenda, particularly for some of our young Israeli friends. It can be comforting to pigeon-hole people, to think that we have them sussed: this person works in the city, another is a lawyer, another an estate agent, a graphic designer, a vicar, as though that is all there is. I often feel claustrophobic in the 'vicar box' and never have felt at home in a dog collar. Labels are easy, it is really quite tough getting to know someone.

Expeditions are littered with disaster stories where the relationships of participants are concerned. By the end of that lunch, by a gut reaction and an affinity with his relaxed and caring philosophy of life, I knew that I was going to enjoy George's company. Whether or not he would find my company bearable remained to be seen. I may be the organizer; I may have more experience on the ground; yet in terms of individual maturity I was certainly the junior of the team.

It took me by surprise when Roy, a volunteer at the hospice who helps with collecting patients, running our computers and doing clock repairs, asked to join us; and yet it shouldn't have done because he fitted the bill perfectly. He is quiet and dependable, exactly the sort of person you want to have behind the scenes, someone who wouldn't panic in an emergency. We had visions of him waiting for us by the side of the road with the eggs and bacon cooking over the gas burner. Upon reaching the Egyptian border he planned to continue with me by foot and then camel for the remainder of the journey. Roy's great love is sailing, which he seemed able to combine with fitness training though I have yet to work out how.

A month before departure Sr Deidre Jordan, (the first nun to be appointed chancellor of an Australian university – Flinders in Adelaide) was passing through London and we arranged to meet for lunch. She was once a student at St George's College. We became life-long friends in a matter of 45 minutes when traversing the Colour Canyon in Sinai. Deidre has a chronic back condition and was convinced that she could not make the walk. I arranged for her to be at the front of the group with myself so that no one else could have an excuse for backing out. Being a remarkably strong and confident person, the humiliation of being led through this sandstone obstacle course was either going to make or break our friendship. 'I am not used to having to trust someone like that,' I remember her saying. She made me feel good about my ability to lead and she was not hesitant in giving encouragement that I would remember for years to come.

I called for her at London House in Mecklenburgh Square, a trust that provides accommodation for Commonwealth students. It had been nearly five years since we last met. We wandered back to Bloomsbury in order to meet up with Sarah. Deidre was wonderfully concerned to hear all our news and it felt good to talk. Her questions were astute and to the point. 'How are you feeding the contemplative side of your character', she asked as we hit Russell Square. I stumbled around looking for an answer mentioning in the process that my formal links with the Church had almost disappeared. She wasn't interested in that. She knew how to live within institutions without being of them or owned by them and she was not at all bothered by my confession. 'Are you giving yourself the space to be the person I met in Sinai: tell me?' I was embarrassed. Within the space of half a mile she had found me out. 'I am no longer leading quiet days on the desert fathers', I said; 'I have started to feel fraudulent.' The truth is that I was living off old experiences and though I had developed the necessary coping methods for life in the city I had not succeeded in bringing the desert stillness with me. 'I have started to walk around the city, as part of my training for a sponsored walk I am about to undertake', I said; and I explained the plan to her, commenting that it had 'had the effect of slowing me down, taking me out of the city without leaving, if you know what I mean'.

The words 'Solvitur ambulando. It is solved by walking', from Bruce Chatwin's Songlines sprang to mind. I adopted them as my motto the moment I read them. Even so, working long if rewarding hours for a charity, driving 30 miles through London each day and responding to the delightful demands of modern fatherhood make them easy to forget. Five days after this encounter I decided to walk half-way to work and then repeat the exercise on the return journey. I left Wandsworth at 5.45 a.m. and headed for Baker Street via Chelsea Bridge, Sloane Square, Kensington and Hyde Park. The sun began to rise over the Thames as I entered Battersea Park, alone with the water, the greenery and the majestic Buddha perched in his peace pagoda. I could have stayed an hour on Chelsea Bridge watching London wake. The Blue Guide had me discovering sights I had only ever before rushed past at more than 30 miles an hour. Even cyclists travel too fast and are distracted by their concerns for safety and pot holes. Why is it that I had to wait until driven by this crazy walk to discover the restorative experience of walking through London at the break of day.

The final weeks before departure went far too quickly despite our impatience to be off. I was frightened of it beginning because already I was fearful of the end.

CHAPTER TWO

The Short Step to Jerusalem

A journey of a thousand miles starts from beneath one's feet

LAO TZU

Consciously taking one's journey, setting out to confront the unknown, marks the beginning of life lived at a new level. For one thing, the Wanderer makes the radical assertion that life is not primarily suffering; it is an adventure.

CAROL PEARSON: *THE HERO WITHIN*

Before Rebbe Zusia died, he said: When I shall face the celestial tribunal, I shall not be asked why I was not Abraham, Jacob or Moses. I shall be asked why I was not Zusia.

ELIE WIESEL: *SOULS ON FIRE*

26 September, Day 1

BEFORE DEPARTING I had hoped to produce 40 entries in a diary so that Sarah might have one to read each day I was away. It was an attempt perhaps to salve my conscience for leaving her alone with the girls for such a length of time. As it was I only managed ten days' worth, squeezed between the many demands made upon me as D-Day approached. Life was beginning to reach a feverish pitch, I was overtired and stressed and I knew that I would be setting out with little in the way of either physical or emotional reserves.

Despite the months of planning it all felt strangely unreal until that moment early on the morning of 26 September when George arrived to collect me from a drizzly Wandsworth.

Day 1 of the journal for Sarah:
How was the send off? I suspect that for me the pain of separation will be equalled by nervousness about the journey ahead. In my imagination you seem very lonely and unrealistically strong, facing six weeks of commuting to work and family responsibility alone. . . . How was last night? Did we fight? Had I left all my packing until the last moment? What did I rush out for at the eleventh hour? How did we cope as the moment of departure dawned?

I write this on Wandsworth Common, remember? The day of *Wild Swans* and Laurens van der Post. I sat on the grass next to Phoebe as Polly took you in tow back to the play area . . . and you made the mistake of trying to return without her permission. You faced down as you moved, steps heavy and shoulders bent. Phoebe was attempting to eat leaves, turning her back to me as I prevented the fun.

These are the moments I will miss most. The inconsequential, normal ones.

It was the earliest family breakfast that we had ever had, and the quickest. Little was said as I was sent on my way with two gifts. The

first, a small clenched fist pendant which was found in an excavation in
Israel and is supposedly of ancient Egyptian origin, symbolized the
struggle involved in this venture – physically, emotionally and spiritually – for Sarah as well as myself. All too little is heard of the long
suffering family members of those driven to pursue, under the aegis of
adventure, what is usually little more than selfish personal ambition. In
this I was no exception though the fund raising helped disguise the fact
both to myself and others.

With the pendant came the second gift, a notebook to be used as a
journal, my 'camera' by which I hoped to capture an occasional
moment. I find words to be more demanding than photographs but they
carry the possibility of proportionally greater rewards. More opportunities exist for recreating the intensity and nuances of an event while
leaving the mind free to add its own pictures. The moment thus evoked
can have a history and future explained. It has to be a work of genius for
a photograph to succeed in doing this and I am no such genius. I always
find the camera an obstacle that comes between me and my surroundings and it never seems to be ready or available at the right moment. I
found the following note scribbled on the inside cover:

Dearest One, We wish you well on your journey. Tonight the girls
sat on my lap and we read the story of the ugly duckling who
couldn't find a place where he belonged. He too set off on his own
journey to find his place and his self. He ends up on a frozen lake
all alone where no one can bother him. He meets three friends
who show him his beauty and they remain together for ever. We
all adore you and are very proud of you. We hope you will return
safely and we'll remain together forever. Truly, madly, deeply:
we love you and miss you.'

I was on the plane when I read this for the first time and it triggered a
dull ache that was to remain with me each step of the way. It was almost
as though a part of me had been amputated. Six weeks seemed a mighty
long time. I could not begin to comprehend what it might be like to

have indefinite separation thrust upon one by war or sickness or death. Having successfully negotiated a window seat my mind was able to wander into the clouds and snow capped mountains that marked our route south and Sarah, Polly and Phoebe felt very close. Polly had suggested that their names be written large in my note book so that I shouldn't forget them. As an afterthought she wondered whether my name ought also to be added in case I forgot myself! (Out of the mouths of babes and infants.) When you let go of all that anchors and gives identity — family, work, friends, books, routines — even if only for a few weeks, it is perhaps easy to forget who you are or, rather, fail to recognize yourself apart from the reflection that such activities give. Life's ephemera don't create memories but they help to frame them. It was strange to be reflecting on the possibility of forgetting *en route* to a land bloated with memories.

I had taken this flight many times before, always with a sense of expectation, but never with the nervous anticipation that accompanied me now. In my mind the venture had become elevated into a major expedition though in cold reality it was little more than a good length sponsored walk. The most that might be said for it is that it is, as far as I am aware, a route never before tackled in this way. The terrain might be rugged and the climate inhospitable but we could hardly pretend to be crossing the Antarctic. A personal Mt Everest perhaps, but in the overall scheme of things nothing to boast about. I had to keep reminding myself of this. I set out with the unrealistic hope that this might be an opportunity for the disparate strands of my 36 years to be drawn together, some old ghosts laid to rest and a more recently discovered self affirmed. Just to see and understand myself a little better would have been sufficient! This desire for self-knowledge seems to be a constituent element of the desert wanderer. The search for a hidden life away from daily distractions. 'What can we gain by sailing to the moon if we are not able to cross the abyss that separates us from ourselves. This is the most important of all voyages of discovery.' (Thomas Merton: *Wisdom*)

There were three brothers one of whom became a doctor, one a lawyer and the third a hermit. After a few years, the lawyer, exhausted by the ever increasing mountain of litigation that he was having to deal with decided to visit his brother, the doctor. This brother was equally worn down by the never ending demands made upon him so together they decided to go and visit their brother, the hermit. Upon reaching him in his small, dusty cell in the desert they were invited to sit and pour themselves some water. Upon doing this they were asked to look into the water and describe what they saw and they replied that it was cloudy with silt and they could see nothing. After leaving the water a while they were asked to look again whereupon they were able to see their own reflections in the water. 'And so it is with us', the hermit explained. 'Unless we make time to stop occasionally we can never see ourselves clearly and understand the forces that control our lives.'

RETOLD FROM MEMORY

I am not sure whether, strictly speaking, we had a right to think of ourselves as pilgrims. Our intention was not primarily to visit the holy places, and ritualized prayers were never on the agenda. We were there to complete a clearly defined task with the intention, thereby, of raising money for charity. But for me it was always going to be more. It was an exploration of the Holy Land, its history and stories. It was an opportunity to reflect at a personal level, and I expected it to be a significant part of my own life's pilgrimage. I thought of *myself* as a pilgrim, albeit a slightly unconventional one.

As the plane circled over the sand dunes south of Tel Aviv, lining itself up to approach Ben Gurion Airport, I felt as though I was entering a dream and I thought myself capable of walking to the moon if need be. The heat of the runway's tarmac quickly brought me down to earth. The glare of the sun was too persistent and the surroundings too concrete. It didn't feel like the correct setting for the commencement of an adventure such as ours. Everything was so sterile and totally lacking in romance.

It would have been more appropriate to have begun our journey at the ancient port of Jaffa, said by one tradition to have been founded by Noah's son Japheth after the flood had subsided. Under King Solomon it became Jerusalem's seaport and some years later Jonah set off from there on his fateful journey to Tarshish. Here, thousands of pilgrims have, through the ages, reverently stepped on to *terra sancta* for the first time, many kneeling to give thanks and kiss the ground as they did so. Such signs of reverence have yet to develop at Ben Gurion and there is something about the clinical nature of modern travel that makes me doubt whether they ever will. The nearest to this that I have experienced is the impromptu round of applause that always seems to take place on El Al flights upon landing safely! To kneel on the runway would be to risk arrest at the hands of the security police that surround each plane in order to scrutinize carefully all arrivals. Worse still it could lead to a messy encounter with an Egged bus (or airport equivalent) driven by a frustrated fighter pilot whose daily goal is to get you to customs before you have had any chance of taking stock of your new surroundings. You don't arrive at Ben Gurion, you're processed.

The modern traveller has arrived at his goal almost before he has had time to take leave of his home. From home to airport to plane to airport to air-conditioned bus to hotel, all in the twinkling of an eye. The next day when he wakes up he could be anywhere in the world. The goal is attained too quickly, without time to assimilate and with little personal cost, other that is than a brief dent in the bank balance. This may be fine for the businessman but it is disastrous for the pilgrim. Instant delivery on such a grand scale is rarely capable of provoking spiritual renewal.

In 1914 Stephen Graham travelled in disguise with Russian peasant pilgrims, many of whom had walked 'a thousand miles and more in Russia before reaching a port of embarkation'. It is not that they were totally without means, for hidden within their rags would often be more money than the tourists in the hotels would have, but it was strictly for 'God's purposes'. It is only the degenerate peasant who pays to have himself conveyed to Jordan, to Nazareth, to Bethlehem. 'Oh, what good is it to come', I heard a peasant say in the Dead Sea Wilderness, 'if we take no trouble over it?' They landed at Jaffa after two weeks at sea:

> As we neared Jaffa the excitement of the pilgrims was tremendous, their hearts beat feverishly. The pilgrims were all attiring themselves in clean shirts, and many were putting on new boots, for they counted it a sin to face in stained garments the land where the author of their religion was born, or to tread it in old boots.
>
> STEPHEN GRAHAM: *RUSSIAN PILGRIMS*

Jaffa is surrounded by history and legends that help to provide an appropriate jetty for the would-be pilgrim. An ambience exists that assists the transition from 20th century traveller to 20th century pilgrim. Ben Gurion Airport, despite (or is it partly because of) the large welcoming signs allows no space for such an internal metamorphosis. It is all too clear that it is the tourist dollar that is really being welcomed. I'm not much good on that front; indeed they would be better off fishing, for (as the Jewish sages used to say of the Sea of Jaffa)

> All the silver and gold and precious stones which are wrecked with the ships in all the seas flow to Jaffa. In the days of yore the sea offered up its treasure to King Solomon, hence all his wealth. Since then, however, the treasure has been accumulating and it will be yielded up in the fullness of time with the advent of the Messiah, who will apportion it to each righteous man according to his merits.
>
> ZEV VILNAY: *ISRAEL GUIDE*

Not far from Jaffa's shore it is possible to see a number of dark and unspectacular rocks protruding from the waves. There is a tradition that sites the following story of Perseus and Andromeda here.

> Cassiopeia, wife of King Cepheus of Ethiopia, boasted that she was more lovely than the Nereids, 50 beautiful sea nymphs who were daughters of the old man of the sea, Nereus, a divinity who lived in the ocean and helped sailors in distress. Poseidon, angered by the boast, flooded his kingdom, and sent a sea monster to ravage the land. Cepheus consulted an oracle and was told to sacrifice his daughter Andromeda to the monster by chaining her to a rock. As she lay on the rock, Perseus flew by and immediately fell in love with her. He offered to kill the monster if he could marry Andromeda. Cepheus accepted the hero's offer, so Perseus took the cap of invisibility, winged sandals and curved sword, and destroyed the monster. He released Andromeda and took her for his wife. She bore him a son, Perses, who became the heir of Cepheus.
>
> ROY WILLIS: (ED.) *MYTHOLOGY*

Perseus managed all this having just decapitated Medusa – the gorgon whose face turned all who looked at her into stone. The recent extension of the pier required the dynamiting of some of these rocks so it may be that the site of Andromeda's captivity will soon be seen no more. The story though will not so easily die and the determined explorer will be rewarded inland by the sight of Medusa's head smiling from an architectural fragment of the ruined synagogue at Chorazin in Galilee.

Jonah, Russian pilgrims, sunken treasure, Greek mythology: how can Ben Gurion begin to compete? Little wonder that Near East Tours (one of the more imaginative pilgrimage organizers) is considering developing a hostel on the sea front in Old Jaffa.

It was a relief to see a friendly face in the customs lounge. Steve has security clearance and seems to spend most of his waking hours meeting groups and trying to make them feel as though they are the first visitors ever to arrive in Israel. He did not appear over excited by an exceptionally overweight group of Christian Zionists who had just arrived from Arizona for the Feast of Tabernacles. They had that keen aura about them that seems to surround those on a religious mission, though I am prepared to admit that it may have been jet lag. An earlier encounter with the Christian participation in this Jewish feast left me both angry and bewildered. It seemed to me then to be verging on the idolatrous as thousands of people from all over the world worshipped the state of Israel, in the best charismatic fashion, confusing it for God.

Ben Gurion Airport's clinical friendliness is not improved by the presence of the mountainous Hiriya, an enormous garbage dump that greets you minutes after setting off for Jerusalem. It is a rude reminder of the realities of modern urban life that is guaranteed to shatter any lingering romantic images we may have of the Holy Land. There are fears that Hiriya is so full that heavy winter rains will one day cause a landslide that would block access to the airport. Our detritus fights back. Hasten, Sinai! It could be argued that the greatest pilgrimage of the late 20th century is the search for ecological balance and sanity. As a driving force it appears to many to be far more compelling than meandering in the 2,000-year-old footsteps of a fisherman.

It is only forty minutes by car from Tel Aviv to Jerusalem, a road on which many visitors doze and dream of a comfortable bed in which to recover from the journey. ('What journey?' our Russian peasant might have asked.) I have always found it a most frustrating road, always wishing to slow down and explore, to make detours, but rarely is there the time to do so. Merely a distance to be covered as quickly as possible. Sadly this occasion was no different but while half listening to Steve's update on life in Jerusalem since the dramatic White House signing of the Israeli–Palestinian Peace Accord I allowed my mind to wander out into the passing countryside.

I couldn't help thinking about all the sites we were missing out on. To set out on foot from Jaffa would repay tenfold the physical effort involved. The tragedy of this mad dash for Jerusalem is that we thereby allow so many stories to slip by. Every stone would have told us a story if we had but made time to stop and listen. The surrounding country-side strains to contain the burden of its history. The very soil seems to be alive with the past. It all takes a bit of getting used to, particularly coming from a culture whose present and future seems to be so removed from its past and where the art of story telling is lost, or at best lying dormant.

The historic semitic concept of 'The Land' (Hebr. *HaEretz*) is not just that of rocks and soil or even plants, animals and humans. Above all it is about stories and the right to retell them and re-enact them at the places of their making. It is rarely simply terra firma pure and simple that is fought over in this part of the world. Memories, given life by the refined art of story telling, can be explosive: and doubly so when claimed by more than one teller. What, for example of George of Lydda (now Lod), patron saint of England, whose birthplace and tomb we passed within minutes of leaving the airport. Theoretically it should be a must for every English visitor.

In the third century George was conscripted into the Roman army and while serving in Cappadocia (now part of Turkey) he was executed for tearing up a copy of the Emperor Diocletian's decree that forbade the practise of Christianity on pain of death. Until then he had kept his faith a secret. This occurred on the 23 April 303, 1680 years, to the day, before Sarah and I married. His body was returned to Lydda, which in some sources subsequently became known as Georgiopolis, that is the 'City of Georgios'. A Byzantine church was built over his tomb, though it was later destroyed by the famous Mameluke Sultan Baybars in 1273 and the stones used to build a bridge over a local stream. This bridge still stands and today constitutes part of the main road from Ben Gurion Airport to Lod. A mosque named 'al-Khadr' now marks his burial site. The Greek Orthodox community managed to obtain a neighbouring portion of land where they erected the present church of St George. Al-Khadr (Arab. *The Green One*), a popular figure of Islamic folklore, is an abstract character who over the centuries has been associated with both the Jewish prophet Elijah and the Christian saint George (who is known as Mar Jirjis by Arab Christians). The idea of George as a dragon-slaying knight seems to be the much later addition of the Middle Ages. One story from Beirut tells of young maidens being attacked and even devoured by a fierce dragon while collecting water from a nearby well. Enter the wandering knight on horseback, called George, who defeats the dragon and deposits him in the well. No more dragon and no more water from the well either — which would not have been appreciated. This story sounds like a retelling of the Greek myth of Perseus and Andromeda already mentioned. Coincidence perhaps, who knows.

This was the picture of St George that won international acclaim. The Crusaders brought the legend back to England but it doesn't explain why he should have become our patron saint. Has it something to do with the fact that he was also known as a healer of sleepwalkers and the insane?

> In the nineteenth century, anyone suspected of belonging to either of these categories was tied with iron chains to the outside walls of any church named after St George. The unfortunate person was left there without food or water in the heat of the day and the cold of the night. If he didn't go crazy from the cure, the demon which was lodged in him would eventually leave his tormented body.
>
> YEHUDA ZIV: *GREEN ONES*

Such chains are still to be seen inside the church in Lod and I can vouch for the fact that they remain well used — though only, it would seem, ritually. On the occasion of the feast of St George local Christians and (it seems) Muslims turn out in their thousands at Lod. The Orthodox Patriarch of Jerusalem was celebrating the Liturgy on the one occasion that I made it to the party, not that anyone seemed to be taking any notice of him or his bishops or clergy or choir. He looked on with more than a slight air of disapproval as we queued to kiss the metal yoke chained to the wall which fitted so neatly around the neck. Three times the chain would be lifted and the ancient slender iron collar kissed after which it was placed around the neck and briefly closed. It was hard to imagine what words were being gently uttered as this rite took place – a prayer perhaps for protection from madness.

I despaired of attempting to understand the celebrations at Lod within the matrix of perception and inheritance that I brought with me, when, upon leaving St George's church (after kissing the chains – well you never know) I noticed a goat having its throat cut over a sand pit to the side of the main entrance. The absence of priestly vestments and appropriate invocations meant that it could hardly be called sacrifice; but amidst the noise, crowds and general confusion of a thousand worshippers all doing their own thing it felt like the next best thing. So much for Lod.

Similarly, we passed the ancient city of Gezer without so much as a by your leave. Travellers fortunate enough to spot the small mound of earth sitting to the south of the highway are unlikely to appreciate its significance, which is not surprising given that it has been abandoned for 2,000 years. During the 1600 years prior to that it was a major fortified city that controlled this section of the coastal plain and guarded the vital junction where the east–west road from Jerusalem to the coast crossed the broadly speaking north–south 'Way of the Sea', the main commercial link between Egypt and Mesopotamia. Gezer changed hands a number of times and in its day it could never have been so easily ignored. The Israelite King Solomon only ever took occupation of the site because he received it as dowry upon marrying the Pharaoh's daughter. Even as recently as 14 November 1917 the site was deemed to be of sufficient strategic importance for it to be rushed and taken from the Turks by a brigade of English yeomanry with a battery of machine guns.

The name given to such an abandoned hill, consisting of layer upon layer of destroyed levels of occupation, is a *tel*. Tel Gezer makes an ideal site for historical and geographical orientation, unspoilt as it is by tourism. It is a site for getting to grips with the long and complex history of the country, for getting the lie of the land, for breathing-in the atmosphere and indulging in the beauty of its surroundings. Why dive straight into the city of Jerusalem?

Moving off the coastal plain we climbed slightly into the foothills or Shephelah — a loose gathering of chalk and limestone hills, round and featureless — that once acted as a buffer zone between Israelites and Philistines, Maccabees and Syrians, Saladin and the Crusaders and, more recently, the infant Israel and Jordan, and which now led us towards the hill-country and Jerusalem. The main road to Jerusalem enters the mountains at Shaar Ha Gay (Hebr.; Arab. Bab al-Wad) which appropriately means gateway to the valley. The sudden incline, together with the presence of roadside shrines made out of the shells of vehicles destroyed during the fighting in 1948, clearly marks the spot. The area between the Latrun junction, where our road crossed the Aijalon Valley, and Shaar Ha Gay is littered by more recent memories: a Trappist monastery famous for its wines; a (British) Taggart fortress; the Palestinian village of Imwas destroyed in 1948 and now hidden beneath the beauty of the 1980's Canada Park; the 'Burma Road' and Jewish Jerusalem's fight for survival in 1948; Neve Shalom with its attempts to enhance Arab–Jewish coexistence. We had only travelled 22 km., not quite half-way to Jerusalem, and already I was struggling to absorb the stories and history that came flooding to mind. I had to keep reminding myself that it was only a matter of hours ago that I had been in Wandsworth! Within minutes I felt as if I had been here all my life, if not longer.

Israel is not a large country, about 10,000 sq. km. including the regions Gaza, the West Bank and the Golan Heights, yet within this area you can find more varieties of plants, animals and geological structures than almost anywhere else in the world. If you want to you can ski on the snows of Mt Hermon in Alpine conditions and float on the Dead Sea in the midst of the desert, within the same day. Throughout its long history, in which for up to 1.4 million years people have left discernable traces, stability does not seem to have been an enduring factor. I once calculated that over the last 4,000 years there has been an invasion, or undesired incursion, on average once every 40 years. It has served as a corridor between the greater powers to the south (Egypt) and north

(Babylon, Assyria, Persia, etc), the western powers adding to the turmoil from Alexander the Great (333 BCE) to this century.

It is little more than a narrow strip of fertile land lying between the Mediterranean Sea and the desert that provides a convenient bridge between Africa and Asia. A 'land between' as James Monson suggested, noting that it is only when the powerful cats are distracted that this particular mouse can play! Only in three distinct periods has there been an independent state here: ancient Israel–Judah (c1020–587 BCE), the Hasmonean kingdom (134–63 BCE), and the modern state of Israel (from 1948). Only in recent years has military and agricultural technology permitted the necessary balance of defence and sustenance for the population to be large, secure and prosperous.

I was relieved to reach Jerusalem and the overwhelming immanence of the city. The lights brought my thoughts back into focus and the adrenalin began to flow as the last U-bends gave way to the city's western outskirts. I wanted to drive through the centre of town, say hello to old haunts and check on new one way systems or building developments, but there wasn't time. Steve deposited us and our mountain of luggage just north of the Old City at St George's Anglican Cathedral, a neo-Gothic, early-20th-century institution that gives the initial impression of being more English than England. Fortunately for us Canon Bill Broughton, chaplain to the cathedral's visitors, was at home in his small flat above the main entrance and we were able to invade and deposit our goods. Bill, once a chaplain to the US marines in Vietnam, has to qualify as one of the world's genuinely good and cheerful individuals who always has an amusing story to hand out with his hospitality. He always seems to have time for you, whoever you are, Jew, Arab or foreigner, a skill heavily underrated amidst the frenetic pace of Jerusalem life.

The original intention of the Anglican mission in Jerusalem was to seek converts from among the Jews and Muslims but when these failed to materialize attention was turned to members of other Christian communities, some of whom seem to have been dissatisfied with the restrictive practices of their hierarchies and were keen to move. Today's Palestinian Arab Anglicans are almost entirely the descendants of these 19th-century converts.

Naji, a Muslim inhabitant of the nearby village of el Jib (biblical Gibeon) and night gatekeeper at St George's for as long as I can remember, was on hand to greet us. The years haven't brought much in the way of change to his working life, apart for the automation of the gate, yet he appears one of the most content individuals within the compound. The various intrigues of the community pass him by as he sits in the wind tunnel of an entrance wrapped in his heavy blue parka silently observing the various comings and goings. I can't pretend to have other than mixed feelings about the cathedral close and it felt strange returning. It is an explosive mixture of church politics, nationalistic sentiments and expatriate intensity. Though it was home for five years most of our sustaining friendships were made outside its walls. It was good to notice that the glint in Naji's eye hadn't died and the warmth of his welcome was restorative.

Jerusalem is full of characters. From all over the world, of all faiths and none, people seem to be drawn to this most perplexing of cities. A melting pot of passions and eccentricities. Many a person's sense of being has become so tied up with the city that it is nearly impossible to imagine them elsewhere. They feed off its beauty, history, archaeology, faith, suffering, divisions. They come alive when in Jerusalem; a part of themselves is left behind when they leave. It is said proverbially that of ten portions of beauty given to the world, nine were given to Jerusalem and one to the rest. So also it seems, with ten portions of suffering.

Soon after moving to Jerusalem in 1985 we were warned by a local shopkeeper of the dangers of staying too long. 'Those who come for a week will leave to write a book about it. Those who stay a month will write an article. Those who make it their home for three months or more will never want to leave and they will find it hard to write anything because the complexities of the city will have become theirs.'

Mark and Simon Khano, old friends whose family own the aptly-named Guiding Star Travel Agency, had kindly agreed to put us up for the night on the floor of their flat in Beit Safafa, a suburb of Jerusalem that lies immediately south of Emeq Refaim (Hebr. valley of the ghosts) which, from 1948–67 marked part of the border between Israeli West Jerusalem and the Jordanian-controlled West Bank. So, grabbing the bags that we needed for the night and leaving the remainder with Bill, we moved on. One final surprise awaited us before we could settle with our thoughts and growing sense of anticipation into the secure confines of our sleeping bags. Simon and Mark had arranged to take us out for supper in Bethlehem.

The journey to Bethlehem is more intense even than that from the airport with a bewildering variety of stories, memories, traditions and religious practices clamouring at you from every turn in the road, every building block. It was all that I could do to stop myself going into 'guide overdrive' but one glance made me realize that now was not the time to introduce Roy or George to the complexities of Jerusalem. They already looked mildly shell-shocked and resigned to the stream of alien stimuli that unrelentingly bombarded their tired senses. Swinging out of St George's in Simon's Volkswagen Golf that had obviously seen better days, we quickly cut across what was, between 1948 and 1967 no man's land. Driving south we skirted the ultra orthodox Jewish Hasidic quarter, the Mea Shearim (Hebr., one hundredfold) which in 1875 was one of the first Jewish quarters to be developed outside the Old City walls. Residents here have retained a way of life and dress that was common in Eastern Europe in the last century before the eradication of Jewry there.

> Jewish Daughter!
> The Torah obligates you
> to dress with modesty.
> We do not tolerate
> people passing
> through our streets
> immodestly dressed.

COMMITTEE FOR GUARDING MODESTY

Yiddish is still spoken by many and some go so far as to say that Hebrew should be reserved only for worship and the coming of the messiah. To enter the Mea Shearim on shabbat (Hebr. pronunciation of sabbath) is to pass through a time warp as men with long beards and side curls, wearing knee-length black caftans and the *shetraimel* (round, fur bordered hat) which date back to the Middle Ages, walk purposefully to synagogue followed by a cluster of pale sons each wearing his black *kippur* (skull cap) and protruding *peot* (side curls). Sarah used to travel daily from St George's Cathedral to the art college in the centre of West Jerusalem on the number 23 Egged bus. Boarding in East Jerusalem the only other passengers would be Palestinians, yet within a matter of minutes an orthodox contingent from the Mea Shearim would enter. Secular Israelis would soon follow and there in a confined fast-moving vehicle she would be confronted with this microcosm of modern Israeli life. On one occasion a heightened sensitivity to the human dynamics of this everyday Jerusalem journey was too much and she returned home, in tears and emotionally exhausted.

Upon reaching the north-west corner of the Old City we turned south towards Bethlehem just glimpsing in the process the convex frontage of City Hall. Daylight would reveal the scars of war on a building held on to by Mayor Teddy Kollek in the face of attempts early in the 1960s to relocate further West. For Kollek it is said to have 'stood on the border as a symbol of the future reunification of Jerusalem'. I was struck by the building activity immediately west of the Old City which included a significant widening of the main road.

Because of the high-density projects already approved, and because the officials in Jerusalem can hardly be expected to take steps to limit the use of private cars, some new roads must be built. For economic reasons these will be sited wherever possible on public open space and in parks. Since the Old City area is the largest reserve of open space near the centre, its landscape has become one of the road planner's favourite sites; it is felt to be particularly suitable for giant interchanges. But because of strong public criticism of these schemes, the municipal authorities have recently announced that no road of more than four lanes will be allowed in the vicinity of the Old City.

Previously, rights of way of up to eight lanes had been proposed for the area. Four-lane roads are for the most part inconceivable in the delicate textures and scale of the Old City's landscape; yet the public is supposed to be grateful for the reduction of a hideous proposal to one that is merely grotesque.

ARTHUR KUTCHER: *NEW JERUSALEM*

As we pulled away from the Old City and crossed the Hinnom Valley I tried explaining to Roy and George that our traditional image of Hell as a fiery furnace possibly finds its roots in this landscaped valley now more famous for its open air concerts than the rubbish, filth and furnaces of Gehenna (Hebr. ge Hinnom). The thought of travelling from Jerusalem to Bethlehem via Gehenna, and all this on day one, was all too much and I could see their eyes beginning to glaze over. From here our road followed the line of the watershed that marks the separation of the east and west drainage basins of the land. Hell drains east into the desert, which may be thought appropriate. The Old City is perched between the Mediterranean world to the west and the desert to the east. The climate, geology, soils and vegetation all reflect this fact. Only three kilometres east the yearly rain fall drops to less than 400 mm. along a north–south line known locally as the starvation line. Jerusalem combines short, mild, rainy winters typical of the Mediterranean region, with the blazing summer sun typical of desert highlands. There is an unusually high percentage of cloudless days. It is possibly among the sunniest places anywhere, and the sky has become famous for its bright deep cobalt blue colour. Mediterranean limestones meet desert chalk and the heavy fertile *terra rosa* confronts the light, friable, greyish, barren *Rendzina* which is barely capable of supporting life.

On the outskirts of Bethlehem the heavily-guarded tomb of Rachel stands by a fork in the road. A site once considered so sacred by the

Muslims that they would not allow the Christians near is now very definitely a centre of Jewish devotions. Each time I have visited it has been full of wailing women seeking comfort for their inability to bear children or for the loss of a child. It is possible to imagine Rachel, who is evoked by the prophet Jeremiah to bemoan the fate of those children taken into exile by Nebuchadnezzer, empathizing with these modern women in their timeless plight. Few pilgrim groups stop here today. The road to Bethlehem has become, for the modern traveller, no more than a 20-minute coach journey broken only by an unwanted visit to a religious trinket supermarket where the guide and driver get a cut.

The left-hand fork took us into Bethlehem and immediately our senses were jarred by the cold metal fronted shops lining the street in stark contrast to the soft natural stone covering of Jerusalem's residential areas. On *intifada* strike days and at night the shops are barred shut, the road is quiet and a sombre, almost frightened mood descends upon the place. Road blocks and the occasional shadowy foot-patrol serve to reinforce the occupation that has existed since 1967. If not for the fact that I had eaten at Abu Shabab's restaurant before I would have despaired at us finding anywhere open in this ghost town. As it was we were the only customers and the owner was keen to shut up as he had to get to a wedding. I thought he appeared inappropriately smart against the backdrop of his plain café interior. They don't go out of their way to attract custom by their decor (that's for sure) but the unperturbed are richly rewarded by some of the best Arabic food available. George, who used to own his own restaurant, was disturbed only by the total lack of wine, a problem that was to haunt him for the next few days.

Mark Khano, together with another old friend, Neil Hawkins, soon joined us. Neil was responsible for setting up and managing the field organization behind the now famous survey of living conditions in the occupied territories known as FALCOT 1992; famous because of its Norwegian sponsorship at the same time that Norway was quietly hosting and brokering talks between Israel and the Palestinians. It was exciting to hear Neil talk of the project and how its results will help development agencies focus their support in areas of greatest need as well as help provide the commonly-accepted ground of primary statistics, for demographics, health, education, work, income, consumption and housing, that is necessary for the dialogue to be effective.

Both Palestinians and Israelis hold firm views concerning the nature of Palestinian realities, and these views are often diametrically different. For example, Israeli official statistics state that unemployment in Gaza is around 5 to 6%. UNWRA has suggested that the real figure is somewhere around 60%. Some Palestinian figures for infant mortality are almost three times higher than Israeli figures. The same disparity exists in almost all other spheres, from Palestinian housing standards to political attitudes. In fact, there is no agreement on how many Palestinians actually live in the Occupied Territories. This gap in perceptions of reality stimulates a war of images, a form of discourse whereby Israelis and Palestinians, while trying to talk to each other, end up talking past each other, partly because they have no shared view of the facts. The search for common ground becomes almost intractably difficult when there is no agreement even on what the ground looks like.

In his section of FALCOT 1992 Neil used the following quote from Sir Henry Gurney, then chief secretary of Palestine, which brilliantly sums up one of the major problems facing the researchers and indeed anyone who would seek to understand any aspect of this country today:

Palestine as you know is full of uncertainties. The first thing you have to do here in Jerusalem is to find out which particular century anyone else is living in. There are people who still think it's the Middle Ages and claim to have been living in the same house for 1700 years. To us it is 1947, but the Jews are in 5707 and the Arabs have it that it's 1366 . . . On the other hand there are several people living in the next century or two and much ahead of the facts, such as some politicians and press correspondents. So we have given up bothering very much about what year it is, and anyway many of the things that happen in Palestine would be unusual at any time.

Our conversation fell into Bethlehem's empty streets as we were hurried from Abu Shabab's. I was exhausted by the evening's stories and memories which insisted on retelling themselves throughout the night with the assistance of convoluted images contraposed one upon another. Despite this I slept well and Roy and George were introduced to my propensity to snore.

CHAPTER THREE

✧

To the Starting Line

To those bred under an elaborate social order few such moments of
exhilaration can come as that which stands at the threshold of wild
travel. The gates of the enclosed garden are thrown open, the chain at
the entrance of the sanctuary is lowered, with a wary glance to right
and left you step forth, and behold! the immeasurable world. The
world of adventure and of enterprise, dark with hurrying storms,
glittering in raw sunlight, an unanswered question and an
unanswerable doubt hidden in the fold of every hill. Into it you must
go alone. . . . The voice of the wind shall be heard instead of the
persuasive voices of counsellors, the touch of the rain and the prick of
the frost shall be spurs sharper than praise or blame . . . like the man
in the fairy story, you feel the bands break that were riveted about
your heart as you enter the path that stretches across the rounded
shoulder of the earth.

GERTRUDE BELL: *THE DESERT*

The call that stirred you must torment all men. Whether we dub it
sacrifice, or poetry or adventure, it is always the same voice that calls.
But domestic security has succeeded in crushing out that part in us
that is capable of heeding the call. We scarcely quiver; we beat our
wings once or twice and fall back into our barnyard. We are prudent
people. We are afraid to let go of our petty reality in order to grasp at
a great shadow . . .

Even so did you feel yourself swept away by that inward migration about which no one had ever said a word to you. You were ready for a sort of bridal that was a mystery to you, but in which you had to participate. 'Do we or don't we? We do.'

ANTOINE DE SAINT EXUPERY: *WIND, SAND AND STARS*

27 September, Day 2

As IF MY SENSES HAD not received enough stimulation last night I unexpectedly found myself confronted by the early morning light, sounds and smells of Jerusalem. There is a quality to the air of Jerusalem that is unique. A blending of the untamed austere winds coming in off the desert with the lavish lascivious breath of the Mediterranean. Jerusalem sits uneasily between the wilderness and civilization. She may have embraced the latter but her spirit looks east to the source of her inspiration. This tension resonated within me explaining perhaps why I felt so much at home.

A process of metamorphosis had begun in Wandsworth when I climbed into my travel clothes which ever seem to have a tang of the desert about them. It was the ritualized removing of the city that occurs at the beginning of every adventure. The pulse increases and adrenalin begins to pump each time I pull my wanderer-rags from the bottom of the rucksack. This morning in shorts and sandals the transition was complete, though you wouldn't have known it looking at me. After completing the mandatory photographs of our first night's billet, Simon and Mark returned us to St George's via the back roads of Abu Tor, the Kidron Valley and the excavated City of David where the history of Jerusalem began: a short cut through Palestinian East Jerusalem that Jewish Jerusalemites might hesitate to take.

Though we were impatient to be on our way we took a few moments to gather ourselves at Bill's flat before setting out in search of the promised vehicle. All went surprisingly smoothly though we had to reject the Fiat Uno first offered because it was too small. It was almost lunch-time before we had all the papers signed and the car loaded. Setting our eyes towards Mt Hermon we departed.

Choosing to go via the Jordan Valley in order to get a sense of the terrain through which, in a few days' time, we would be returning (this time on foot) we drove to the northern edge of Jerusalem and joined a relatively new road that quickly took us east from the city into the

Judean Desert. It dropped steeply away towards the Dead Sea and joined the old Jerusalem–Jericho road a few miles east of Bethany. As we approached the junction of these two roads we were confronted by the view of the squatting fortress condominiums of Ma'ale Adummim planted squarely atop the steeply-banked hill in front of us. Ma'ale Adummim's population of around 30,000 is among the largest of the Jewish settlements on the outskirts of Jerusalem and is, to all intents and purposes, a satellite city. The loaded word 'settlement' is, strictly speaking, an Israeli civilian development on land that pre-1967 was controlled by Jordan, Egypt or Syria. Discussion about the settlements is always guaranteed to arouse strong emotions. An Israeli friend once commented that he and his neighbours only continued to live peacefully together because such topics were never aired. I doubt that this is universally true but it illustrates well the fact that there are a number of issues lying just beneath the surface concerning which modern Israelis are seriously divided.

After capturing the Old City of Jerusalem in 1967, Moshe Dayan, then minister of defence and soon to be made responsible for administering the newly occupied territories, said, while visiting the Western ('Wailing') Wall: 'We have returned to our most holy places; we have returned and we shall never leave them.' (Meron Benvenisti: *Conflicts*) The perception of the West Bank and Gaza as liberated rather than occupied territories slowly spread among Israelis and, reflecting this, titles in both official and common speech have changed from 'occupied West Bank' to 'administered Judea and Samaria' to simply the 'areas of Judea and Samaria'. Views on the territories define whether you are a 'Hawk', a 'Moderate' or a 'Dove' in the Israeli political spectrum. Hawks are those who don't wish to return any of the territories; moderates talk of autonomy or confederation for densely populated Arab areas but insist on keeping the River Jordan as the strategic border if not the political one; doves support the return of all the territories.

It was a Labour minister of housing who suggested in 1974 a plan for 'thickening Jerusalem' which involved the establishment of satellite towns within a radius of ten to fifteen miles. Thus the establishment, in

1978, of Ma'ale Adummim. According to Meron Benvenisti (*Conflicts*) in 1977, the hawkish Likud, upon winning the national election, inherited a situation where no less than 40% of the West Bank was designated as 'settlement areas ultimately to be incorporated into Israel proper'. The foundations had been perfectly, if unwittingly, laid by the Labour governments between 1967 and 1977 for the fulfilment of Likud's goal to secure title over the whole of Eretz Israel. To this end all means were seen as justified, be they 'wholesale confiscation of land, profiteering' or the 'destruction of nature reserves'.

The Likud realized that the future of the territories depended on internal political facts and the development of large suburban settlements would create a reality from which there could be no withdrawing. This would prevent a repeat of the Sinai scenario where settlers were bought out in order to facilitate a withdrawal and the implementing of the Camp David Accord between Israel and Egypt. Suburban settlements such as Ma'ale Adummim are filled mainly by Israelis in search of a better standard of living, not by idealists. Land values have differed by as much as ten to one between plots only a few yards apart but separated by the now invisible 1948–67 border, known as the 'armistice' or 'green' line. The new road we travelled down was built as an arterial highway to enable the residents of Ma'ale Adummim and other such settlements nearby, to be able to commute to Jerusalem with relative ease.

It is not usually realized that as a result of the increasing number of settlers a dual state of law has come into being in the Occupied Territories. Jewish residents are treated according to Israeli law, though without the land upon which they live being incorporated into the state of Israel, whilst the Palestinians are ruled by a military government. The latter is not an organization well equipped for ruling a civilian population. The settlers enjoy their own services coordinated by their own local and regional councils funded directly by the appropriate Israeli ministries. They can expect the same standards as those living within the pre-1967 borders. In stark comparison the Arabs are entitled according to Benvenisti 'only to what the military government sees fit to provide under the strict budgetary constraints of the Ministry of Defense'. The Arab population may be 20 times that of the settlers but this does not prevent the Jewish councils in the West Bank from 'monopolizing the environment (including water sources), and planning land-use zones, roads, and nature reserves' without consultation.

As we travelled east from Jerusalem I was provoked by a new set of issues and questions. Yesterday's thoughts of pilgrims landing in Jaffa were replaced by bewilderment at the complex background of the problems facing today's would-be peacemakers. Though the creation of small semi-autonomous enclaves around Jericho and in the Gaza strip is a mountainous achievement, it has arguably been straightforward when compared with the thought of what to do next.

Putting the settlement, together with the questions it provokes, behind us, we headed out into the desert. Almost half-way to Jericho we reached the ancient Ma'ale Adummim (Hebr., lit. Red Ascent), a stretch of road so named because of the reddish iron oxide showing from the limestone hills. In Arabic it is known as Ta'alat ed-Damm, the ascent of blood. A small hill to the north of the road was the site of a fortress, positioned there for the protection of travellers. Opposite this, to the south, lie the restored ruins of a Turkish police post on the site of a Mamluk caravanserai. It has been restored for tourists as there is a tradition that suggests this is the inn of the Good Samaritan. No doubt the parable (Luke, 10:25–37) is located here because of the iron oxide which, for those with an active imagination, could appear as the blood of the traveller who was beaten up and left for dead by robbers. That such an attack should occur in this area is attested as recently as 1857 by William Thomson, who describes a group of pilgrims with a large armed guard passing nearby. One traveller who fell behind was 'attacked, robbed and stripped naked'.

I enjoyed stopping here when it was no more than a ruin because it was a good example of what an ancient caravanserai was like. Today's sanitized bedouin tent – with their purchased hospitality, up, round and down, two-dollar, camel-photo opportunity, together with the usual

over-priced trappings of the modern tourist industry – make me happy
to keep on driving. Our route to Jericho now lay on a road built with
the assistance of American aid granted to the Hashemite kingdom of
Jordan just prior to its changing hands in 1967. Not far beyond the 'inn
of the Good Samaritan' we could distinguish ruined sections of the old
British road which now have bedouin encampments clinging to the
cracked tarmac. There is little romance about these communities with
their flimsy livestock pens standing against goatskin or sack tents that
always seem to be caked in dirt and dust. The sides were rolled up in
order to catch every passing breeze thereby revealing stacked mattresses
and the few other material possessions to all passers by. Water was
stored in a rusty tanker and a tractor, looking forlorn and broken, stood
nearby. The Subaru pickup seems to be something of a status symbol
and most tents had television aerials attached. Children ran around
barefoot lost in play worlds of their own making, the stick and hoop as
popular as it ever was.

It would be wrong to suggest that all the bedouin living thus are poor
or miserable, but there was no avoiding the harsh impression. It stood
in sharp contrast to the clinical comfort of Ma'ale Adummim.
Somehow, isolated in the Sinai Desert, such surroundings seem more
acceptable, more a part of the environment. The Judean Desert, a long,
narrow strip bounded by the Judean hills and the Dead Sea, is now full
of modern urban developments and hot tarmac roads which seem to
portend the passing of a once noble and still idealized way of life. The
situation is not improved by the restrictions placed on the bedouin's
movements as a result of the use of large tracts of the desert by the military for training purposes.

We opted to leave the main road in order to follow the ancient route
to Jericho via the Wadi Qilt and the monastery of St George of Koziba.
(*Wadi* is the Arabic term for the bed of a river valley that is usually dry
but liable to flood. *Nahal* is the Hebrew equivalent.) Turning from the
main road we stopped within minutes to climb a small bank offering
spectacular views to the north across the Wilderness of Judea. The
Wadi Qilt, a steep-sided gorge, lay immediately before us, a snake-like

horizontal band of green along the far side marking a still operative aqueduct carrying water from the spring of 'Ein Qilt to Jericho. Beyond, layers of barren rolling chalk hills continued unbroken to the north until they touched the intense blue of the sky. It completely took our breath away and by descending a little way into the valley it was possible to leave the noise of the main road behind and be confronted by the stillness and space of the desert. The loudest noise was my heartbeat and breathing, neither of which I ever hear in the city. Time slipped by as we fell under the desert's hypnotic spell and we began to attune ourselves to our setting.

Abba Arsenius said, 'I have often repented of having spoken, but never of having remained silent.

HENRI NOUWEN: *THE WAY OF THE HEART*

Archbishop Theophilus visited Abba Pambo who did not speak to him. The brethren finally said 'Father, say something to the archbishop, so that he may be edified'. He replied: 'If he is not edified by my silence, he will not be edified by my speech'.

BENEDICTA WARD: *SAYINGS*

It was said of Abbot Agatho that for three years he carried a stone in his mouth until he learned to be silent.

BENEDICTA WARD: *SAYINGS*

Standing atop our small hill we could see two Egged buses waiting for their occupants to ascend from the western reaches of the gorge where 'Ein Qilt is to be found. It is a perennial spring with surrounding pools that are particularly popular in the hot summer months among those foolish enough to enter the desert then. Sarah and I would take picnics there in the winter in order to escape the wet and cold of Jerusalem. Within minutes we would be in a different world where it was possible to be cheered by the sun. Would that such were possible in London!

There are three springs in the valley, 'Ein Farah (nearest to Jerusalem), followed by 'Ein Fawwar, and finally 'Ein Qilt. The British installed pumping stations at the first two in order to take the water up to Jerusalem, a city that has throughout history been restricted in size by its inability to make enough water available. 'Ein Farah saw the beginning of the monastic movement in the Judean Desert when in 275 Chariton, a pilgrim from Turkey, decided to settle in a nearby cave. The cave he chose was one of a complex that was used in the first century as a base for the Jewish rebel leader Simon Bar-Giora. Chariton's biographer tells us that he was kidnapped by robbers and taken to their cave in Pharan, near 'Ein Farah. Upon being 'miraculously rescued he inherited the cave and the treasures hoarded in it and founded his first monastery there'. This community of recluses called a *Lavra*, was unique to Palestine and it

offered the advantages of living in solitude in individual cells most of the time, but of meeting for communal prayer and Mass at weekends. The community provided for the material and spiritual needs of the solitary cell-dwellers without interfering in their daily routine or self-discipline. The word *lavra* means 'lane' in Greek and probably refers to the paths linking the hermits' cells with the community church. Monks were accepted into a *lavra* only when they were mature and experienced and had developed strong self-discipline.

YIZAH HIRSCHFELD: *DESERT MONASTERIES*

'Ein Fawwar similarly became, at a later date, a *lavra* of 12 cells (Pharan had 15) covering an identical area of 30,000 sq. m. 'Ein Qilt did not attract a *lavra* to itself, though between there and Jericho the compellingly attractive monastery of St George of Koziba came into being.

Tearing ourselves away from this first taste of solitude we drove on to the base of a small hill marked by a cross on its summit and a drinks stall at its base, operated from an ice box in the boot of a car. Here sightseers by the busload stop to stare at St George's Monastery clinging precipitously to the cliffs on the far side of the *wadi*. It was restored between 1878 and 1901 (having been abandoned for at least 500 years) and its fortress-like walls, balcony openings protected by black iron railings, domes and bell tower have earned it a place on every visitor's itinerary. Between 420 and 430 five hermits settled there and the church that they built was developed into a monastery by John of Thebes from 480. Its heyday came in the sixth century under the direction of George of Koziba, hence its name. The Persian invasion of 614 resulted in a great deal of turmoil on which local Saracens were quick to capitalize; the site was temporarily abandoned. The Muslim conquest followed in 638 and it was only in 1179 that the monastery was restored for the first time. According to Fr Murphy O'Connor it was at this time that other stories became attached to the place: Elijah is meant to have stayed here on his way to Sinai and St Joachim, weeping because of the sterility of his wife St Anne, was met here by an angel who announced to him the conception of the Virgin Mary.

George of Koziba's story is of a type told about the holy men of the day. Yizah Hirschfeld (in unpublished research material) writes of George coming from Cyprus to join his brother at a *lavra,* but because he was still without a beard he was not allowed to stay within the *lavra* and was sent to 'the monastery of our holy Lady, the Mother of God' where he was placed in the supervisory hands of the hegoumen or abbot.

The hegoumen, remarking on George's great steadiness and his monastic discretion, after a short time shaved his head and clothed him in the monastic habit. Then he called one of the solitaires, a man already advanced in asceticism, who was entrusted with the care of the so-called 'new garden', and gave him George as a helper. This elder was a hard man, a Mesopotamian by birth. Now, one day he sent the youth to the torrent to bring water; but after having gone there, he came back with empty hands, for with all his clothes on he had been unable to draw the water, which was smothered under a tangle of reeds and wood. The old man made him take off his garment, gird himself with his apron and go down and bring the water. Then, since the youngster was a long time coming out of the stream, the old man hid his garment and went off for eating time. When the boy returned and did not find either his master or his garment, he went back to the monastery naked, except for the cloth around his loins. When he knocked, the hostel keeper opened the door and, seeing him naked, asked him whatever was the matter. George told him what had happened, and the hostel keeper brought out a garment, gave it to the boy to put on, then let him into the monastery. When his master came down from his meal, he met George in front of the chapel of the five holy fathers who are buried there, and seeing him, angrily and threateningly slapped him, saying, 'Why did you loiter?' And immediately (the old man's) hand withered.

George's prayers cured the hand and then fearing the renown that this act was likely to bring he left secretly and returned to his brother. After his brother's death he returned to Koziba, where he received a warm welcome and was at once given a cell.

Nobody was able to observe his way of life . . . he used no wine, no oil, no bread, and had no garment except one sleeveless tunic, the one he wore for the Divine Office. Instead, he would go about the refuse heaps and collect rags, and stitching them together, he would make himself a garment. From those rags he also made his bedding. George used to ask the men who in turn were in charge of the store-chamber to keep for him, from Sunday to Sunday, the waste wiped off the tables of the fathers and the guests, were it vegetables, pulse or kernels; then he took these scraps, pounded them in a stone mortar and made them into balls, which he would put in the sun to dry for two or three days, and if he wanted food at all, he would eat in his cell some of those balls, soaked in water.

When asked for advice about whether or not to flee to Arabia at the time of the Persian invasion he said:

> My son, it is best for us to stay, for life or for death, in the place where we renounced the world, and rather to die in this country than to escape. For even if the Lord reprimands us for our sins as a merciful and loving father, he will not forsake his Holy City, and his eyes will forever watch over this city and this land, the promised land, until the end of time, as he promised.

By the end of the fifth century a steady stream of pilgrims travelling between Jerusalem and the River Jordan caused the gates of the monastery to be opened even to women. Giving hospitality to travellers was a high priority among the monks as is well illustrated by the following anecdote, told of one of the old monks of Koziba.

> When he lived in his village, as a layman, he used to follow this practice: if he noticed that one of the villagers, on account of extreme poverty, had no means to sow his field, he would go by night, unknown to the owner of the field, bringing his own oxen and a suitable quantity of seed, and would sow the field of the other man. When he retired into the desert and took his abode in the cells of Koziba, the elder kept his old compassion and feelings unchanged: thus he would go out to the road leading to the Holy City, carrying loaves of bread and water. And whenever he saw somebody tired out, he would carry his burden and ascend with him as far as the Mount of Olives; then he would come back by the same road, carrying the burdens of others, if he found such as needed his help, as far as Jericho. You could see the old man sometimes bearing a big load and sweating, sometimes carrying a child on his shoulder: on occasions he even carried two. At another time he would sit and mend the torn sandals of men and women, for he used to carry with him all that was required for this work. To some people the old man would give of the water he

had brought to drink; to others he would offer bread. If he found one who had no covering for his body, he would give him even the robe he wore. And you could see the old man toil all day long. Also, if he ever found a dead man on the road, he would recite the funeral office on the body and bury it.

Beyond St George's Monastery the road meanders on its way towards Jericho with precipitous drops into the gorge on the left. We could see caves in the northern cliffs, some of which looked as though they had once been occupied. Those with a fear of heights would never have been numbered among the visitors to such dwellings, which would have counted me out. Such a view as this forces you to put aside any lingering romantic ideas about the eremitical life.

There is the famous story told of George returning to his cell late at night, against the advise of the gate keeper, after a prolonged conversation with one of the brothers.

'Reverend Father, I am afraid to be blamed, if something should happen to you on the way'.

'There is God who helps, my son', said the elder. So the gate keeper, after many efforts to detain him, not being able to persuade the holy man, finally let him out. The old man went out and began to walk along the narrow path, where only one man can tread at a time, towards his cell. And an evil spirit came, and tried to throw him headlong into the precipice. When he perceived this, the old man ordered the spirit, 'Stay away from me.' But, after this had happened several times, since the devil did not give in, the old man finally said to him, 'As in your impudence you refuse to be off, blessed be the Lord! You will carry me and bring me to my cell.' And the spirit at once bent down, and, carrying George on his back, took him to his cell. Then the old man said, 'Now go and never behave impudently and contend with us, the humble sinners'.

We entered the plain of Jericho to the wondrous noise of water from the aqueduct flowing beneath the road and filling a pool from where it proceeded to give life to the surrounding soil. After winding our way round the little-known Herodian fortress, Kypros, named after Herod the Great's mother, the glory of Jericho was revealed before us. The fortress sits in a dominating position on Tel el-Aqaba overlooking Tulul Abu el-Alaiq, Herod's winter palace complex, which sits astride the Wadi Qilt. Beyond, the intense green of Jericho shines as a pearl surrounded by barren desert and hills.

Josephus described the soil of Jericho as 'the most fertile in Judea, producing an abundance of palms and balsam. The stems of the latter are slashed with sharp stones and the resin, which exudes from the incision, is collected drop by drop.' This 'juicy balsam . . . the most valuable of all the local products', was used to produce a perfume, the secret of which has long been lost. So valuable was this parcel of land that Cleopatra had Anthony expropriate it from Herod and give it to her. Herod, never one to miss a business opportunity, leased back the land for an annual rental of 200 talents, and I imagine still made a healthy profit.

Just prior to reaching what little remains of the ancient centre of luxury where Herod the Great died just five days after killing Antipater, his eldest son and heir, we passed the dilapidated outposts of present-day Jericho consisting of mud brick dwellings where human accommodation blends into that of the animals and brightly-coloured Palestinian drapes hang over makeshift lines, drying in the desert heat. Young children play barefoot among the sheep dung on the hard baked soil, faces glued up with seeping eyes and running noses: numerous flies accepted as a part of the order of things.

We stopped briefly in Jericho, at the fruit stall beside the Mount of Temptation Restaurant, so named I imagine because from here you can clearly see Jebel Quruntul (Arab. mount of temptation) which since the 12th century has been the customary place to commemorate the temptations of Jesus. Hanging precariously to the rock face is yet another monastery, which like St George's, was rebuilt at the end of the last century. This location was chosen because it was the site of a medieval cave church where, it was thought, Christ fasted and refused to turn stones into bread. The monastery blends in with the rock face and you have to know that it is there in order to see it. Its architecture is not as romantic as that of St George of Koziba. These two facts, location and architecture, have helped preserve it from the tourist invasion.

Ancient Jericho, Tel es-Sultan, is to be found on the other side of the fruit stall, and the famous spring, 'Ein es-Sultan (which feeds the oasis at a rate of 1,000 gallons per minute) was just across the road from us.

This spring, it is said, at first not only blighted fruit crops, but produced miscarriages in women. Indeed it proved unwholesome and destructive of everything, until it was reclaimed and transformed into a salubrious and life-giving stream by the prophet Elisha, the disciple and successor of Elijah. . . . With prayers, accompanied by many ritual acts with his hands, using his skill, he changed the nature of the spring so that the water that had hitherto brought childlessness and famine, from then on became a source of fertility and plenty. Indeed, such are its powers that if the irrigated water but skims the soil, it is more salubrious than other sources of water that soak in and saturate it.

FLAVIUS JOSEPHUS: *JEWISH WAR, IV*

We had our first taste of *falafel* (deep fried balls of crushed chick peas) surrounded by Egged buses and military patrols, at a hot, dirty café situated on a crocodile farm north of Jericho. We calculated that if all went according to plan we would pass this way again in eight days' time. A cold beer enjoyed on the shores of the Sea of Galilee and a brief visit made to the Mt of Beatitudes were our only other stops on our drive north before reaching the slopes of Mt Hermon late in the afternoon.

Driving through the 'pan-handle' — that part of Israel that has Lebanon sitting on its western flank and Syria to the east — towards Kiryat Shemona, Israel's northern capital, I suffered my first, and only, attack of nerves. This was it. No more losing myself in the planning and no more being distracted by old friends or allowing my thoughts to be absorbed by all the sites we were missing in our rush to the starting line. What on earth am I doing? I would gladly have taken the opportunity of returning to the security of home, our comfortable Wandsworth flat overlooking the circular tower and mock Greek facade of the 'pepperpot' church of St Ann. I felt lost among the open spaces of the Hula Valley with its eucalyptus trees and cotton fields. The hills of Naphtali west of us weighed down on me. The landscape that I know and love so much felt strangely threatening. We really were about to begin.

CHAPTER FOUR

Mt Hermon to Kibbutz Gonen

Whoever walks four cubits on the Land of Israel is assured of a place in the world to come.

TALMUD: KETHUBOTH 111A; FROM ZEV VILNAY: *ISRAEL GUIDE*

A man on foot, on horseback or on a bicycle will see more, feel more, enjoy more in one mile than the motorised tourists can in a hundred miles.

EDWARD ABBEY: *DESERT SOLITAIRE*

I T WAS REASSURING to see a familiar face, hospitality should never be undervalued. There is a world of difference between being greeted by a receptionist, however friendly and professional, and a family eager to welcome and share their home with you. We happily paid for our accommodation when required to do so, but to be someone's guests the night before we started walking provided a much-needed psychological boost. I first met Michael Cohen and her family in a rented apartment in St John's Wood while they were on holiday in London. The setting could not have been less like their home on the foothills of Mt Hermon. Kibbutz Snir was founded immediately after the Six Day War on land that had previously been a part of Israel's border with Syria. It benefited from a near alpine climate which came as welcome relief after the heat of the Jordan Valley. I had lost the battle over whether or not to use the car's air-conditioning. Comfort won out against my purist ideas for acclimatizing. There was a freshness to the air, the prolonged heat of the summer months having just been broken by the briefest of rainfalls. Michael had arranged for us to have a room in the guest quarters beside an ancient carob tree that seemed to embody in its gnarled form the anguish of the warring communities that have competed for the region. After emptying the car we were drawn by the coming sunset to a vantage point at the rear of the guest quarters where, enveloped by an almost ethereal stillness, we watched Israel's Lebanon border dissolve slowly in the twilight.

The tranquillity of the scene gave no hint of the continuing tensions between Israel and her northern neighbours even as the neatly-packaged fields below us belied the years of toil involved in taming the once swampy and malaria-infested Hula Valley. Behind and above us the dominating Crusader fortress known as Qalaat Nimrud (originally Subeibe), sentinel to the memory of previous inhabitants, reflected the glory of the setting sun long after we had passed into shade.

Michael had collected sundry items of food from the kibbutz kitchens and we ate beneath the veranda of her functional yet appealing home. We shared a relaxed evening of traditional Israeli cuisine spiced with conversation about changing attitudes within the kibbutz movement that would allow for greater individual freedom. The appearance of community, camaraderie and shared purpose is very appealing. I appreciate that all is not as it seems on the surface and though ideal places for the young and the old it can be frustrating during the energetic and independent middle years.

Michael's husband Maurice was studying for an exam the next day in the one space where he could escape from the activity of his three sons and daughter: the laundry room! Immediately after his exam he had to leave for his annual military service, a month's night duty in Rosh Pinna. We sat the other side of a thin wall, enjoying the strange smells and noises of the night as the flickering of water jets made music with the cicadas. Despite the moon's dominant presence the stars appeared brighter than I have ever seen them in England. There is little in the way of light pollution in this part of the country. The sky was clear, the air invigorating and I quietly absorbed the sense of freedom and space that the environment offered. At that moment I was well able to concur with Shelley's description of hell as 'a city much like London – a populous and smoky city'.

Our sense of anticipation grew sharply when we participated in some last minute map reading in order to capitalize on local knowledge. Yossi, a small wiry kibbutznik, who works for the nature reserves authority, met us late in the evening. My ingrained suspicion of experts was confirmed by the tones of foreboding that arose as we told him of our plans. We gained useful information about the restrictions on walking on Mt Hermon, it being in a militarized area, but he also left us with more than a nagging doubt that we were biting off more than we could chew. We later surmised that his calculations must have been based on having a school group in tow and stopping at regular intervals for stories about the flora, fauna, geology and local history. He tried to divert us from our intended route in order to take a more interesting path that followed the river. But expediency forced us to keep to our original plan. He seemed to be more excited by my map than our walk. Taking it in both hands he aggressively began to screw it up. My heart sank. Then, straightening it out, he extolled the virtues of the waxy, waterproof material on which it was printed. 'They no longer make them like this', he moaned. His creases are still there but the map did survive.

Israelis have a reputation for being curt and brash. The sabra syndrome: spiky on the outside but refreshingly honest and welcoming within. They tell the following story about themselves:

A survey was taken in Israel to ascertain people's views about meat shortage. Arriving at each house the person taking the survey said, 'Excuse me please, what is your opinion of the meat shortage?' The first house approached was owned by Polish Jewish immigrants who replied: 'What is meat?' The second house approached was owned by Russian Jewish immigrants who replied: 'What is an opinion?' The third house approached was owned by American Jewish immigrants who replied: 'What is a shortage?' The fourth house approached was owned by sabras, native born Israelis who replied: 'What do you mean by "Excuse me please?" '

28 September, Day 3

The highest point on Mt Hermon accessible to visitors can only be reached by a ski lift which was unlikely to be running before nine o'clock so we did not have to rush our preparations. Our kit, consisting mainly of water, sandwiches and first aid items, was double-checked, feet were well powdered, muscles were warmed up and every minute of the drive into the mountains was savoured. Since 1967 Israel has controlled 104 sq. km. of Mt Hermon's western and southern flanks during which time skiing has developed as a popular sporting activity. As it was the lift did not come to life until ten o'clock and after being informed that we would not, in any case, be allowed to descend by foot we decided to commence the walk from the base of the ski-lift. The resort's parking lot doubled up as a military camp and it was more reminiscent of the setting for a James Bond film than the imagined mountain top start that I had hoped for. But compared with the excitement of finally being on our way such details were insignificant. After photographs in front of the chair-lift and once George had recovered from the shock of being stung by a wasp, which might easily have been seen as a bad omen, we were off. Thirty seconds later I found a discarded staff of perfect walking-stick length which was to accompany me throughout the whole of the journey.

At a height of 1,650 m. we were 1,200 m. below the summit of Mt Hermon, which is in Lebanese territory, and 575 m. below the highest peak controlled by Israel. By the end of the day we had dropped to a mere 400 m. above sea level, a height that we were not to regain until well into Sinai. Ours was a journey through the world's lowest places. The Hermon range covers an area of almost 932 sq. km., and it dominates surrounding countryside in Lebanon, Syria and Israel. The highest reaches have an annual precipitation of up to 1500 mm. and many of the peaks are covered with snow for up to two-thirds of the year. Water readily penetrates the mountain's sedimentary limestone and is channelled via a complex internal drainage system through to a number of springs in the foothills. Banias, the most famous of these, was our goal on this first day.

After the almighty had given the Holy Law from Mount Sinai, all the other mountains appeared before the Lord with plaints and quarrelsome words, crying together,
'Why didst thou give the Holy Law from Mount Sinai and not from other mountains?' The Lord answered,
'Set yourselves in an orderly row and let me hear each mountain in turn.' The mountains tussled among themselves until they stood in order, from the most powerful to the weakest.
    Mount Tabor approached first, and said to the almighty,
'Why was the Holy Law not given upon me? See my rounded peak. Am I not lovelier than all the mountains of the world?' And the Lord answered,
'Indeed you are more beautiful; but I foresee that in days to come

churches of the Gentiles will rise on your summit. I cannot give the Law to Israel from a mountain upon which there will be churches.' Tabor went forth with bowed head, and Mount Gilboa drew near, saying,

'Why didst thou not give the Torah from me?'

'Because I know that Saul, first of the kings of Israel, will perish upon you', replied the Lord. Thus did all the mountains pass before the Lord of the Universe and were turned away. Last of all came a small, lowly hill, and the Lord said,

'Tell Me your name.' In sorrow, it answered, 'Hermon. Why didst thou not give the Torah from me? At the borders of the Holy Land am I, and from my feet flow the fountains of the Jordan that is so dear to thee.' And the Lord said,

'Verily, it would have been fitting that the Holy Law should be given from you; but since it was not, I give you another gift. I shall make you loftier than all the mountains of the land, and upon your highest portions shall eternal snows rest. And all the mountains shall envy you.' Since then, Mount Hermon is the highest of the mountains of the land, and its summit is covered with an eternal cap of snow.

ZEV VILNAY: *LEGENDS*

Visible from a distance of 100 km. the mountain exerts an impressive hold on its surroundings and it is hardly surprising that from earliest times it has been credited as the seat of a god. In the books of Judges and Chronicles it is called Baal-Hermon and the name Hermon is derived from the root word *hrm* (Hebr. sacred). Deuteronomy informs us that it was also known as Sirion by the Phoenicians and Senir by the Amorites, which explains the name of our host kibbutz.

The Israeli army was even hesitant about allowing us to walk from the parking lot but after assuring them that we wouldn't leave the road until just above the resort village Neve Ativ they allowed us to proceed. Security demands are such that you need to have a group of at least eight people plus an official guide before you can hope to visit the more isolated regions of the mountain and even then your itinerary has to be agreed in advance. This is perhaps understandable given the closeness of the Syrian and Lebanese borders. Our first steps were thus on Route 98, that is, along the side of the road we had earlier driven up.

Many of Mt Hermon's peaks are of such a height that even the hardiest trees cannot survive. Typical of Middle Eastern mountain ranges, it suffers from hot dry summers followed by severe winters, and anything that would grow in the area must be able to adapt to both extremes. The predominant plant group of the upper reaches is known in Hebrew as *karkotzim*, meaning thorny pillow. These tragacanths are also found in other parts of the world where similar conditions prevail. The brightly coloured leaves are shed in winter leaving behind a pillow shaped clump of thorns upon which the snow settles but fails to penetrate. Similarly, its compact round shape protects it from the summer winds. In both climates it provides a protective environment for small creatures beneath.

The heights of the Hermon are a huge mosaic of soil, rock, climate, snow, altitude, exposure to wind, intensity of sunlight, and evaporation, and each different configuration and variation is accompanied by its own vegetation. The plant groups which thrive in each situation are those which are best at exploiting that combination of conditions and overcoming other species in the struggle for survival.

DAN PERRY: *BACK TO SPRING*

I never cease to be amazed by the ways in which wild plants adapt to their own specific locale. It is impossible (even if it is simplistic) not to make comparisons with our attempts to change the environment violently to suit our own needs.

To an untrained eye such as mine the upper reaches of Mt Hermon seemed extremely barren. I don't remember any birds of note and I was too distracted by the fact that we were at long last on our way to notice whatever lay immediately beneath our feet. When the naturalist, Henry Tristram, ascended to the highest peak, Qasr 'Antar (Arab. The fortress of 'Antar', a negro hero of Arab legend) in the early 1860s he came across three new species of birds: 'a very beautiful little finch, allied to our canary, a new warbler, and a very beautiful and remarkable bird, *Bessonornis albigularis*. Who can say there is nothing left to be discovered in natural history, when on hackneyed Hermon, in a single spot, three new species could reward our search?' He also came across the Alpine yellow-billed chough, the English brown linnet, the common whittear, the snow finch and the Persian horned lark, not to mention 50 species of plants new to him! Why though the phrase 'Hackneyed Hermon'? I can't help wondering what we missed. Leaving the confines of the coach for the freedom of the feet is obviously not all that there is to it. A complete relearning is needed and yet I had no teacher, or indeed, on this occasion, the time for one.

The 'dry heart' of Australia, she said, was a jigsaw of microclimates, of different minerals in the soil and different plants and animals. A man raised in one part of the desert would know its flora and fauna backwards. He knew which plant attracted game. He knew his water. He knew where there were tubers underground. In other words, by *naming* all the 'things' in his territory, he could always count on survival.

'But if you took him blindfold to another country,' she said, 'he might end up lost and starving.'

'Because he'd lost his bearings?'

'Yes'

'You're saying that man "makes" his territory by naming the "things" in it?'

'Yes, I am!' Her face lit up.

Wendy said that, even today, when an Aboriginal mother notices the first stirrings of speech in her child, she lets it handle the 'things' of that particular country: leaves, fruit, insects and so forth. . . . The child, at its mother's breast, will toy with the 'thing', talk to it, test its teeth on it, learn its name, repeat its name — and finally chuck it aside.

'We give our children guns and computer games', Wendy said.
'*They* gave their children the land.'

BRUCE CHATWIN:*SONGLINES*

Roy had driven ahead of us in order to find a suitable place in which to
park, from where he could walk back to join us. This was to become a
recurring pattern until we entered Sinai. We were soon absorbed by
our surroundings, by the need to discover a comfortable walking pace
and the thrill of being on the move. It was perfect walking weather with
just the slightest of cloud-cover and a cool tang in the air, which we
could ominously feel to be disappearing as we descended.

The road was being widened and large items of mechanical equipment, lazily watched over by an occasional tank, marked our way. The
loose underlay, or 'oggin' as George insisted on calling it, was springy
and easy to walk on. The only vehicles to pass us were a couple of
Subaru vans collecting workers who had completed the early shift. The
only two men still at work were elderly members of the Druse community, immediately recognizable by their long silver moustaches, baggy
black trousers and white turbans. They were sitting astride kerb stones
chipping away fragments of cement that were protruding from the
joints. In sharp contrast to the efficiency of the heavy equipment now
lying silent their routine appeared to be painfully slow, more of a
monastic discipline than an income earner.

There are over 15,000 Druse inhabitants on the Golan Heights today
and more in Galilee. In 1967 when the Golan Heights came under
Israeli control the number was only 6,700, hence the majority of
today's population must be under 25 years of age. I have no idea what it
is that provoked this baby boom but together with increased educational
opportunities it has led to the frustrating situation in which there are
more qualified graduates than there are job opportunities. (This
problem is also faced by the Palestinian community throughout the
Occupied Territories.) The Druse are a complex and secretive society,
so much so that many of their own number never discover the inner-
most traditions and tenets of the community. According to Fr Murphy

O'Connor any adult Druse, male or female, can ask to be initiated but only those who pass a 'severe test' become wise. The remainder, numbered among the 'ignorant' may have another go in the next incarnation. The wise are immediately identified by their clothing and white turban. Known as the 'uqqal (lit. the knowers) they have access to the central teachings and are able to participate fully in the religious ceremonies that take place on Thursday nights. It has been suggested that the Society of Freemasons was influenced by these rituals but not being an initiate to the secrets of either I am in no position to judge.

Sheikhs, who are responsible for giving spiritual direction to the ignorant and presiding at marriages and funerals, are chosen from among the wise. In each Druse district one such sheikh is recognized as the supreme religious authority. Thus Mt Hermon, known as it is as Jebel al-Sheikh, must itself be numbered among the wise! It is perhaps surprising that the Druse communities have managed to survive over the centuries given this limited participation in their self-defining rituals. A ban on inter-marriage with other religious groups as well as on conversion into or out of the community must have helped. Equally important perhaps is the common sense concession that they can deny their faith in times of persecution if their life is in danger. I have always found the cult of martyrs difficult to relate to and wondered why it is that those Christians who denied their faith in order to protect their skin were given such a rough time by their peers.

The Druse trace their name to one Muhammad ad-Darazi, a missionary who taught that al-Hakim Bi-Amr Allah, the sixth Fatimid Caliph, was 'the incarnation of the Divinity'. Al-Hakim obviously holds a pivotal position in their tradition as does Jethro, Moses' father-in-law. Despite holding a complex mixture of Jewish, Christian, Gnostic, Neoplatonic and Iranian ideas together with Isma'ili teachings (a division of the Shi'ite branch of Islam) they see themselves as strict monotheists.

Al-Hakim, who came to power in 996, is an interesting figure who was nicknamed the Mad Caliph. He is remembered for the bizarre action of killing all the dogs in Cairo because he could not abide their barking; and for banning, for no logical reason, certain vegetables and shellfish. He cruelly persecuted both Christians and Jews, a practice which sometimes extended to Sunni Muslims as well. It was he who in 1009 systematically destroyed the original rock-tomb of Jesus within the Church of the Holy Sepulchre in Jerusalem. On the other hand, however, he also distributed food during famines, founded mosques and supported poets and scholars. Al-Hakim mysteriously disappeared on the night of 13 February 1021 while taking a night walk. The Druse believe that he will return one day in order to inaugurate a golden age.

Their dress told us that the elderly Druse whom we passed were numbered among the wise. They methodically chiselled away, hardly noticing us. We passed in seconds but it would have taken years to cross the cultural barriers that separated us. Learning Arabic would be the easiest of the hurdles to be negotiated. Their world-view, based on centuries of inherited stories and traditions, would be impossible to enter empathetically however skilful an anthropologist I might become. This thought saddened me as we passed. Physically we could come so close and yet we might just as well have been from different planets. It takes so much effort to understand those different from ourselves and so little to create irreparable divisions.

It had been agreed with the army that we could leave the road on the south-westerly track that leads towards the ski resort Nevi Ativ. If we had stayed on the road we would have entered the largest of the Druse villages, Majdal Shams, that is 'tower of the rising sun', so named because it is the first place to be illuminated by sunlight in the morning. At a height of 11–1200 m. it is also the highest community in all Israel. Just prior to joining the track the road passed within a mile of the Syrian border. Some of Majdal Shams' lands are located on the Syrian side of this 1967 ceasefire line and as there is no border crossing point it has to be cultivated by relatives or other landowners in Syria. Many Druse families are divided by this border and it is customary for them to communicate with each other by shouting, with the assistance of mega-phones, at the appropriately named 'hill of shouts'.

Surrounding Majdal Shams, particularly in the Ya'afori valley that we

drove through on our way up, there are numerous orchards, each with
its own iron water tank. Apples, which were brought to the area in
1945 from the Druse villages of Lebanon are the major crop. Cherries,
blackberries, pears, peaches and quinces are also harvested, but none is
as lucrative. Near by, 'Ein Kinya, the oldest of the Druse villages, also
cultivates sabras and olives. The Ya'afori valley is named after a
prophet, a friend of Mohammed, who is buried in the valley. The Druse
travel here on pilgrimage on 25 August each year.

Neve Ativ is a *moshav*, that is, a community that subscribes to collec-
tive principles rather like a kibbutz yet also makes room for 'individual
initiative and independent farm management'. Built to simulate an
alpine ski resort, it felt strangely out of place in the parched dryness of
late summer. Being so close to the Lebanese border it is protected by
heavy-duty lattice wire fencing and plenty of rolled barbed wire but the
gates across Road 989, which runs through the centre of the *moshav,*
were open and unguarded. My English reticence made me wish to ring
a bell and request permission to enter but there wasn't one. The fence
does not delineate private space as it would have in London, making it
requisite for permission to be sought prior to access. Not being a security threat we were welcome to come and go as we pleased and though
I knew this I remained uneasy entering the *moshav* without even talking
to someone. The ease of access seemed to deny the function of the
fencing. We sat and ate sandwiches on a manicured grass verge relishing
the feeling of finally being on our way. We then left the out of season
alpine ghost *moshav* as we had entered, without seeing anyone. Olive
groves accompanied us on the road west towards the impressive
Crusader castle Nimrud. The village of 'Ein Kinya, where Sat Shuana
the tomb of Jethro's sister is said to be situated, could be clearly seen
nestling on a small promontory of the Hermon foothills just south of us.
And there is a tradition that says that God's conversation with Abraham
(as recorded in *Genesis* 15) which ends with the politically troublesome
words 'to your descendants I give this land, from the river of Egypt to
the great river, the river Euphrates', took place somewhere in these
hills.

Upon reaching Nimrud I sat and caught up with my journal while George and Roy explored the castle. The overpowering Crusader presence at the site reminded me of a conversation I had in 1981 with a Muslim shopkeeper in the Old City of Jerusalem. It was August, I was hot and thirsty and intent on purchasing an ice cold Coca Cola.

'You're English aren't you?' he suggested as he reached down into the bottom of the fridge. My accent always has been something of a giveaway.

'What have you got to say about the Crusades?' he continued, as though it were an everyday topic of conversation. This caught me totally unprepared, and, wondering whether he might be talking to someone behind me, I looked round. What did he mean? What do I have to say? Why should I have anything to say? He handed over the Coca Cola and finished with the timeless comment,

'You may have forgotten, but we haven't.'

This dialogue has haunted me ever since. Should I have had something to say? An apology perhaps or maybe just the acknowledgement that I knew what had gone on, that I wasn't ignorant of the atrocities that my forebears had committed. It felt as though he was implying that I was party to their crimes – which is of course nonsense – unless, that is, ignorance and lack of sensitivity to the consequences of their actions in some way makes me culpable. The past is never neutral and I was beginning to wonder whether the passage of time ever truly succeeded in diminishing its effect. I know that to ignore the past is to risk repeating it but I had never before been so directly confronted by the immanence of history.

That same year I visited the prison in Acre where British Mandate forces had executed Jewish terrorists. A noose hung from the ceiling above a closed trap door. It wasn't hard to imagine the scene: blindfolded prisoner led meekly in, noose laid over head, thump as the trap door falls open, the neck suddenly and fatally bearing the full weight of the body. We've all seen the movie versions but they did not prepare me for the sickness that began to rise in my stomach. I had never been to a site of execution before. An elderly Jewish gentleman who came in after me must have noticed my reaction for he went out of his way to say how that was in the past, a finished episode. He remembered, but not in the same way as the Muslim shopkeeper.

As a youngster the Crusades only ever meant one thing to me — Richard the Lionheart. King John and Robin Hood may have got a look in but that was about it. The murderous destruction of religious communities throughout Europe, and the massacres in the Holy Land: these were never taught in school. Discovering later that Richard was not the hero that I had been led to believe made me wonder whether I could trust anything that I had been taught in those formative years. The question played on my mind, 'What do you have to say about the Crusades?' Very little it would seem and mostly inaccurate at that. Though not responsible for their actions, I must by now be responsible for my own ignorance.

Nimrud is the best preserved and most impressive of all the Crusader fortresses within Israel's borders. The views it offers of the northern reaches of the Hula Valley, the hills behind Kiryat Shemona and the northern border with Lebanon make it the ideal location for a geography lesson. To stand on top of the keep when the wind comes up at the end of a hot summer's day, overlooked by Mt Hermon, with steep ravines to either side and the lush fertility of the Hula Valley spread out below, is to bare yourself to the full magic of this land. When cooped up in the crushing density of London, I can mentally transport myself there and invariably return refreshed! Nimrud acted to guard the Crusaders' north-eastern frontier. Its sister castles, Beaufort on the Litani River (of South Lebanon), and Chateauneuf above Kiryat Shemona, are both visible, which would have been essential for communications. This was a critical strategic site and no one could control the upper Jordan who did not also hold this fortress. When the Crusaders lost control and retreated to Chateauneuf they were obliged to arrange a division of the fields with the Saracens.

The castle stands on land that was handed to the Crusaders during the reign of Baldwin II by the infamous sect known as the Assassins who, like the Druse, have their roots in the Isma'ili tradition of Islam. Founded towards the end of the 11th century by the Persian Hasan as-Sabah this 'Order, united in strict obedience to himself as Grand Master' (Runciman: *Crusades*) became famous for its use of assassination as a political weapon. The devotion of his followers, who were prepared to go to any length to carry out his orders, meant that no political adversary in the Muslim world could rest secure. Murder of the sect's enemies was seen as a religious duty. It is suggested that the term assassin comes from *hashshashin* meaning hashish smokers. However, Marco Polo's stories of taking hashish before departing on a mission, thereby obtaining visions of the paradise that awaited them should they have to face martyrdom, is not collaborated elsewhere.

The fortress was originally called Subeibe, and it changed hands a number of times including one occasion, in 1139, when a joint force of Crusaders and Muslim Damascenes (inhabitants of Damascus) retook it from Zengi, atabeg of Mosul and Aleppo. Intrigue was such that your enemy today could be your ally tomorrow, particularly if a greater power threatened you both.

Israel has a superb network of footpaths which are, as a rule, very well marked by two coloured bands separated by a white band painted on the face of a rock, the side of a gate, wall, or other such location, at regular intervals. Such a path leads from Nimrud's car park down the steep slope of the hill to Banias. The terrain is rocky, overgrown with thorn bushes and the path was not easy to follow but we couldn't go far wrong so long as we kept descending. Before we knew it we were standing beside a *weli* on the cliffs above the cave of Pan enjoying a panoramic view of the major source of the River Jordan. Local pronunciation has converted the 'p' of Pan to a 'b' and thus the name Banias. *Weli* is the name given to the tomb of a Muslim saint, in this case our mysterious friend, el-Khadr, Elijah, St George again. It was appropriate that he should be here to greet us at the end of our first day's walking.

Pan, the goat god of nature, patron of goatherds, music, homosexuals and nymphs, has been described as the embodiment of the living, creative force of nature, which would explain why he was venerated in this cave where a spring, the principal source of the River Jordan, once burst forth. As a result of seismic disturbances the torrent of 20 cu. m. per second now appears from a crack just below the cave's entrance. A Greek inscription tells us that it was the inheritors of Alexander the Great's conquests who initiated the cult of Pan here, perhaps because, as Dean Arthur Stanley suggested, this site 'both in itself and for its romantic situation' was 'the nearest likeness that Syria affords of the beautiful limestone grottos which in their own country were inseparably associated with the worship of the sylvan Pan'.

In 20 BCE Herod the Great was given the town by the Emperor Augustus, in gratitude for which Herod dedicated a temple of white marble to him near the spring. This was the second time that Herod had raised his head on our journey and it was only our first walking day. Given the fact that, apart from Hadrian, he was the greatest builder that the Roman world ever knew, it should not have surprised us. He may have had no more status to the Romans than that of any client king but he became an accomplished diplomat who succeeded in holding together, in relative peace and prosperity, a culturally and religiously diverse populace.

After Mark Anthony's defeat at Actium in 31 BCE, Herod had to face the victorious Caesar Augustus (Octavian) in Rhodes. Were it not for a Nabatean invasion into his kingdom and a calamitous earthquake, which destroyed countless cattle and 30,000 people, he would have been fighting alongside Mark Anthony. Appearing before Octavian in the clothes of a commoner 'but with the proud bearing of a king' Herod delivered a speech that included the following shrewd words.

I am defeated with Anthony and with his fall I lay down my crown. I have come to you, basing my hope of safety upon my integrity, and presume that you will ask yourself not whose friend, but how loyal a friend, I have been!'
Caesar replied:

You may rest assured of your safety and reign now more securely. A champion of the claims of friendship such as you deserves to rule over many subjects. Try to remain as loyal to those who enjoy better success; for my part, I have the brightest hopes for your bold spirit.'

FLAVIUS JOSEPHUS: *JEWISH WAR, I*

It was his ability to be both ruthless despot and astute politician that enabled Herod to succeed.

After Herod's death Banias and the surrounding area passed to his son Philip who made it his capital. He named it Caesarea after the emperor and Philippi after himself in order to prevent confusion with the port of Caesarea Maritima on the coast.

Now when Jesus came into the district of Caesarea Philippi, he asked his disciples, 'Who do men say that the Son of man is?' And they said, 'Some say John the Baptist, others say Elijah, and others Jeremiah or one of the prophets.' He said to them, 'But who do you say that I am?' Simon Peter replied, 'You are the Christ, the Son of the living God.' And Jesus answered him, 'Blessed are you, Simon Bar-Jona! For flesh and blood has not revealed this to you, but my Father who is in heaven.'

MATTHEW, 16:13–17

There is a good argument for also siting the Transfiguration, which in Matthew's gospel follows the above encounter, in the area. The slopes of Mt Hermon certainly fit the bill by being 'a high mountain apart'. Mt Tabor, near Nazareth, has become the more convenient pilgrim memorial for this most mysterious of events when Jesus' face 'shone like the sun, and his garments became white as light' and Moses and Elijah appeared talking with him. Perhaps the authenticity of Hermon is assured by the fact that no buildings are to be found commemorating the event here. A further tradition claims that the woman 'who had suffered from a haemorrhage for twelve years' (*Matthew* 9:20) and who was cured upon touching the fringe of Jesus' garment, came from Banias. In memory of this the Christian inhabitants of Banias erected a statue of Jesus that was later seen by the Church historian Eusebius in the fourth century. St Willibald, the English traveller, recorded that he saw it in 954, after its destruction by Julian the Apostate who replaced it with his own image.

Banias is thus, understandably, a crucial stop on the pilgrim itinerary. Greek mythology, el-Khadr, the Herods, New Testament events and beautiful natural surroundings provide all the ingredients for an evocative holy place, which perhaps makes it all the more surprising that it has never particularly appealed to me. Arriving on foot and succeeding in gaining entrance without paying helped on this occasion. I resent the extortionate rate charged to visit a cave, river and barbecue site. There are few remains to be seen. Though this is rapidly changing as two archaeological excavations work at the site, one of which has uncovered Herod's temple. My reaction may also have something to do with buried memories of evangelical sermons that often build on the Banias story by pointing a finger out into the congregation (and every time without fail, it seemed, directly at me), saying 'and who do *you* say that I am?' Twenty years on, ordained priest, and I'm still not sure that I'm any the wiser. The question remains as confusing as ever. The answer seems to depend on who it is that asks the question – the evangelical answer, the catholic answer, the liberal answer, the socialist answer, the existentialist answer, the historical answer.

In order to cool the back of my head I climbed onto a dam-like wall that crosses the river soon after it surfaces and soaked my white *keffiyeh* (the traditional Arab head-dress) in the icy cold water. George went to buy postcards and Roy had not yet caught up with us. While there the question continued to echo inside of me. How can we pretend to give an answer, clouded as our judgement is by years of interpretation, theology and the interests of formalized religion? Two thousand years and controversial records make an enormous barrier. Even the Druse workman suddenly felt closer. How can I make sense of the factions who each claim Jesus as their own while hinting at damnation for their opponents? It struck me that I had run out of patience, and religious energy. At that moment I no longer felt any desire to associate myself formally with any particular group. It is too easy to conform and mimic Peter's reply 'You are the Christ, the Son of the living God' but it is far from straightforward to understand what it means. I now find myself focusing more on what he did than who he was, or indeed is. Early Christians were known as 'Followers of the Way' which has an appealing ring to it, a more immediately practical emphasis. Followers of one who was to quote Bonhöeffer 'a man for others', preferring the company of society's outcasts to that of the religiously respectable. That I can relate to. Lost among such thoughts I sat, almost level with the water, and observed a group of Asian Christians from England holding a brief service in the shade of the trees opposite.

These headwaters of the River Jordan are the life blood of Israel, forming as they do the major source of water for the Sea of Galilee which itself serves as feeder to Israel's national water carrier. Appreciating the significance of this the Lebanese and Syrians began to divert water from the tributaries of the Jordan River. Banias, with its annual provision of 122 million cu. m. of excellent quality water, then controlled by Syria, became a major focus of attention as the Syrians sought to build a canal to divert its waters into the River Yarmuk in Jordan. Long-range Israeli artillery and tank fire sought to disrupt these 'diversionary works' and in November 1964 Israeli aircraft were used as well. 'Israel's activities ultimately brought the work to a halt for it became clear to the Syrian leadership that pursuit of the diversion ultimately must mean war with Israel . . .' (Chaim Herzog: *Arab–Israeli Wars*) Such is the importance of water in a parched Middle East that it is often said that future wars in the region will be fought over water, not oil.

The sun sat low in the sky as we returned to Kibbutz Snir flush with the satisfaction of having completed day one. As if to welcome us back a coterie of butterflies were performing a ritual dance over the tennis courts against the backdrop of Mt Hermon's constantly changing colour. A gentle breeze added to the magic of the moment.

29 September, Day 4

We left Kibbutz Snir at four o'clock determined to get into a rhythm of early starts. There was heavy cloud-cover and only the slightest hint of dawn as we set off due south from Banias along a jeep track on the Golan Heights, just above the floor of the Hula Valley. Looking behind us we could see Nimrud and the heights of Mt Hermon romantically shrouded in clouds. We passed a signpost to Tel Faher, scene of heavy fighting in 1967, and barbed wire fences bearing notice of mine fields – a red triangle on a yellow background with an explicit warning in both Hebrew and English. The land beyond the fences looked seductively tranquil, undisturbed by any signs of life. The signs are easily blown from the fencing so the general rule is never to climb over a barbed wire fence unless 100% sure about what lies on the other side. There was heavy hand-to-hand fighting at Tel Faher back in 1967:

> The approaches to the Syrian lines were completely dominated by formidable concrete emplacements and positions at Tel Azaziat, which covered by fire the entire north-eastern area of the Huleh [sic] Valley. The only way to overcome this position was to outflank it, to capture the Syrian positions behind it and then advance on it from the rear. To do this it was essential to overcome another formidable position in the rear, Tel Faher. . . . Surrounded by three double-apron, barbed wire fences and several minefields, it was criss-crossed with trenches, machine-gun and antitank positions and dug-outs. It was cleared only after fierce hand-to-hand fighting. . . . Under withering fire, some of the Israeli troops, many of whom died in the process, threw themselves on the coils of concertina wire, creating a human bridge over which their comrades could cross and attack.
>
> CHAIM HERZOG: *ARAB–ISRAELI WARS*

Perhaps this goes some way towards explaining the slightly eerie nature of the Golan Heights today. Recent history, harsh basalt hills and dark wide open spaces where the sky sits low.

I told George the story of Eli Cohen, 'Our Man in Damascus', Israel's most famous spy who socialized with Syria's military élite. On a private tour of the Golan Heights, hosted by the military, he overheard complaints from the soldiers about the heat whereupon he suggested that trees be planted to provide shade for the gun emplacements. This was promptly done and thus it was that the Israeli airforce was able to identify the Syrian positions. Eventually he was uncovered and publicly hanged in the central square of Damascus, a scene that was televised and could be seen in Israel. The clumps of trees that we passed took on a new meaning as I retold this tale.

We crossed the TAP line — the world's longest pipeline (at least it used to be) that passes through the Golan Heights. Starting its journey in Bahrain it used to carry 320,000 barrels of oil a day over a distance of some 2,000 km., 30 of which are in Israeli controlled territory. I assume that modern politics means that it no longer operates.

George was later to recall this as his most enjoyable day, spent on dusty tracks away from tarmac roads with occasional bursts of plant life breaking up the rocky barrenness, and sightings of gazelle, hyrax, foxes, eagles and vultures adding to the scene. The hyrax or rock badgers, agile, fast, teddy bear like creatures were in plentiful supply. I met someone in Turkey who had devoted three years of his life to observing the play habits of the hyrax for his doctoral thesis. In order to attract them for observation he had to leave out bananas to which they promptly became addicted. The net result of all his labour was the discovery that they probably don't play at all!

We did not get to see the fruitbats, wild boar, wolves (is the Tibetan wolf to be found on the Golan?) or packs of wild dogs whose howling had so unnerved us the previous evening. Neither did we see as much of the bird migrations as we might have hoped. As many as 150 million birds follow the migratory paths through Israel each spring and autumn. We did, however, confront large numbers of longhorn cattle through which we had to negotiate our way because minefields lay to either side.

There was not a moment of the day without spectacular views, either behind us towards Mt Hermon or westwards across the Hula valley to the hills of Naphtali which rise to a height of more than 800m. above the valley's floor. 'The beauty of the world is almost the only way by which we can allow God to penetrate us. . . . A sense of beauty, although mutilated and distorted and soiled remains rooted in the heart of man as a powerful incentive.' (Simone Weil)

All 177 sq. km. of the Hula Valley could be seen spread out beneath us. There is an abundant flow of water into the Hula basin as a result of heavy precipitation in the west (900 mm. on the Naphtali ridge), north and east (1,000 mm. on the Golan plateau and 1,500 mm. on Mt Hermon). Total inflow into the Hula basin is estimated at 740 million cu. m. annually! Vast quantities of alluvium, carried by the water, are deposited as it reaches the flat ground. This used to cause water levels to rise and the narrow outlet through the Rosh Pinna sill to the south to become obstructed, thus creating swampland.

The whole marsh is marked in the maps as impassable, and most truly it is so. I never anywhere else have met with a swamp so vast and so utterly impenetrable. First there is an ordinary bog, which takes one up to the knees in water, then, after half a mile, a belt of deeper swamp, where the yellow water-lily flourishes. Then a belt of tall reeds; the open water covered with white water-lily, and beyond again an impenetrable wilderness of papyrus . . . which extends right across to the east side. A false step off its roots will take the intruder over head in suffocating peat mud. . . . In fact the whole is simply a floating bog of several miles square — a very thin crust of vegetation over an unknown depth of water, and if the weight of the explorer breaks through this, suffocation is imminent.

HENRY TRISTRAM: *LAND OF ISRAEL*

The Hula drainage scheme, carried out between 1951 and 1958 succeeded (at a cost of 22.4 million dollars) in lowering the water level as a result of which 15,000 acres of dark, rich alluvial soil were reclaimed, and a remaining 30 sq. km. of lake were preserved as Israel's first nature reserve. The idea of draining the Hula basin originated with the Turks and similar plans developed by the British were shelved upon the outbreak of the Second World War. Soon after the project was inaugurated by Israel on 20 January, 1951, the Syrians, a few kilometres away from the proposed drainage channels, claimed that the project would give Israel a strategic advantage. They even succeeded in getting the United Nations to halt operations temporarily. Objections were also raised by a number of nature enthusiasts and environmentalists. One unexpected side-effect has been the increased amount of pollution entering the Sea of Galilee. Prior to drainage the whole area served as a giant sump, filtering the water as it proceeded on its way to the Sea of Galilee but numerous peat fires and the increasing use of poison to control rodents have now become serious causes of water pollution. A poet, noticing that the Hula and Kinnereth lakes are both heart-shaped and observing the River Jordan flowing from one to the other exclaimed:

'O God! You have joined the Kinnereth and Hula by a rope – your River Jordan – but to link the hearts of men you have not found among all your treasures even a thread.'

ZEV VILNAY: *LEGENDS*

Massive roadworks on Route 959's steep ascent to the central Golan plateau prevented Roy from driving up to meet us, so, making the most of the opportunity, he legged it – a sight for sore eyes though he looked disturbingly fresh. Tempting as it was to call it a day we decided to push on for another 6 km. and time ourselves in order to gain some idea of our pace which proved to be almost 5 km. per hour. We took the minor road south towards Gadot to a point due east of the Hula nature reserve, level with the junction of the western and eastern drainage canals.

The road was shaded by eucalyptus trees and we saw Egyptian papyrus in some abundance, particularly in Nahal Khamdal. This is the furthest north that this papyrus grows though no one seems to know how it reached here. Before the area was drained Arab and Jewish inhabitants used it for making mats and rafts upon which they would fish in Lake Hula. According to Zev Vilnay the Israelite tribe of Naphtali learned to make paper out of the papyrus by cutting the 'pliant long stems into thin strips' and then twisting and weaving them into sheets. Proof of this lies in their very name for, say the sages, 'Naphtali is derived from the Hebrew root *phatol*, meaning to twist'.

We had forgotten that we were in the middle of the major Jewish feast of Sukkot, one of the three pilgrim festivals which celebrate God's bounty in nature and his protection. We joined all 500 members of Kibbutz Gonen, where we were staying for one night, in eating beneath a *sukkah*, a makeshift booth whose roof is made of branches or vegetation thin enough to let the rain in. This is meant to remind us of the booths that the children of Israel dwelt in during their exodus years in the wilderness, and the fact that it is not bricks and mortar that provide us with ultimate protection but God himself. Ours was a decidedly secular affair, the highlight being some singing by young children surrounded by flashing cameras. There was a reading of sorts though it was all but ignored.

The festival of Sukkot teaches us to give thanks to God for the harvest of fruit and grain and to share these and all nature's blessings with our fellow men. Let us praise God with this symbol of joy and thank him for his providence which has upheld us in all our wanderings and sustained us with nature's bounty from year to year. May our worship help us to live this day and all days in the spirit of this festival of Sukkot with trust in God's care, with thanksgiving for his goodness, and with determination that all men shall enjoy the blessings of the earth.

FROM: *SERVICE OF THE HEART*

The reading for the sabbath in Sukkot is taken from Deuteronomy 8 and 10 and includes the following words: 'The Lord has brought you into a good land, a land with streams and springs and lakes issuing from plain and hill, a land where you may eat food without scarcity, where you will lack nothing. When you have eaten and are satisfied, give thanks to the Lord your God for the good land which he has given you.'

With hindsight it all seemed very relevant – to celebrate the fruits of the land and the providence of God near the beginning of our journey. There was a restorative process going on inside of me, a renewing of my relationship with the earth that had been numbed by the concretization of the city.

For thousands of years men have been tillers of the soil, living and working in tune with the rhythms, cycles, and seasons of the earth. Men invested themselves in the earth, caring for it, nurturing it, preserving it, because they knew firsthand that its fruits were their source of life. In a real way, part of a man's identity lay in his relationship to the land. If a man's identity is (at least in part) tied to the earth, what happens to him when our technological society tears him away from the earth, perhaps even forces him to abuse it? Something in the man is killed, I think, or at the very least paralysed. As our involvement with nature and its rhythms stops, our awareness of being part of a world much larger than ourself is numbed; we are unable to be nourished and taught by the land, unable to see the handiwork of God in the earth, and therefore unable to act effectively as its stewards.

VERNE BECKER: *REAL MAN*

It is estimated that by the year 2000 nearly all human beings will live in a more or less urban environment.

Without wilderness (or alternative wilderness – parks and gardens), man could evolve, as some men are doing, into a variant species: urban man for whom food begins in plastic at the hyper-market and life is unthinkable apart from the noise of his *alter ego*, the car . . . man may loose his capacity to wonder and to love all the living. . . . An urban world without wilderness would be a global prison.

EDWARD ECHLIN: *OF WILDERNESS*

In July 1987 Pope John Paul II took his first holiday away from Castelgandolfo, six days walking in the mountains north of Venice. That Sunday when saying Mass for the villagers he preached on the Christian duty to care for the environment. On one of his walks a passing hiker asked him if he appreciated the wilderness freedom after life in the Vatican to which he replied thoughtfully, 'You have to know that prison to appreciate this freedom.'

CHAPTER FIVE

Around the Sea of Galilee

In the last century, a tourist from the States visited the famous Polish rabbi, Hofetz Chaim. He was astonished to see that the rabbi's home was only a simple room filled with books. The only furniture was a table and a bench.

'Rabbi, where is your furniture?' asked the tourist.

'Where is yours?' said Hofetz.

'Mine? But I'm passing through. I'm only a visitor here.'

'So am I.'

(SOURCE UNKNOWN)

There is no quiet place in the white man's cities. No place to hear the unfurling of leaves in the spring, or the rustle of insects' wings. And what is there to life if a man cannot hear the lonely cry of the whippoorwill or the argument of frogs around the pool at night? . . . What ever befalls the earth befalls the sons of the earth. If men spit upon the ground, they spit on themselves. This we know: the earth does not belong to man, man belongs to the earth. All things are connected like the blood which unites one family. Whatever befalls the earth befalls the sons of the earth. Man did not weave the web of life; he is merely a strand in it. Whatever he does to the web, he does to himself.

(SOURCE UNKNOWN)

30 September, Day 5

IT WAS UNNERVING setting out before light into our eucalyptus avenue yet the heat was such that it was the only sane way of reaching the northern shore of the Sea of Galilee on schedule. After about an hour we crossed the Jordan River which at this point looked more like a French canal than a mighty river, an impression enhanced by beret-clad fishermen breaking first light with their melancholy patience. Today was a holiday and what better way to spend it than quietly on the bank of the drainage canal through which the once mighty Jordan now flows. I could easily have been tempted to give up the day's walk and join them in their passive tranquillity. We soon reached Kibbutz Gadot where we turned east towards Benot Ya'aqov (Hebr., the bridge of Jacob's daughters). Considering that Jacob, according to the Bible, only had one daughter, Dinah, the name is problematic. A popular guide's tale says that the name does not refer to daughters of the patriarch Jacob at all but rather to nuns from a Crusader convent in Safed who had been raped, as was Dinah. A number of stories relating to Jacob circulate the area but accurate details are lost in the haze of time.

The famous traveller Burckhardt relates the story of the tears of Jacob's daughters which goes some way to explaining the rugged terrain of the area.

When the daughters of Jacob, coming from the east, were crossing the Jordan at the spot where today stands the bridge named for them, tidings reached them that Joseph had been mauled by a wild beast. The maidens began to stray to and fro, and wandered amid hills and dales, seeking traces of their unfortunate brother. They wept and wailed and hot tears fell from their eyes. These tears were changed to black stones, and these are the blocks of dark basalt scattered through the numerous hills and vales of Galilee.

ZEV VILNAY: *LEGENDS*

The little-known Crusader castle, Chastellet, that guarded the border with the Muslim kingdom to the east, was built in 1178 by Baldwin IV. It was meant to control the river crossing and prevent any serious incursion by Saladin's forces into the Crusader kingdom. Appreciating its strategic significance, Saladin offered 100,000 dinars to the Crusaders to halt its construction. They should have accepted the money, for on 25 August 1179 Saladin's forces laid siege and after only five days succeeded in undermining the fortress's only tower, storming the defences and massacring 1,000 Christians whose bodies they deposited in a well. A gory story to remind us that we were still on border territory.

The importance of this crossing was enhanced when travel north on the west bank of the Jordan was made impossible by the Hula Lake and swamps. This was the furthest that Napoleon reached with his troops, when he hoped to prevent Turkish forces from relieving Akko which he was besieging. A century later, in 1918, after defeating the Turks the road lay open for the British and Australian forces to move on to Damascus. It was also at this point that British forces broke through in the Second World War when they sought to wrest control of Syria from the Vichy French. In 1948, there was heavy fighting here between Syrian forces and the small Jewish colony of Mishmar Hayarden (Hebr., guard of the Jordan) which resulted in the survivors of the colony spending 14 months in a Damascus jail and the colony being totally destroyed. A memorial to those who died marks the site today. Two Bailey bridges now span the river just north of the ancient crossing.

We succeeded in walking blithely by without taking note of all this history. There was a long day ahead of us and if we sought to overturn every stone we would need twice as long. Having said that I was later disturbed by the degree of my ignorance about this critically important location. Perhaps that is the price I must pay for there not being a tourist development near the bridge inviting me to explore beyond the superficial. Tourism or ignorance, not the easiest of choices to be presented with.

From Benot Ya'aqov we entered 'the mountainous Jordan' as the section of the river between it and the Sea of Galilee is known. No longer diverted through modern canals it follows its original course through the hilly Rosh Pinna sill that separated us from the Kinnereth. Here it drops rapidly, 270m. in only 14.5 km., giving it a great deal of power to erode even basalt. We were walking high above the river and it was lost from view to us until it reached the bottom of its run.

It was at about this time that, much to my surprise and horror, blisters first began to appear. I had had no problem when training and I could only think that it was the heat that made the difference. Despite the expected swelling my feet were beginning to slip within the light-weight boots. They began beneath the balls of my feet, quickly followed by the tops of my toes and before long on my heels as well. There were to be days when I would be walking with twelve such distractions. Add to this a throat infection which led to a partial loss of voice, followed by a course of antibiotics to which I proved to be allergic, and you will understand why the next five days passed in something of a blur. There were moments when I doubted my physical ability to keep going but my mental resolve never let me down. Only upon returning to England did I discover that Roy hadn't expected me to make it.

We kept thinking that the next corner would bring us our first view of the Sea of Galilee but it seemed to take for ever to arrive. Finally, after we had given up looking the sudden opening up of the gorge on to the plain of Bethsaida beneath us took us quite by surprise. From our vantage point we were able to follow the course of the river, now meandering through densely overgrown fields, into the lake.

The Sea of Galilee (also known as the Sea of Kinnereth, Lake Genneseret, or Sea of Tiberius) is an impressive sight when approached from above. Surrounded as it is by the Galilean hills to the west and the Golan Heights to the east it appears as a sparkling jewel sunk deep into its setting. You don't need to start digging into the religious and histor-ical significance of the place to be impressed. 'Few can fail to have been struck by the sudden flash, as from a rent in the bowels of the earth, when this view of the lake rises from below, and greets the traveller in his steep downward journey.' (Arthur Stanley: *Sinai and Palestine*)

The rabbis said: 'The Lord hath created seven seas, but the Sea of Genneseret is his delight.' (George Adam Smith: *Historical Geography*)

> One ridge after another had been surmounted, when on a sudden the calm blue basin, slumbering in placid sweetness beneath its surrounding wall of hills, burst upon us. The first gaze on the Sea of Galilee, lighted up with the bright sunshine of a spring after-noon, was one of the moments of life not soon or easily forgotten.
>
> HENRY TRISTRAM: *LAND OF ISRAEL*

The lake covers an area of 165 sq. km. and its height varies between 209 and 214 m. below sea level depending on the season and amount of rainfall. 'The surface of the water of the lake is so low that, if St Paul's Cathedral were set upon the shore, and Westminster Abbey on the top of the dome, the summit of this pile would still be lower than the Mediterranean Sea.' (John MacGregor, 1868; from Linda Osband: *Famous Travellers*)

Though a freshwater lake the high degree of evaporation brought about by the climate, together with mineral springs that rise near the shore and on the bottom of the lake, mean that the water is very slightly saline. In any case, given the number of visitors camping on the shores and swimming in high season, you would not want to risk drinking the water directly. It has also been said that the waters of the River Jordan succeed in passing through the Kinnereth without mixing with it! 'Do not wonder thereat, for lo! the Jordan passes through the Lake of Tiberius yet does not mingle with it. The thing is indeed miraculous! (Bereishith Rabba 4:5; from Zev Vilnay: *Legends*)

It is an image that Naphtali Imber, composer of Israel's national anthem, Hatikvah, uses to describe the wanderings of the children of Israel who do not mingle with the nations among whom they dwell:

To Lake Kinnereth, with a roar,
The Jordan enters lonely.
Its waters do not mingle
And proudly it steers its way through.
So my wandering people Israel,
Who settles in all countries
But yet remains solitary,
Among the nations unaccounted.

ZEV VILNAY: *LEGENDS*

We met up with Roy beneath the impressive villas of the village of Karkom, each of which must have the most staggering views across the lake. Prior to this we spent some time looking east across the Bethsaida plain towards Nahal Daliyyot and Gamla, otherwise known as the Masada of the north.

Perched on a rocky, camel-shaped ridge, with deep valleys dropping sharply away on either side, the ancient city of Gamla (Camel) gave birth to a dynasty of zealot leaders who roused much patriotic fervour throughout the area during the Roman rule in Israel. They taught that God alone was the ruler of Israel, not the Roman emperor, and therefore one ought not to pay taxes. Such a view was bound to prove popular with the people at a time when over-population was causing many peasants to lose their independence as farmers, forcing them to join the fast growing ranks of impoverished, poorly-paid labourers. Social conditions were ripe for revolt. The zealots awaited a political messiah who would lead them to victory over the Romans. That some of the disciples initially saw Jesus as such a messiah is hardly surprising given the closeness of Gamla to the village of Bethsaida from which Peter, Andrew, James, John and Philip came. It has been suggested that the reason Jesus took them as far away as Caesarea Philippi (Banias) before tackling the issue of his identity was to remove them from the dominating influences of their home environment.

As was invariably the case for those opposed to Rome, Gamla finally came to a sticky end; but not before inflicting a major defeat upon

Vespasian's forces. This took place during the First Jewish Revolt of 66–70. Flavius Josephus, the Jewish historian, records the episode in some detail and he has a loquacious attempt at reconstructing Vespasian's speech to his troops after their initial set back.

> If it is vulgar to be elated at victory, it is just as cowardly to be despondent under adversity; for the transition from one to the other is rapid; and the best soldier keeps his self-control when successful, so that he may still remain cheerful when meeting with failure. . . . Recklessness in war and mad impulsiveness are foreign to us Romans, who owe all our victories to efficiency and self-discipline. That is the vice of backward peoples and the chief cause of Jewish defeats . . . the best encouragement each of you will seek is in your own right arm.
>
> FLAVIUS JOSEPHUS: *JEWISH WAR, IV*

Leaving the view behind us we followed the road away from Karkom until we were able to cut through to Moshav Almagor via a rocky field densely packed with thistles. It was late morning by the time we descended on to a pitted tarmac road that passed through mango plantations to the lake. My feet were foul, I was exhausted and miserable. It felt good to be through for the day.

We drove directly to Kibbutz Ma'agan on the southern shore where we were expecting to stay but because of the influx of Israeli tourists over the holiday period we were moved to the Golan Hotel in Tiberius. The owners, a Palestinian Christian family, made us extremely welcome and even allotted us single rooms. We had four nights here with views in all directions over the lake and never anything but the most courteous service. The restorative nature of these surroundings kept me going while I was physically at a low. After a nap we visited Capernaum arriving just before it closed, which is invariably the best time as there are not too many groups around. I went into 'guide overdrive' which was the final straw for my throat. To my surprise George lapped it all up. I had made the mistake of assuming that because he had clearly stated his lack of religious practise he would have little interest in such sites.

Historically there may only have been one Capernaum (Kafr Nahum, lit. the village of Nahum) but today there are most definitely two. Less well known is the Greek Orthodox site marked by the red cupula of its small chapel. Few people bother to visit here despite recent archaeological work turning up some interesting remains including a Roman bath house. The Greeks have not made any effort to court visitors and one bath house is hardly able to compete with the monumental synagogue and house of Peter found next door. The Franciscans, who own this larger portion, have it made; they know how to make a few pence out of it and who can blame them. What I don't understand is their priggish insistence on modest dress which is taken to such an extreme that they even ban boats from landing at their jetty if they see bare knees approaching! Demanding a certain standard of clothing will not, of itself, encourage reverence or respect for the site. I wonder what Jesus would have been wearing.

The incongruous white stone of the fifth-century synagogue, which may have been built on the site of an earlier one, stands out from afar. Why white stone in the midst of this dark basalt area? It must have involved an enormous amount of work carrying it here. What statement were the builders trying to make? One interesting theory speculates that it was the result of rivalry between the Jewish and Christian inhabitants of the town. The synagogue was built to overshadow the nearby basilica that covered the house of Peter. An alternative possibility is that it was built by Christians in order to show pilgrims the synagogue where Jesus taught. Whatever the reason there can be no doubting the fact that it has, for centuries, successfully dominated the area.

The house of Peter, argued to be one of the earliest sites of Christian veneration, was, for many centuries lost among the basalt walls of the ancient town. More recently the balance has been redressed by the erection of a large basalt basilica (shaped like a flying saucer). Inside you can look down, through the floor, to Peter's house while the windows above the tiered rows of seats offer superb views across the lake. Its scale, like that of the synagogue, is overbearing and inappropriate. Rather than enhancing the importance of the site it neutralizes it. To stand outside where the wind can be felt against the face and the water heard breaking on the shore is far more evocative of the memories of the site. The building does nothing to help me in my attempt to recreate the environment in which Jesus and his followers might have lived. It is plainly designed more for the liturgical ritual than the provocation of memory. Only these few Latins and Orthodox Christians, separated by an eight-foot basalt wall with mesh fencing on top, live in Capernaum today.

1 October, Day 6

Our day around the lake should have been among the most enjoyable of all but my feet and throat schemed to ensure otherwise. The sudden flow of adrenalin that kick-started me first thing in the morning enabled me to build up sufficient momentum to get round. That and my stubborn determination which was at last finding a positive outlet. At the last minute we changed our plans and opted to follow the western shore as it offered us longer stretches next to the water's edge which we thought would be good for morale. The eastern shore may be quieter but it is also more tedious for the hiker who is simply intent on covering the ground. We were 200 m. below sea level and it was dark and cool though a little sticky. We were off again, sustained by the thought of a rest day ahead.

For the first three kilometres the road sat slightly back from the lake but contact was made soon after Capernaum where the road almost touches the water. Here we saw a large wooden boat moored beside a scruffy makeshift restaurant. Made in Egypt, the boat was brought via the Mediterranean Sea to Haifa and then overland to the Sea of Galilee. The aim is to create the impression of a first-century fishing boat – an aim which is not enhanced by a toga-clad native throwing out a net by way of imitating ancient fishing habits. The size of the sail appears to be far too small ever to succeed in powering the boat, but I was assured otherwise. For all my cynicism I can see why it appeals, confirming as it does the romantic picture that many pilgrims bring with them. It may be preferable to the modern ferries that ply the lake though they can't be accused of creating a pretence. A genuine first-century boat was recently uncovered when poor rainfall reduced the level of the Kinnereth to an all time low. Known as the 'Jesus boat' it soon became a popular addition to the pilgrim itinerary. One of the archaeologists working at the site asked me what I would say to a group of Eskimo pilgrims who explained that they had come all this way to see the Jesus boat!

Pilgrimage has become an opportunity to confirm images, assumptions and beliefs already held rather than an opportunity to be provoked or stretched. A large industry has grown up in support of this process and clever guides and tour operators change the nuances in order to suit the specific religious background of the group be they Baptist, Anglican, Catholic, Orthodox, Mormon or whatever. It forms a natural progression: comfortable flights, comfortable coaches, comfortable hotels and now comfortable sites, comfortable holy places and comfortable experiences, all for would-be comfortable pilgrims. There was certainly nothing comfortable about the way I felt. Perhaps I secretly envied them.

Between Capernaum and Tabgha, beneath the Mount of Beatitudes, there are a number of small bays whose shores serve as natural amphitheatres. A scientist pushed out a boat into the centre of one and discovered that the water, when still, acted to project the noise of even a whispering voice over a good distance. Is this why Jesus was in the habit of pushing his boat out a short distance from the shore before addressing the crowds? Perhaps it was possible for hundreds, if not thousands, to hear him at the same time after all.

The name Tabgha comes from the Greek name Heptapagon, meaning seven springs. Again, we have here two sites in close vicinity. The first, 'Mensa Christi' (table of our Lord) is also owned by the Franciscans. It recalls the Resurrection appearance of Jesus during which he cooked breakfast for his disciples who were out fishing. Their nets were empty until they followed his instructions to throw them out on the other side of the boat.

Next door the German Dominicans have faithfully reconstructed the Byzantine basilica that commemorated the story of the loaves and fishes. This is a site at which I find myself wanting to spend time; it has an integrity about it. The church authorities request modesty but there are no frocked bouncers hidden in the shadows waiting to enforce it. To come with an appropriate attitude seems more important. In a small room off the atrium of the church there is a slide presentation of some of the wider concerns of the community that is based here. Camps are held throughout the summer for young people and in particular disabled youngsters. Paralleling the miracle of the loaves and fishes is the belief that if we each give of ourselves, the little that we have will prove enough to go round. Idealistic? Perhaps, but it is just the sort of vision I want to be presented with.

I was tempted to stop and join them for their early morning Mass but it would have been too difficult to get going again. I discovered that blisters are manageable if you keep walking on them but it is fatal to halt and disastrous to remove the boots. If they became particularly painful I would jump and land heavily on them which had the effect of shooting a bolt through the nervous system, which in turn would then cut out, as insignificant, any subsequent pain waves.

It is argued that the area around Tabgha is the *eremos topos* (Gr., desert place) of the gospels where Jesus sought refuge from the crowds. Capernaum, whose population may have numbered thousands is not that far and the main road to Syria was but a stone's throw away so it can't have been that isolated. This observation aside it is an ideal site for reflection.

Just beyond Tabgha we hit Route 90, the road that runs from Metulla on the Lebanese border all the way south to Eilat. It was to be our daily companion for the next two and a half weeks. We soon discovered kilometre markers that were decreasing as we walked south and it seemed a fair deduction that they finished on zero in Eilat. This was a particular stroke of good fortune for Roy as it stopped us taunting him with 'how much further?'

Counting off each day's 30 km. became an invaluable psychological aid. We would pretend not to notice them for as long as possible in the hope of having walked further than we realized. Kilometres 10–20 were always the toughest of the day as it began to get hot, breakfast was finished and the end was not yet in sight. After 20 km. it was a steady count down to the 30 mark when we would collapse into the car. Well, I collapsed, George invariably looked as though he had hardly begun.

Our first steps on Route 90 were something of a novelty as they involved climbing a hill that reached the dizzy height of 125 m. below sea level. To this point we had only descended, one small slope near Benot Ya'aqov excepted. Our interest increased when we realized that the hill housed the pumps that draw water from the lake to a height of 256 m., before sending it south through conduits, tunnels and siphons for a distance of some 142.5 km. into the Negev Desert just west of Beersheva. With a capacity of almost 3 billion cu. m. the Sea of Galilee is the obvious choice as Israel's main reservoir though the initial pumping costs must be horrific. The only evidence for all this activity is the cluster of electricity pylons that cling to the western side of the hill together with the fencing that prevents any further exploration.

We quickly descended into the fertile Genneseret plain and four kilometres of straight tarmac road. Potentially the most tedious stretch of the day, it was lightened by the fact that we had somehow managed to lose Roy when coming over the hill. We crossed Nahal (valley) 'Ammud, which can be followed all the way up to Zefat and Nahal Zalmon, which also twists its way up into the hills of Upper Galilee. They have so flattened out by the time they reach the road that they are hardly noticeable. Nahal 'Ammud is best known for the two caves in which prehistoric human remains have been found. One had the complete skeleton of a young male who had been buried on his side with his knees drawn up. It is dated somewhere between 80–35,000 BCE, a sign perhaps of the fertility of the region that has attracted settlers through the millennia. Josephus described the plain in the following way:

The plain of Gennesar, skirting the lake, which takes its name from the lake, is an area whose natural property and beauty are very remarkable. Thanks to the rich soil, there is not a plant that does not flourish there, and the cultivators in fact grow every species; the air is so temperate that it suits the most diverse varieties. The walnut tree, which is the most winter loving, grows luxuriantly beside the palm tree, which thrives on heat, and side by side with the fig and olive, which require a milder air. One might deem it nature's crowning ambition to force together, in a single spot, the most discordant species, and that, by a healthy rivalry, each of the seasons, as it were, wishes to claim the region for her own. For not only does the region produce the most surprisingly diverse fruits, but it maintains a continuous supply: for ten months on end it supplies those royal fruits, the grape and the fig; the rest mature on the trees all the year round.

FLAVIUS JOSEPHUS: JEWISH WAR, III

Dominating the southern end of the plain are the cliffs of Arbel, pockmarked by more than 100 caves which first saw human occupation back in the second century BCE. Herod the Great went to the length of lowering his men down in baskets in order to ferret out supporters of a rival who had holed up there. To assist them they used grappling hooks with which they pulled 'the brigands' from the caves to send them hurtling to their death.

Wishing to save some of them, Herod's herald summoned them to him, but none surrendered voluntarily. Of those who were brought out forcibly, many preferred death to captivity. In one case, seven children and their mother begged the father, an old man, for permission to come out, as their lives were guaranteed; but he ordered them to come forward one by one, and standing at the mouth of the cave, he killed each son as he emerged. Herod, watching the spectacle from a convenient position, was cut to the heart; he stretched out his hand toward the old man, begging him to spare his children. The man treated Herod's words with contempt, and even taunted him as a cowardly person. After his sons he killed his wife, then threw their bodies down the cliff and threw himself after them.

FLAVIUS JOSEPHUS: *JEWISH WAR*, I

By looking long and hard at the cliffs it is also possible to discern the remains of fortifications around the caves that were added by Fakhr-ad-Din II, a Druse who ruled Galilee in the 17th century.

To the south-west, beyond Arbel, and equally visible from many miles are the Horns of Hattim, a double-crested mound which from the right angle can appear as a pair of animal horns. It was here on 4 July 1187 that Saladin annihilated the largest army ever assembled by the Crusader kingdom, thereby effectively bringing to an end their hegemony of the country. It is a sombre tale that well suits the barren windswept surroundings.

In 1185 a four-year truce was negotiated between Saladin and the Crusaders. Saladin needed the time to consolidate his powerbase and the Crusader kingdom required peace in order to recover from poor rains and potential famine. Civil war nearly broke out in August 1186 upon the death of the nine-year-old Baldwin V as agreement could not be reached concerning his successor. Eventually the young king's mother, Sibylla, was crowned queen and she, herself, then placed a crown on the head of her unpopular husband Guy. Towards the end of 1186 a wealthy Muslim caravan travelling from Cairo, with but a few soldiers to protect it from the bedouins, was attacked by Reynald of Chatillon from his castle, Krak, in Moab (now Jordan). This was a clear breach of the truce and war was certain to follow.

On 1 July 1187 Saladin crossed the lower Jordan near the Sea of Galilee, with the largest force that he had ever commanded. He camped with half of his army between Mt Tabor and the lake while the other half laid siege to Tiberius. The town fell after no more than one hour's fighting though the Countess Eschiva, wife of Raymond of Tripoli, was able to hold out with a small garrison in the castle. Raymond had led the opposition to Sibylla and Guy's enthronement but he now made his peace with them and the Crusader forces began to gather at Acre. Everyone rallied round and the relic of the True Cross was brought up from Jerusalem.

The future now depended on the debates that took place among the Crusaders concerning which military strategy to adopt. Raymond of Tripoli argued that the kingdom should not be risked for the sake of his wife in Tiberius and that they should stay put as the army that advanced in this summer heat would be severely disadvantaged. It would seem that most of the knights supported this argument but a few others, led by Reynald of Chatillon, who had provoked the crisis, accused him of cowardice and a lack of chivalry. King Guy, renowned for indecision ordered the march towards Tiberius.

This debate was repeated the following night when they were camped at Sephoria, just north of Nazareth. This time Raymond argued even more forcefully and they retired at midnight having resolved to travel no further. However, the grand master of the temple, Gerard of Ridfort, a long-time opponent of Raymond of Tripoli, crept back to the royal tent and persuaded Guy to change his mind. Thus was the fateful decision to march on Tiberius made.

The morning of Friday 3 July was hot and airless, as the Christian army left the green gardens of Sephoria to march over the treeless hills. . . . There was no water along the road. Soon men and horses alike were suffering bitterly from thirst. Their agony slowed the pace of the march. Muslim skirmishers continuously attacked both the vanguard and the rearguard, pouring arrows into their midst and riding away before any counter-attack could be made. . . . Guy, moved by the weariness of his men, decided to halt for the night. On the news Raymond rode in from the front crying: 'Ah, Lord God, the war is over; we are dead men; the kingdom is finished.'. . . Saladin, waiting with all his men in the verdant valley below, could hardly restrain his joy. His opportunity had come at last. The Christians passed the night in misery, listening to the prayers and songs that came from the Muslim tents below. . . . Under cover of darkness Saladin moved up his men. When the dawn broke on Saturday 4 July the royal army was encircled. Not a cat, says the chronicler, could have slipped through the net.

STEVEN RUNCIMAN: *CRUSADES*

It does not take a great deal of imagination to envisage what happened next. The Christians fought with great bravery but weakened by thirst they stood little chance. Raymond of Tripoli, at the king's command, attempted to burst through the Muslim lines but when he charged with his knights the line simply opened allowing him to pass through unhindered. There was then nothing he could do but depart and leave the others to their fate. Balian of Ibelin and Reynald of Sidon also managed to break out, they were the last to escape. The Holy Cross, borne into battle by the bishop of Acre fell into the hands of the infidel. The king and many of his followers were captured and taken to Saladin's tent where they were well treated. The king was seated next to Saladin and he was handed

a goblet of rose-water, iced with the snows of Hermon. Guy drank from it and handed it on to Reynald (of Chatillon) who was at his side. By the laws of Arab hospitality to give food or drink to a captive meant that his life was safe; so Saladin said quickly to the interpreter: 'Tell the King that he gave that man drink, not I.' He then turned on Reynald whose impious brigandage he could not forgive and reminded him of his crimes, of his treachery, his blasphemy and his greed. When Reynald answered truculently, Saladin himself took a sword and struck off his head.

STEVEN RUNCIMAN: *CRUSADES*

All the other prisoners were spared except the knights of the military orders who were given over to a band of fanatical Muslim sufis to be slayed, a task they 'performed with relish'. So many prisoners were sent to Damascus to be sold as slaves that the bottom fell out of the market and one Muslim 'thought it a good bargain to exchange a prisoner for a pair of sandals.' 'A militant and truculent Christianity, as false as the relics of the 'True Cross' round which it was rallied, met its judicial end within view of the scenes where Christ proclaimed the Gospel of Peace, and went about doing good.' (George Adam Smith: *Historical Geography*) Thoughts of the battle provided a welcome distraction and before we knew it we were up against the Arbel cliffs where they tumble into the lake forcing the road to climb above the shore line.

It is an attractive road that enters Tiberius from the north but it is not particularly safe for the walker. There are a number of sharp bends and vehicles are upon you before they see you. In the first century there were nine cities around the lake, each with a population of at least 15,000. Today there is only Tiberius with its close, oppressive climate. Founded between 17 and 22 by Herod Antipas it quickly became the capital of Galilee. Initially religious Jews would not enter the city because it was believed to be defiled by the fact that the foundations were built upon an ancient cemetery. This inhibition did not last long for a rabbinical school was founded here in 220 and the Gemara, which together with the Mishnah constitutes the Jerusalem Talmud, was completed here. Today the tombs of the great Jewish sages, Rabbi Yohanan ben Zakkai (first century), Rabbi Eliezer ben Hyrcanus and Rabbi Akiva (second century) and Rabbi Moses ben Maimon, better known as the Rambam or Maimonides (12th century) are all to be found within the city. Together with Jerusalem, Safed and Hebron it is listed as one of four Jewish holy cities.

A few miles north of the city centre George decided that he wanted to return to the hotel for breakfast so I continued on my own for a couple of hours. Tiberius is built on three levels: the shore, the hillside and the top of the hill. It was the tourist centre that I walked through, shops, markets and numerous cafes selling either beefburgers and ice cream or St Peter's fish. Newly laid paths shaded by well-positioned trees took me out of the city towards the hot baths of Hammat Tiberius. The southern shore has laguna's hugging the water's edge and water-slides of unbelievable size dominate the skyline. Fortunately, I was sufficiently early to miss the day's hedonist invasion! Abandoned and quiet these monstrosities of modern amusement appeared as the handiwork of some futuristic sculpture garden. Roy caught up with me near the Bereniki Beach at the junction with a minor road that climbs the hillside to the best positioned youth hostel in Israel. Breakfast was prepared and sitting in the boot. I was just finishing my second mouthful and reflecting on the fact that I would probably finish the day half an hour ahead of George when an apparition passed in front of me. I don't know what George had for breakfast but there he was jogging serenely past. Roy had been caught up in traffic in Tiberius and George had very nearly beaten him to me. The sight was an enormous boost to the morale, and by way of response my blisters grumbled louder than ever!

Just before finishing for the day we crossed the River Jordan at Yardenit which has been developed as a baptismal site. The traditional baptism site used by John the Baptist, near Jericho, is, for security reasons, only accessible on special feast days. There was therefore, for many years, nowhere on the River Jordan where pilgrims could readily commemorate Jesus' baptism or be baptized themselves. Appreciating the aesthetically pleasing nature of this stretch of the River Jordan, an entrepreneur, aware of the needs of pilgrims, developed an accessible alternative. A small area of water is railed off so baptism by immersion can safely take place. Plenty of room is provided for onlookers and fellow worshippers. Clean bathroom facilities, showers for those wishing to remove the physical effects of Jordan's water, a café and souvenir shop all add to the amenities. Plastic bottles can be purchased so that you can carry home your own sample of Jordan water for the next child's baptism. It was sure to be a success. Rumours are leaked that St Peter himself was baptised here and, behold, you have the birth of a new holy place! If trade is slow incentives can be offered to guides and drivers according to the amount that their groups spend.

The motives of the founders of this site are unlikely to have been other than commercial but does that matter if it has the desired effect? A number of now very respectable and ancient holy sites probably began in this way. I once saw a bus-load of elderly, female, Greek pilgrims washing their burial shrouds here, an act which I suspect would have taken place whether or not the surrounding amenities were present. Apart from its convenience the only redeeming feature, to my mind, is the frozen yoghurt, which, being a group leader, I used to receive free on a good day. The site provokes questions as to the purpose of modern pilgrimage.

Beside Yardenit is the country's first kibbutz, Degania Aleph, which was founded by Russian immigrants in 1910. The entrance is marked by a Syrian tank that was stopped in its tracks by kibbutz defenders during the 1948 War of Independence. Famous to the outsider as the birthplace of Moshe Dayan it is also remembered by Israeli's as the place where Aaron David Gordon worked and died, though without becoming a kibbutz member.

Brought up in the depths of a Ukrainian forest Gordon became well known as an intellectual and writer before moving to Palestine, aged 48.

Gordon was modest, sociable, tolerant. He worked to exhaustion, and he never saved a penny, as though the purpose of his work were not money but the work itself. I used to watch him, face running with sweat and his expression like that of a man in prayer, and when he rested he made me think of a pious Jew during the Neila prayer on the Day of Atonement. . . . He had a great love of manual labour and he thought that everybody should work with his hands. . . . 'You see,' he said, 'when you stand in a field and you use your pitchfork like this . . . and this . . . you feel well and you feel you have a right to live.' *He used to say that by work a man is healed.* [emphasis mine]

JOSEPH BARATZ: *A VILLAGE*

Gordon believed that

> the source of evil, as of good . . . was within man. The evils of
> society were manmade. It is man, the individual, who must
> 'preserve the image of God' in himself. . . . Nothing could make
> men happy unless they found the source of happiness, and this,
> according to him, lay in their relationship to the universe and to
> nature.

> Men should be drawn together and held by the same power that
> holds together everything in creation. It wasn't just a matter of
> living in the country or in town. A man could live in the country
> and be a stranger to it; then he would begin to feel a void inside
> himself and he would begin to fill this void with artificial satisfac-
> tions.

> What we know is merely a fragment of what we are. A man
> becomes an individual by the way in which he opens himself to the
> immediacy of the experience of life.

He argued that religion helped one to feel again an essential part of
creation though he accepted the sad fact that the formal expression of
religion had lost much of its vitality. 'The content of religion originates
in the religious individual; it is the expression of his sense of cosmic
unity and purpose. But men tend to sanctify religious forms at the
expense of religious content.' God, 'a mystery to the intellect, . . .
cannot be known, but he can be experienced and lived', indeed, though
'He is a hidden mystery, yet we encounter him in all we experience'.
The problem is that man's relationship with his fellow beings as well as
material things and the natural world has become purely utilitarian and
'authentic religion cannot survive in such an atmosphere'. His suggested
answer was 'the return to nature through labour', a religion of labour
perhaps, strongly influenced by Tolstoy, but, unlike Tolstoy, put into
practice.

Gordon further argued that, even as the individual is created in the image of God so should 'the people', that is the state be. This was the challenge faced by Eretz Israel.

We were the first to proclaim that man is created in the image of God. We must go farther and say: the nation must be created in the image of God. Not because we are better than others, but because we have borne upon our shoulders and suffered all which calls for this. It is by paying the price of torments the like of which the world has never known that we have won the right to be the first in this work of creation.

Prophetically, perhaps, he saw the crucial test to be found in the attitude of the Jews towards the Arabs:

Our attitude toward them must be one of humanity, of moral courage which remains on the highest plane, even if the behaviour of the other side is not all that is desired. Indeed their hostility is all the more a reason for our humanity.

'How shall this nation', he wrote, 'throw off two thousand years of the Diaspora?' And he answered, 'We, an alienated people with no roots in the soil and who are thus deprived of the power of creativeness, a people who have lived as parasites in towns and to whom by force of circumstances this has become second nature, we must return to the soil, to independence, to nature, to a regenerated life of work.'

Gordon died in 1922, before the horrors of the Holocaust and the 1948 battles for statehood. One can only speculate whether he would have found such high ideals too much of a burden given the demands of the hour. Many an Israeli voice has been raised since expressing the wish to be treated, and thought of, no differently from any other nation. Gordon's vision may not be completely lost at an individual level but it did prove to be too much for the structures of a modern state to absorb.

It is easy to understand why he was held in such esteem. A mystical philosopher whose musings found a spiritually hungry audience among those seeking to reclaim the land through their own labours. Joseph Baratz, one of the founders of Degania, was himself deeply effected by Gordon for similar ideas can be seen in his own writing:

> For what had happened while we were in exile? The land lost its fertility and it seemed to us that we ourselves, divorced from it, had become barren in spirit. Now we must give it our strength and it would give us back our creativeness. . . . What we wanted was to work ourselves, to be as self-supporting as we could and to do it not for wages but for the satisfaction of helping one another and of tending the soil. We knew that we needed one another's close and constant help because in the harsh conditions of the new country neither a person nor a family could stand alone, and it seemed likely that if we worked more closely together we should produce more. But we were not only thinking of producing big crops, though this was important since the country must support more people; the fact of producing – growing things – had for us a meaning which was related to the whole of human life. It was this wholeness we had lacked in exile.
>
> There we had been cut off from nature, from our roots, and everything had been distorted by the need for security – even the family had become a little fortress. We had to buy security with money and make money with whatever are the money-making faculties of the brain, we had lived on our brains and we hadn't used them properly because we had been cut off from the growing, natural side of life. That was why we had become so dry, so barren.
>
> JOSEPH BARATZ: *VILLAGE*

So it was that undergirded by these twin pillars of practical need and spiritual idealism that the kibbutz was born.

A kibbutz is not an organization, not a party grouping, it is a life lived together. It is not just a question of agreeing about principles, but of give and take, of understanding, of putting aside selfishness; we learned that it wasn't easy and that it didn't suit everybody. Such a community always started with a small group of friends, people who knew each other, who had worked together; it developed little by little, organically, gradually absorbing newcomers.

BARATZ

The emotions of this story fill me with an ill defined longing and remind me of the immense satisfaction I gain from activities as simple as the raking of leaves and freshly mown grass. I wonder whether English farmers ever express themselves in such a manner as Aaron David Gordon did or indeed could relate to such a spirituality of labour and land. Is it perhaps the soil of Palestine, sanctified as it is by the blood of the centuries, that is the prerequisite to fire such primordial passions?

The last six kilometres proved to be as difficult as any on the walk. It was the end of our fourth day's walking, about 110 km. done. To make matters worse I lost my hat along the way. So focused was I on finishing that I had not even noticed its falling from my head until caught by the sun. Roy and George returned to chivvy me along. The cold beer at the café beside the information booth where Route 90 turns south into the Jordan Valley tasted like nectar! The Sea of Galilee was really too much to absorb in one day, we could have done with a week exploring the area.

2 October, Day 7

A free day and an opportunity to do a little exploring. We had planned to visit as many of the Israeli hospices as possible so we started today with a trip to Nazareth. The Nazareth Hospice is a ward within the

Scottish Hospital that has been set up and is run by an Australian nursing sister Berris Bird. She took time out of a busy day to show us round and she spoke candidly about the seemingly endless problems they faced. Everything seemed to be a fight and despite having just returned from a four-week holiday she looked weighed down by the size of the task. There are no district nurse teams, enormous cultural differences exist within the various communities they seek to help and traditional medical practice seems content to say goodbye when there is no longer any potential for cure. Resources are stretched and the needs of the dying are not high on the agenda. Berris's husband works as a doctor in the outpatients' clinic and he kindly took a look at my throat. He reckoned that a course of antibiotics was essential if I was to have any hope of continuing to walk. I proved to be allergic to his prescription.

Nazareth is a busy car-jammed city famed for its Arabic sweets. Tucked away behind the popular Church of the Annunciation are the Sisters of Nazareth who run a pilgrim hostel and a residential school for blind and deaf girls. Sister Veronica's enormous drive and determination is inspirational. She and Diane, the gentle but efficient house mother of the hostel, gave us lunch and regaled us with stories of the community and school. Soon after moving in to their present premises a workman fell through the floor into an old cistern. Archaeologists were called in and to everybody's surprise one of the best examples of an ancient rolling stone tomb was uncovered. Above this is an area that some argue shows the remains of a first-century Nazareth home. Nazareth was certainly much smaller then, a couple of dozen families only. Might this have been the site of Joseph's home? It may be little more than romantic desire that links the two but it is without doubt a preferable location for remembering than the nearby St Joseph's church.

On the way back to Tiberius we stopped at Cana in order to buy the obligatory bottle of wedding wine. The church commemorates Jesus' first miracle, the turning of water into wine at a wedding party. After supper at our hotel George received a phone call from home with the news that his daughter would be getting married two days after he returned from the walk. I also heard from home though the message was very different. Sarah's dry sense of humour did a great deal to lift my spirits. 'The wardrobe door has collapsed. There is water coming through the kitchen roof. It has not stopped raining all day. We all went to Sainsbury's, 2 children and a mother who is still deaf in one ear. So did everyone else in Wandsworth. I screamed at three drivers and two people pushing trolleys. I hope you are having a nice time.'

3 October, Day 8

Fresh from a day's break we set off enthusiastically into the lower Jordan Valley. The area immediately south of the lake is lush and fertile, nourished as it is by the Jordan River, the Yarmuk River joining it from the east and a number of underground springs. We soon approached the entrance to Afiqim, one of Israel's wealthier *kibbutzim* from where we enjoyed a spectacular view across the Jordan and on into the Yarmuk Valley. Layer upon layer of hills stacked up against a pre-dawn sky. The air was fresh and we were determined to push on as quickly as possible before having to compete with the sun from which there promised to be little shade. The days would be getting hotter the further south we travelled.

Apart from one brief showing the Jordan River was to remain hidden from view. The southern Jordan is not as old as that feeding the Sea of Galilee, as there was once a lissan lake that covered the length of the valley as far as the Dead Sea. As this slowly dried up two unconnected lakes remained, the Sea of Galilee fed by the northern Jordan River and, isolated to the south, the Dead Sea. In the intense heat of the valley the waters of the Dead Sea evaporated thus creating the high salt content for which it is now famous. Then, about 15,000 years ago the Sea of Galilee burst its banks and began to find its way south towards the Dead Sea through the then dry bed of the ancient lissan lake. At that time the height differential between the Sea of Galilee and the Dead Sea was not as great as it is today and thus the river had to meander its way slowly through 193 km. of desolate valley before covering the 104 km. direct distance. Mark Twain once described the River Jordan as 'so crooked that a man does not know which side of it he is on half the time.'

The waters of the Dead Sea continued to evaporate causing the height differential with the Kinnereth to increase. This in turn made the river flow faster leading to the deepening of its channel. Thus today the Jordan Valley has two heights, the main valley through which we walked, known in the Bible as *kikar hayarden* and the lower valley, *gaon hayarden*, that is 'the Jordan's flood area'. It is this lower area with its dense undergrowth and wild animals that modern politics has sadly put beyond reach.

We finished walking just south of Beth Shean and but a few miles from the West Bank territory. The morning had passed quickly and there was a definite smell of desert in the air. It would not be long before the greens of Galilee were but a faded dream. Apart from spending 45 minutes queuing at three separate locations in a bank in Beth Shean (Israel's financial bureaucracy has to be experienced to be believed) we decided that we were too hot and exhausted to explore the extensive archaeological remains. Thus, apart from a brief visit to the Crusader fortress of Belvoir with its impressive views over the lower Jordan Valley we returned to Tiberius to pack and sleep.

It is Beth Shean's geographical position, at the meeting of the Jordan and Harod Valleys, the latter leading west into the Jezreel Valley and thence to the Mediterranean, that has given the town its importance. Ancient roads generally followed valley systems and Beth Shean, once known as Scythopolis, found itself at the hub of a network of Roman roads. The surrounding area was also famed for its agricultural productivity. Rainfall may be erratic as a result of its proximity to the desert, but this is more than compensated for by over 30 natural springs which between them are estimated to produce more than 130 million cu. m. each year.

If you look up Beth Shean in the *Encyclopedia Judaica* you read the following note, 'In the War of Independence, Beth Shean capitulated on 12 May 1948 to Jewish forces, who found it deserted by its former inhabitants. The settlement of Beth Shean by Jewish immigrants began in 1949.' However, Canon Naim Ateek, for many years our next door neighbour in Jerusalem, has written his version of events that day:

> I had just turned eleven in 1948 when the Zionists occupied my hometown, Beisan (Beth Shean). We had no army to protect us. There was no battle, no resistance, no killing; we were simply taken over, occupied, on Wednesday, May 12, 1948. . . . The state of Israel was proclaimed two days later. We lived under occupation for fourteen days. On May 26, the military governor sent for the leading men of the town; at military headquarters, he informed them quite simply and coldly that Beisan must be evacuated by all of its inhabitants within a few hours. My father pleaded with him, 'I have nowhere to go with my large family. Let us stay in our home.' . . . I remember vividly my father's return from headquarters to give us the bad news. With great anguish he said, 'We have been given no choice. We must go.' The next two hours were very difficult. I can recall with great precision what happened, almost minute by minute. . . . As people gathered at the centre of town, the soldiers separated us into two groups, Muslims and Christians. The Muslims were sent across the Jordan River to the country of Transjordan (now Jordan). The Christians were taken on buses, driven to the outskirts of Nazareth, and dropped off there, since Nazareth had not yet been occupied by the Zionists. Within a few hours, our family had become refugees, driven out of Beisan forever.

> NAIM ATEEK: *THEOLOGY OF LIBERATION*

If they can't agree on what happened in 1948 what hope is there that the more distant history of this land was accurately recorded?

As far as I know they never received any compensation for the loss of their home and subsequent displacement. It was ten years before they had the freedom to travel without a military permit and thus on Israel's Independence Day in 1958 the Ateeks returned to visit Beisan.

Some homes had been pulled down. Our little church was used as a storehouse. The Roman Catholic church and its adjacent buildings had become a school. The Orthodox church was left to rot. The Beisan we knew was left to gradually become a ruin while a new Israeli Jewish town was sprouting on the edge of it. Our homes were still standing and several families were occupying them. I still remember that when we asked permission to go inside, just to take a look, our request was turned down. One occupant said very emphatically, 'This is not your house; it is ours.'

There have been many arguments over the details of what took place in 1948 where the displacement of the Arab population was concerned. In this instance I have no reason to doubt Naim's story. When trying to explain the distance that existed between the Palestinians and Israelis as far as their understanding each other's situation he would tell the following story:

Imagine yourself in your own home and some people arrive with nowhere to live. The rules of hospitality lead you to invite them in and you share your resources with them. As they grow in number you are disturbed by the dawning realization that you are slowly being pushed out of your own home until one day you wake up and find yourself in the garden. Understandably communication breaks down and tempers begin to flare. Eventually the new inhabitants of your home come into the garden and say 'Let's talk about making peace'; to which you reply 'certainly, but first we have to speak of justice'.

Resh Lakish, a third-century scholar, stated 'If paradise is situated in the land of Israel, its entrance is Beth Shean.' How many, I wonder, would agree with him today?

✦

CHAPTER SIX

Through the Jordan Valley to Jericho

We need wilderness whether or not we ever set foot in it. We need a refuge even though we may never need to go there. . . . We need the possibility of escape as surely as we need hope; without it the life of the cities would drive all men into crime or drugs or psychoanalysis.

EDWARD ABBEY: *DESERT SOLITAIRE*

Her being had, however intangibly, undergone a change of course and come under the pull of a mysterious force of gravity in the human spirit which determines that a journey into the unknown in the world without produces a movement towards new and unknown areas in our world within.

LAURENS VAN DER POST: *A FAR OFF PLACE*

4 October, Day 9

WE LEFT TIBERIUS before dawn and were walking by five o'clock. It was beginning to feel as though we were making progress and by the end of the day we would be half-way between the Sea of Galilee and the Dead Sea: one overflowing with fertility and the other capable of bearing no life. As though a presage of this transition from life to death Mt Gilboa dominated the beginning of the journey. Sentinel to the Jezreel Valley, supposed site of Armageddon, that lies due west of Beth Shean it also, in its dignified silence, bears witness to that famous battle when Saul and Jonathan were slain by the Philistines.

> And David lamented with this lamentation over Saul and
> Jonathan his son.
> Thy glory, O Israel, is slain upon thy high places!
> How are the mighty fallen!
> Tell it not in Gath,
> publish it not in the streets of Ashkelon;
> lest the daughters of the Philistines rejoice,
> lest the daughters of the uncircumcised exult.
>
> Ye mountains of Gilboa,
> let there be no dew or rain upon you,
> nor upsurging of the deep!
> For there the shield of the mighty was defiled,
> the shield of Saul, not anointed with oil.
>
> From the blood of the slain,
> from the fat of the mighty,
> the bow of Jonathan turned not back,
> and the sword of Saul returned not empty.
>
> Saul and Jonathan, beloved and lovely!

In life and in death they were not divided;
they were swifter than eagles,
they were stronger than lions.

Ye daughters of Israel, weep over Saul,
who clothed you daintily in scarlet,
who put ornaments of gold upon your apparel.

How are the mighty fallen
in the midst of the battle!

Jonathan lies slain upon thy high places.
I am distressed for you, my brother Jonathan;
very pleasant have you been to me;
your love to me was wonderful,
passing the love of women.

How are the mighty fallen,
and the weapons of war perished!

2 *SAMUEL*, 1

Echoes of this haunting lament followed us as we negotiated some small but vicious dogs in Sede Terumot, the last Israeli village prior to entering the West Bank. The 1948–67 border would have been hard to locate were it not for the army checkpoint and the sudden change in land usage south of the Bezeq River. Surprisingly, this turned out to be a river with running water. A large herd of cattle following its bank passed beneath the bridge as we crossed over.

The calming greens of Galilean fields were now replaced by a harvest of rocks and herds of goats tended by young lads on donkeys whistling wistfully on tin pipes. We were passing from the sown into the desert, from communities that could rely on the seasons and their fields to produce wealth, enabling them to settle, trade and build cities, to a wasteland where you always have to be on the move looking for the next day's food and water. The use of drip irrigation (thin black hoses with pin pricks at selected intervals which only allow water to escape at each seed, thus minimizing waste) makes this transition seem more sudden than in reality it is. Within feet we passed from irrigated extravagance to barren despair. The goats added poignancy, the dream of every pilgrim's camera invoking as they do an imagined biblical past.

If like Daniel Hillel you define a desert as an area with 'a total annual rainfall of less than 250 mm. and a continental type temperature regime of hot summers and often cool winters' then we were not quite there for rainfall here might still reach 300 mm. plus. However, within 48 km. we could be sure that we had arrived at the 200 mm. mark. Every step south took us further into the desert, we were walking towards aridity and into a yawning silence. Upon reflection I can see that this dramatic change to our external environment was balanced by a subtle change within. The Golan Heights were fascinating, Galilee was beautiful, but it was the desert that I craved. This I realized was the driving force behind the whole venture. 'Man was born in the desert, in Africa. By returning to the desert he rediscovers himself. . . . To be lost in the desert was to find one's way to God.' (Bruce Chatwin: *Songlines*) 'I felt drawn to this wasteland, in no way that I could yet articulate, but through a growing sense of excitement within.' (Michael Asher: *Forty Days Road*)

Geographically I knew where we were but within myself I became increasingly disorientated. The lack of external stimuli meant that distractions were few and I found myself with increasingly little on which to focus my mind. I began to count paces even as my eyes searched for the next distance marker. George and I shared a good deal of conversation but I remember little of it. My thoughts frequently turned to home and sex became a disturbingly dominant theme, undiminished even by the relentless heat of the desert sun.

Abbot Cyrus of Alexandria, questioned as to the imagination of lust, made answer: 'If thou hast not these imaginings, thou are without hope: for if thou hast not the imagination thereof, thou hast the deed itself. For he who fights not in his mind against sin, nor gainsays it, sins in the flesh. And he who sins in the flesh, hath no trouble from the imagination thereof.

HELEN WADDELL: *DESERT FATHERS*

Abba Sisoes' disciple said to him, 'Father, you are growing old. Let us go back to inhabited country.' The old man said to him, 'Let us go where there are no women'. His disciple said to him, 'Where is there a place where there are no women except the desert?' So the old man said, 'Take me to the desert.'

BENEDICTA WARD: *SAYINGS*

I would not want to leave the impression that such thoughts worried me or that I thought them wrong in any way. I might have been more concerned had I not felt such lust. Being on a forced diet does not prevent you from focusing on the menu. My concern was that they should not dominate continually as they threatened at one point to do. 'Meeting some nuns on the road, a monk made a detour. The superior said to him: "If you were a perfect monk, you would not have noticed we were women." ' (Benedicta Ward: *Wisdom*)

Near the settlement of Mehola we were overwhelmed by the smell of fresh coffee and warm bread. At first sight it appeared to be little more that a tin shack café but the clean, fresh looking tables and chairs hinted otherwise. Forgetting all our rules about not breaking the journey we halted and indulged in the most delicious hot chocolate croissants that I had ever tasted, washed down with filter coffee. It was almost impossible to get to our feet again. I could not believe it when, upon entering the portacabin men's toilet, I saw religious graffiti on the walls. There was a quotation from Bruce Springsteen that seemed to express surprise at the fact that at the end of a hard day's work people are still able to find time to believe. Believe what? I wondered. Beneath someone had added: 'I try to live my life as best I know how.' Was this also Springsteen or the beginning of a graffiti dialogue?

It was our first day on the desert fringe and I should not have been too hard on my disorganized mind, adapting as it was to the freedom that this external barrenness provoked. I disciplined myself to keep looking out, beyond myself. We passed acres of torn polythene that had once been stretched taut over wire hoops in rows across dusty fields. I assumed that the condensation collected on the inside of these plastic tunnels would be sufficient for the tomatoes, cucumbers, lettuces and melons that we saw being sold on the side of the road. The far side of the Jordan looked to be more fertile with large green fields and a chain of small farming communities for as far as the eye could see.

For a while we were able to enjoy the luxury of walking on half an inch of loess (wind-blown dust deposit that is very fertile when irrigated) which had a good spring to it. Occasional wet patches had to be avoided at all costs as they form an extremely heavy mud. It was this soft surface that made me realize just how badly I was walking – leaning heavily on the instep of my right foot. Calf-strain could now be added to the list of woes.

It is said of the carcasses of meat hanging in the butchers' quarter of the old city of Jerusalem that there has to be something good about them: a million flies can't all be wrong! By the same standard there must be plenty that is good about the desert. (Though we would have been perfectly happy without the flies.) They would arrive with the sun, forcing us to take our breakfast early and refrain from breathing through the mouth. There is nothing quite so abhorrent as swallowing a fly and luckily I indulged only three or four times. Roy bought some Pif-Paf which was sprayed with great abandon within the car, after which he would then not open the doors to us for fear of a fresh invasion so our water and food had to be stored in the boot. I'm surprised that he even let us in at the end of the day. My *keffiyeh* came into its own as a substitute horse-hair swat.

We finished at kilometre marker 345 on a line between Jerash to the east and Netanya to the west and then drove on to Almog where we arrived in time for lunch and a well-earned afternoon by the pool. Almog is well and truly in the desert, framed by the hills of Judea and Moab, just a few miles south of Jericho and overlooking the Dead Sea. A small oasis of paradise in a forbidding and hostile terrain. We were welcomed by a hoopoe bird, with its long curved bill and distinguished black and white stripes on wings and crest, dancing on the lawn in front of our rooms.

Early in the evening another fax arrived from Sarah letting me know that the rain continued to pour in through the kitchen roof. I had visions of the rear extension of our flat collapsing. It was both difficult and frustrating communicating only by fax and telephone, making for unreal perception, and putting a limit on sensitivity. This fax ended, 'My faxes seem meaningless when I look at what I thought I'd sent. . . . Perhaps no communication is better – silence. Words seem empty.'

5 October, Day 10

Setting out while it was still dark along a section of road that sits right up against the border fence made me uneasy and just a little frightened. It was not long before we were stopped by an Israeli border patrol. There is a security track, consisting of very powdery soil, next to the fence that is regularly raked and searched for footprints. It is near impossible to cross without leaving some evidence behind and we were careful to walk on the opposite side of the road. As we crossed over to meet the patrol I must have taken one step too many for they all suddenly jumped from their vehicle and shouted for us to stand still. The force of their reaction almost had me wondering whether we had walked onto an unmarked mine field! I carefully backtracked to the road. Their concern turned out to be no more than a desire not to confuse later patrols.

After this brief episode we were asked the standard questions which produced the same bemused smiles from the teenage soldiers. Their lack of English and my almost non-existent Hebrew added to the slightly ludicrous nature of this encounter. Finally with a shrug of the shoulders they let us continue, making it clear that we were to remain well away from the security track.

The road moved slightly away from the border as we approached the Palestinian community of Marj en-Na'ja beside Wadi Abu Sidra. The village was already bustling with life and everyone seemed to be making their way to the fields in order to work before the heat of the day. The elderly men sat astride donkeys, a few clung to the back of a tractor and some women, wearing traditional embroidered long black dresses, carried the day's requirements on their head. It was an evocative and timeless scene. It was impossible to be inconspicuous and the flag of St George flying from my straw hat didn't help. After explaining our venture in sign language to one particularly curious lady she was adamant that we should stop and take *shai*, tea, with her. It was tempting but again we dare not because the late morning heat in which we finished our day's walking was becoming increasingly intolerable.

Arabs are famed for their hospitality and it went against the grain to refuse. Major C. S. Jarvis, a former governor of Sinai, tells the following sobering story concerning the consequences of rejecting hospitality:

To refuse hospitality without good cause is an offence. On one occasion two Arabs were hurrying to attend a court – they were probably several days late when they started – and passed the tent of a solitary Nekhlawi Arab. He called to them to dismount and take coffee, but they replied that they were pressed for time and could not wait.

'By God,' said he, 'you would not insult me by refusing my hospitality if I had my rifle with me.'

'It would be all the same,' they replied, 'if you had your rifle or not. We are late for the meeting and must hurry.' They then rode off, but the Nekhlawi, feeling grossly insulted, hurried back to the tent of his cousin where he had left his rifle, and, having secured it, gave chase on a camel. On getting within range of the two

Arabs he kept up a running fire till he wounded one in the leg, whereupon the other dismounted and shot him through the head. This case, incidentally, caused a considerable amount of trouble, as such a thing as justifiable homicide does not exist in the Arab world, and, moreover, the Nekhlawi tribe considered they had been grossly insulted — to be shot through the head is bad enough, but to have one's coffee refused is unthinkable.

C. S. JARVIS: *YESTERDAY*

Adam's junction marked the half-way point for the day. This is where Wadi Farah comes down from Nablus (ancient Shechem) and meets the River Jordan at Gesher Adam (Adam's bridge). Large Mercedes lorries packed high with onions were parked at the junction waiting for the opportunity to export their wares to Jordan. It is possible that Abraham crossed the Jordan at this point when on his way to Shechem. Another theory has it that it was here that the waters of the Jordan once stood still, enabling Joshua and his army to cross over 'dry footed', further down. The mud must have been unbelievable. Occasionally earthquakes have been known to cause rock falls that have temporarily blocked the flow of the river.

Beyond the junction is the conical shaped Hasmonean—Herodian fortified mountain Sartaba, otherwise known as the Alexandrium. It is the northern most of a chain of fortresses that guarded the eastern boundary of Herod the Great's kingdom. It was also one of a long line of mountains which was used to signal, by the lighting of bonfires, the beginning of the new month and the arrival of holy days. Thus the modern settlement at the base of Sartaba is named Massu'a, meaning bonfire. 'They used to take long cedarwood sticks and rushes and oleaster-wood and flax-tow: and a man bound these up with a rope and went up to the mount and set light to them and he waved them to and fro and up and down until he could see his fellow doing the like on the top of the next mountain. And so on, too, on the top of the third mount. (Talmud Yerushalmi, from Zev Vilnay: *Legends*)

The valley broadens out significantly beneath Adam's junction and we could see the road ahead of us swinging west to stay close to the Judean mountains which began to drop dramatically into the valley. It was tempting to cut across the fields but a lack of clear paths suggested that a possible shortcut might deteriorate into a major detour and we thought better of it. It was not long before we reached the entrance to Gilgal, another modern settlement, founded in 1970, where we were able to call it a day. As to the site of ancient Gilgal, where 12 stones were laid by Joshua's forces in commemoration of their safe crossing of the Jordan, no one is certain.

Between Jericho and the River Jordan sits the Greek Orthodox monastery of St Gerasimus known popularly as Deir Hajla. From a distance it looks like a small square fortress but the top half of a silver dome breaking the skyline suggests that there is more to be found. Founded by Gerasimus in 455 it grew into a monastery surrounded by 70 hermitages, many of which were cut into the side of the nearby Wadi en-Nukheil. By the 12th century only one monk remained, 'befriended by two lions living among the dense undergrowth along the Jordan', and then for many years the site stood empty before rebuilding began late in the 19th century.

We were booked in to spend a night here, determined to have the genuine pilgrim experience. I had stayed once before and remembered it as exceptionally spartan but even so I was ill prepared for the ramshackle environment we found ourselves in. The courtyard around the main entrance, looking like a cross between a builder's yard and a scrap metal dump, should have warned us of what lay ahead but we thought it was no more than the side effects of renovation works that were in progress. At the sight of the dead budgerigar in its cage we should have turned and fled but it hardly even raised our eyebrows at the time, probably no more than a lucky break for one of the hundreds of half-wild cats that infested the area.

The senior monk was away when we arrived and it seemed to take for ever to find someone who knew that we were booked in to stay. Two labourers couldn't bring themselves to consider this possibility but a young Greek lad finally appeared and pointed to our rooms. It was the most unwelcome greeting that we were to receive on the whole of the journey. Having shown us where we could find some drinking water in the kitchen he returned to his table in the inner courtyard, which doubled up as a packing factory for religious tack, where he continued stuffing cheap icons into cellophane covers.

The kitchen was indescribable, so bad that even after 20 miles of walking we experienced an immediate loss of appetite. However, being British to a fault we kept our thoughts to ourselves and began unloading the car. Roy and George shared a room of six beds whilst I, because of my snoring, placed myself in a small outer room. Paint was flaking from the walls and ceiling and just across the corridor the toilet door was swinging from its hinges. The toilet doubled up as a shower as we discovered when our young Greek neighbour stood there, for all the world to see, making good use of it. He had an attractive young wife and child with him and together they had the room next to ours. Perhaps his frostiness was the result of feeling territorial.

Being exhausted we were all keen to sleep, hoping at the same time that it would all look better when we woke. At least someone had taken the trouble of putting sheets on the bed. It didn't take long for me to realize that this must have been the last occupant and even more disturbing were the hairs he had left behind. Then I started to itch, though this may well have been my imagination. The fact that it was the hottest time of the day, without even a breeze, and that there was no electricity let alone air conditioning, just added to the fun. Although not a word had been said I began to feel the vibes coming through from Roy and George's room.

I had billed this as the real thing, pilgrimage as it was meant to be, simple and without unnecessary luxury. I hadn't banked on all the filth. There didn't seem to be any excuse for it, it was just plain dirty. Being unable to rest I walked through to Roy and George and spoke my mind. Within two minutes we were in the car and on our way back to Almog! On the way out we passed the young mother seated in the corridor with her child, in a pram, beside her. An elderly monk was waving an incense burner around the child whilst making mumbled incantations which regularly included the name of St Gerasimus. To protect the child from us perhaps? No one seemed surprised, or sad, to see us leave.

I imagine that the great Gerasimus would have had little time for us, softened as we are by our comfortable life styles. He was renowned for his asceticism and it is said that throughout lent he went totally without food, content simply with the bread of communion each Sunday.

Cyril of Scythopolis recorded the following anecdote about 'great Gerasimus'.

Some of his anchorites (the hermits who lived alone in their cells) came to him saying: 'Give us permission to make ourselves a hot drink, to eat cooked food and to light a lamp during nocturnal office, so that we can read.' But he answered: 'If you even desire to drink eucration, [a warm drink used by the monks], eat cooked food and read under a lamp, you had better stay in the coenobium [that is the central part of the monastery inhabited by those not thought to be ready for the rigours of the ascetic life]; 'for I shall not permit this while I am alive.'

YIZHAR HIRSCHFELD

Not all the monks were this strict.

Some old men came to see Abba Poemen and said to him, 'When we see brothers who are dozing at the liturgy, shall we rouse them so that they will be watchful?' He said to them, 'For my part when I see that a brother is dozing, I put his head on my knees and let him rest.'

BENEDICTA WARD: *SAYINGS*

It seems to have been generally agreed that 'all bodily comfort is an abomination to the Lord.' (Ward) Occasional outbursts of common sense stand out all the more for their scarcity.

> A hunter in the desert saw Abba Anthony enjoying himself with
> the brethren and he was shocked. Wanting to show him that it was
> necessary sometimes to meet the needs of the brethren, the old
> man said to him, 'Put an arrow in your bow and shoot it.' So he
> did. The old man then said, 'Shoot another,' and he did so. The
> old man said, 'Shoot yet again,' and the hunter replied, 'If I bend
> my bow so much I will break it.' Then the old man said to him, 'It
> is the same with the work of God. If we stretch the brethren
> beyond measure, they will soon break. Sometimes it is necessary
> to come down to meet their needs.'
>
> BENEDICTA WARD: *SAYINGS*

I dread to think what they would have made of us, guiltless as we felt,
resting by the side of the pool attempting to catch the eye of one of
Israel's most beautiful and vain lifeguards. Almog stands in sharp
contrast to the ascetic traditions of this Judean Wilderness, though they
have the healthy precedence of Herod's winter palace to support them.
I know where I was happy to be that night. Not that they offer five-star
accommodation at Almog, far from it, and I wouldn't have enjoyed it if
they did. It is simple, clean, friendly and air-conditioned.

6 October, Day 11

The thought of walking through Jericho, so much the focus of world
attention, followed by a two-day break in Jerusalem, meant that we set
out in high spirits from Gilgal. We had our packing down to a fine art
and we could be on our way within half an hour of waking. This was just
long enough for George to do his exercises, me to bandage my feet, and
Roy to pack the car. Remarkably neither George or I ever finished before
the car was ready. Roy was very long-suffering. It was a relatively short
drive from Almog back to Gilgal, and we were in good time.

Dawn began to break as we approached Niran. To begin with it was no more than a thin strip of light sitting on top of the hills, held down by the full weight of a night reluctant to depart. Then, slowly, a red light began to arrive and darkness was defeated. Opposite the entrance to Niran there are some abandoned earth works which George and I were both drawn towards. It was as though we had a need to climb above the floor of the valley in order to participate in this turning of the night. I don't know exactly what it was that made this morning's sunrise so spectacularly different but it must have had something to do with the view. The vast Ghor el-Katar spread north of us and though the Zor (thicket) of the Jordan could not be seen its route was easily discernable. The outskirts of Jericho's greenery was visible to the south. There was space, a staggering skyline and that invasive pre-dawn stillness.

Once again the hypnotic silence of the desert subtly drew us into its spell. Without realizing it we had stopped, held fast in our tracks, in order to soak it up. The day's walking was forgotten, only that moment existed. Time seemed to stand still, we were caught by the power of the present moment. 'Peregrinatio est tacere. To be silent keeps us pilgrims' (Henri Nouwen, The Way of The Heart)

For the time being, around my place at least, the air is untroubled, and I became aware for the first time today of the immense silence in which I am lost. Not a silence so much as a great stillness – for there are a few sounds: the creak of some bird in a juniper tree, an eddy of wind which passes and fades like a sigh, the ticking of the watch on my wrist – slight noises which break the sensation of absolute silence but at the same time exaggerate my sense of the surrounding, overwhelming peace. A suspension of time, a continuous present. If I look at the small device strapped to my wrist the numbers, even the sweeping second hand, seem meaningless, almost ridiculous.

EDWARD ABBEY: DESERT SOLITAIRE

Who needs so-called holy places I wondered. Just get up in time for sunrise and make your way into the desert.

We finally tore ourselves away and continued, silently at first, on the road to Jericho. Mud-brick houses with courtyards crammed full of goats near the tiny village, Khirbet el 'Auja et-Tahta finally succeeded in breaking the spell. Dust hung in the morning air and dogs noisily made the most of their unusual visitors. From here it was but a short journey into Jericho. We passed flattened refugee camps that once housed as many as 70,000 Palestinians but which were now marked by no more than an isolated UNWRA flag and a store selling clay garden pots. Just west of the road ruins of the sixth-century synagogue of Na'aran, which had a mosaic floor which included the signs of the zodiac, reminded us of an earlier vibrant Jewish community. The site was covered in large Israeli flags and a handful of gun-toting religious nationalists watched us pass. A few yards further on a road led east towards the impressive Islamic hunting lodge, Hisham's Palace. Jericho has always attracted the wealthy during the winter months and though named after Hisham ibn Abd al-Malik (724–43) 'who ruled an empire stretching from India to the Pyrenees' it was probably his profligate nephew and successor Walid ibn Yazid (743–44) who sought the joys of this bath and surrounding hunting grounds. The Zor of the Jordan was once famous for its wildlife, including lions, jackals and wolves.

It seemed like a lifetime ago that we had passed through Jericho on our way north to Hermon and yet we had been walking for only eight days and were not even half-way to Eilat. It was good to be back. The orange juice tasted better than ever and we were given bags of fresh fruit to take away with us. I sat in the back of the shop while Roy and George indulged in a little more bartering. A few early tourists were beginning to arrive on the scene when, totally unexpectedly, Bill Broughton appeared. It was great to see him again and he informed us that he had arranged a reception for us in Jerusalem which would be hosted by the British consul general. Recognition at last!

It was John Garstang who, as a result of his archaeological work in the 1930s, provoked the *Daily Telegraph* headline 'Walls of Joshua found'. He discovered an ancient wall that seemed to have been destroyed by earthquake and fire, which he dated to the 15th century BCE. His method though was primitive and his dating erroneous. Biblical historians have long argued as to whether Joshua was around in the 15th or the 13th century BCE, the latter date being the more popular. The indefatigable Dame Kathleen Kenyon, doyen of modern archaeology, working on the site from 1952–59, concluded that it was unoccupied in the 13th and 15th centuries. She was therefore forced to conclude that there was no walled city at the time of Joshua, whichever date you prefer! Her scholarly integrity led her to be vilified by many biblical fundamentalists whose religious convictions were threatened by her findings. The saddest aspect of this whole affair was that, in the ensuing furore, her dating of a newly uncovered monumental tower to around 8,000 BCE was all but ignored at a popular level. This find provoked a debate about the date, origins and development of urban civilization which is arguably of far greater significance than whether or not Joshua's trumpets blew some walls down. 'Palestine, as represented by Jericho, can therefore put forward a good claim to be one of the places in which there took place the transition from a nomadic way of life to the settled existence that is the prerequisite of all development towards civilization.' (Kathleen Kenyon: *Archaeology*)

Archaeology of itself does not prove or disprove the biblical text. It does though help to provide some background information about the settings of various narratives. That the book of Joshua was compiled 6–700 years after the stories recorded, that the battle for Jericho reads more like a liturgical procession than the record of a military campaign, that it is not set within a wider political context and that the major point being made is clearly that it is God who won the victory and led them into the land can all be made without any reference to archaeology. If Joshua visited Jericho at all I reckon it would have been for the orange juice! That or the balsam trees if they had but existed then.

With ten kilometres still to be done and Jerusalem beckoning we dragged ourselves back out into the sun. Apart from winter weekends when all sensible folk leave Jerusalem and Ramallah for the open air restaurants that line the main streets of Jericho it had always struck me as a sleepy town. It will be interesting to see how it changes during the coming years. Real estate prices have shot up since the announcement that it is to receive a degree of autonomy.

The road going south from Jericho is long, straight and tedious. Another refugee camp is passed, fronted by a large YMCA training centre. Opposite the camp we saw our first camels and to begin with we thought that they were wandering wild. It was only when Roy started to take photographs that a lad, who can have been no older than eight, appeared from behind a suaeda bush ('sea blite') and ran towards us screaming for baksheesh.

Apart from that minor distraction it was sheer slog and though we only walked 26.5 km. it seemed a lot further. It brought us past the 200 km. mark which boosted our morale. We finished close to Kibbutz Almog at the point where the track starts to descend into Nahal Og. By crossing the *wadi* and following a dirt track down to Qumran we would save ourselves ten kilometres on the main road. Fortunately we returned to the kibbutz for lunch since another fax had arrived from Sarah. It brilliantly summed up all that she was feeling.

> I envy your freedom, the sheer physicalness of it all. The clear air, the wind, even the blisters. I envy the difference of it all: the stark contrast to the drudgery of tube, dirty dingy offices, tired worn out, underpaid employees. The tedium of domestic trivia – all is dust, decaying edifices around us, just like Gabriel Marquez. I feel like the elements creeping in from outside would get us in the end if it were not for the toil that pours money to block them out. My solace in the day is sitting on our bed feeding Phoebe and reading to Polly.

We arrived at the Azzahra Hotel in East Jerusalem by half past three. It is a large converted house rumoured to have had connections with the royal Hashemite family. We had a three-bedded room overlooking the patio/dining area and a large Palestinian flag hung from our window.

This took a bit of getting used to as it wasn't that long ago that you would have been imprisoned for such a public showing of Palestinian nationalism. There is definitely a sense of hope and expectancy in the air though no one is getting carried away. 'What's in a flag?' asked a friend in Jericho. 'We must wait five or ten years in order to see what this peace means.' The Palestinians are used to waiting and many are convinced that time is ultimately on their side.

7 October, Day 12

After an early breakfast we set off for the Old City. I had already warned George and Roy that I was in no fit state to guide them round but we initially stayed together. Our first stop was the money changers where we were able to get an exchange rate better than the banks and without commission being charged. That made for a good start. Then it was to a sports shop so that I could buy a pair of trainers as George was convinced that they would be easier on my feet. Though double the price of the same in London they were to more than pay their way.

I had one visit only that I wished to make in the Old City, to the Armenian Pottery. It is a small store hidden off the Via Dolorosa where some of the most exquisite pottery to be found in Jerusalem can be purchased. Everything is made on site and the volume of stock is small so you just have to hope that they have something you like. Most of the pottery sold in the Old City is tacky, touristy and poor quality. So it brings a reward all of its own to discover an artisan among the dross. I splashed out before stopping to think about the logistics of carrying a box of breakables with me over the next four weeks.

Entering the Old City through Herod's Gate I took Roy and George to St Ann's church on the way to the pottery. It is an impressive Crusader edifice with a superb acoustic. We sat near the altar while a Pentecostal group filed in and began to sing. They quickly proceeded from the stock choruses to singing in tongues (which is where they allow the spirit of God to replace their language with a 'heavenly' one).

George had never heard anything like it before and we all sat quite mesmerized. To my surprise it seemed appropriate for the setting with the building's echo adding to the overtones of the impromptu harmonies.

I was glad to have some space to myself. Returning first to St George's College, I looked up the newest member of staff now responsible for running and developing their desert programmes. As well as teaching he was completing a Master's programme on the desert and mid-life crisis.

Returning to the Azzahra I had coffee with Hani Abu Dayyie, joint owner of NET (Near East Tours) one of the two largest tourist companies in the country. He had just returned from delivering a paper (Peace 2000: peace for sustainable tourism and tourism for sustainable peace) in Europe and was fired with enthusiasm for the possibilities that peace in the Middle East could bring. The year 2000 has been declared a year of peace by the Higher Council of the Arab Tourist Industry in Palestine. (I imagine that there will be quite a party in Jerusalem on New Years Eve 1999.) In his presentation he had quoted from the present Pope's message to the World Congress on Tourism in 1988:

Tourism is born of peace and leads to peace. It responds to a desire to meet and to know other peoples and other countries. It presupposes conditions of economic, political and ideological freedom, which make such human encounters with others possible and meaningful. It can and should lead to a better understanding and respect for ways of life different from our own. Tourism has a powerful potential for educational and cultural exchanges that broaden the horizon of the human spirit to embrace the unity of the whole human family. By facilitating more authentic social contact between individuals, tourism can help overcome many prejudices and foster new bonds of friendship and fraternity. In this way tourism strengthens unity and solidarity between individuals and between nations and so builds peace.

Hani is a genuine believer in such possibilities which is partly what makes him such an effective businessman. I confess to being a little more cynical. The vast majority of tourists seem to make no contact at all with indigenous communities other than the staff of the hotel, and they seem to have little desire to do otherwise. Most tourism seems to be about little more than amusement, rest and indulgence.

When I lived in Jerusalem I had dreamed of being able to return on my own terms without obligations to anyone. This walk was very much a fulfilment of that yearning. In all my enthusiasm though, and consumed as I was by the demands of work and the need to prepare myself, I had not taken time to stop and ask how it was going to be for Sarah, who would be working and looking after two children at the same time. The reality of her situation was not to hit me until much later though I was beginning to get a hint of it from the faxes and telephone calls. She had been nothing but supportive because she knew how much it all meant to me. If I had been but slightly more sensitive I may have appreciated what it was that I was asking of her, and the walk may never have happened. Perhaps there has to be something intrinsically selfish about the driven adventurer.

I sat down to pen a fax back to Sarah. Words weren't easy to find and compared to her intensity my musings seemed shallow. I found it difficult to return in my imagination to our flat; and focusing on home made me realize again just how much I was missing them all. In particular I longed for a conversation with Sarah. We are good at solving the world's problems over a candlelight supper and bottle of wine.

I felt slightly fraudulent at the reception that was held on our behalf in the bishop's reception room and hosted by David McClennan, the British consul general. He spoke generously and effusively about the venture, the diverse geographical, cultural and political areas we were walking through and our determination and bravery. I simply felt stubborn and lucky! It was good to see some old friends and a collection of over $300 was made for our hospice.

8 October, Day 13

A day for visiting Israeli hospices. Initially we had only intended to go to the Tel HaShomer Hospice in Tel Aviv but then we heard that they were also expecting us at the Hadassah Hospice on Mt Scopus. It was to be a busy day as we also had lunch arranged with Anna Grace Lind at the American Colony Hotel. An opportunity to eat at the Colony is never one to be spurned, particularly when hosted by Anna Grace who embodies the recent history of Jerusalem and ever has a wealth of interesting stories.

Tel HaShomer Hospice is a part of the huge Tel Aviv hospital. Set within its own buildings it has that atmosphere of care and attention to detail for which hospices are so well known. We were greeted by a parrot which we later discovered to be a close personal friend of the medical director. To begin with I felt that Dr Waller was not sure what to make of us and his manner, typically Israeli, seemed brusque. But after a cup of coffee the conversation warmed up and despite his hesitant use of English we were able to communicate well. It soon dawned on us that palliative care is fighting an uphill battle for recognition as an equal medical discipline in Israel. We were embarrassed by the trouble they had taken in Jerusalem to welcome us. The nursing sister had come in specially and a veritable feast of nibbles was spread before us. It is without doubt the most attractive hospice unit that I have ever visited. Perched on the summit of Mt Scopus it has the most spectacular views across the Judean Desert and down towards the Dead Sea. On the edge of the city overlooking the wilderness, perfect. If I was able to choose where to spend my last few days this would be it. In the security of the known it would help me to contemplate the unknown that lay ahead. I find it hard to believe that we have traditionally left people to die in the impersonal environment of large hospital wards or in soulless side rooms – so that others should not be disturbed. What a send off for the single greatest adventure that we all have to participate in.

✦

CHAPTER SEVEN

The Dead Sea to the Red Sea

Perhaps only those who have willingly submitted to the searing heat of the desert by day and shivered unsheltered in the chill of its nights; suffered the caking dust in their eyes and tasted the saline grit in thirsty mouths; stumbled over the jagged rocks and sought rest in the soft, warm sand; climbed the lofty peaks and gazed over the vast primeval vistas; descended into the shadowy ravines and searched through ancient caves; witnessed the desert gush forth with waters in a sudden flash flood of winter and sprout a carpet of flowers in the brief blossom of springtime; or listened for — and heard — the eloquence of total silence, as in the all-engulfing silence one senses while floating all alone in weightless suspension over the dense blue brine of the Dead Sea, as if hovering between two utterly still skies, can ever truly understand the haunting fascination of the desert.

DANIEL HILLEL: *NEGEV*

9 October, Day 14

WE WERE UP AND on our way out of Jerusalem by half past three, fresh from two days of relative rest and relaxation. Our morale was high and we were pleased to be back on the road. A smashed, rear-side window, was the only evidence of an attempted break-in of the car. It happened but hours before we left and was mildly frustrating because it meant that we had to return to Jerusalem later in the day to have the car replaced. We were given a BMW which more than compensated for the inconvenience.

The descent into the Jordan Valley only takes half an hour but it involves a drop of almost 1,200 m. It is rarely appreciated that this means a change in atmospheric pressure of about 100 mm. which is equivalent to a 'difference of nearly 2.5 tons in the weight of air pressing on the human body'. It has been suggested that those 'who are not constitutionally very strong may therefore feel seasick'. (Eugene Hoade: *Holy Land*) Lightheaded we may have been but not seasick.

Returning to Nahal Og we felt nothing but excitement at being on the move again. The name of this *wadi* is misleading for the Biblical Og, who belonged to a race of giants, was king of Bashan, in the vicinity of the Golan Heights. This is hardly his neck of the woods. Kibbutz Almog is, I assume, named after Yehuda Almog who devoted a lot of his time and energies to various developments in the Dead Sea area. There seems therefore to be no connection between Og and Almog.

It was great to be starting off in the middle of the desert on a stony track well away from the road. It took us from Kibbutz Almog to Kibbutz Qalya, just above Qumran. Were it not for the steep-sided Nahal Og itself Roy would have been able to follow us in the car. A good four-wheel drive could pass through though there might still be problems with the stream of sewage at the bottom. Tragically, sewage is to be seen flowing through a number of the *wadi's* leading down to the Dead Sea. Is it thought that waste products can do no harm to the 'dead' Dead Sea? Might they even be neutralized by its pungent waters? I couldn't help wondering whether, upon reaching the Dead Sea, the waste floats as everything else seems to. It doesn't bear thinking about. It isn't completely true to say that nothing is living in the Dead Sea for research has shown that some micro-organisms seem to thrive there.

Guides seem to enjoy telling the story of the Dead Sea fisherman who set up camp near to Masada. Tourists were bound to see him as they descended on the cable car and the inquisitive would be driven to find out more.

'Excuse me, are you fishing? I thought that there were no fish here.'

'Well, I make a good enough living out of it.'

'Will you tell me your secret?'

'If I did then everyone would be doing it.'

'Go on, I promise to keep it to myself and here is $10 for your troubles.'

'Well, as you are a tourist, and are not likely to set up in competition with me, I will.' He reached out and taking the money, said:

'There you are, my sixth catch today!'

We had to leap across Nahal Og with the aid of strategically placed stones. It was not the sort of soaking with which we wished to start the day. A porcupine, much larger than I would have imagined, was happily wandering alongside the waste in the direction of the sea. We walked in near silence for the first hour allowing the memories of Jerusalem to slip away. Our first view of the Dead Sea came just before sunrise. It is deceptively beautiful and very enticing to overheated walkers. Had the reality been half as good as the promise our progress would have been very slow indeed.

The Dead Sea has almost seven times the saline content of the oceans and is in effect 33% solid substance: a cocktail of magnesium, sodium, potassium and calcium chlorides. It has been calculated that 'in its volume of 157 billion cu. yds. are 42 billion tons of minerals. In other words, each gallon of Dead Sea water contains 2.5 lbs of saline material.' One mouthful and a stomach pump is required. To get any in the eyes, on a sore or open wound is to invite excruciating discomfort. (Neither piles nor blisters seem to be immune!) The sea, sitting at the heart of the Great Rift Valley that runs between Lebanon and East

Africa is, at 405 m. below sea level, the lowest place on the surface of the earth. It is estimated to have been 225 m. higher than this 50,000 years ago and it has dropped 12 m. in the last century alone. Changes have occurred as a result of a drop in the rain fall and the reduced volume of water entering from the river Jordan. The sea has no exit and therefore water only leaves by evaporation, which can, in the summer, amount to as much as 25 mm. in 24 hours.

There are plans, that seem to be resurrected at regular intervals, of digging a canal across from the Mediterranean which would raise the level of the Dead Sea once again. An alternative idea suggests a channel connecting the Dead Sea with the Red Sea. Either option would provide a considerable amount of hydroelectric power which could then be used to desalinate sea water, thus providing much required fresh water for Israel and Jordan. It is estimated that, between them, Israel, Syria and Jordan face a water shortfall of one billion cubic metres a year by the year 2010. This is more than half of Israel's current annual consumption.

The sea, 82 km. long by 18 km. wide, is in effect two seas separated by the Lynch Straits near Masada. If it were not for a canal that has been cut through in order to connect them, it would be possible to walk across this 'tongue' of land and the southern 'sea', being only 5.5 m. deep, would quickly dry up altogether. By contrast, the far larger northern area reaches depths of over 365 m. The geological formation of the two areas is also quite different.

The Dead Sea has been, or is, known variously as: the Salt Sea (Hebr., Yam ha-Melah), the Sea of Sodom (from the Talmud, Yammah shel Sedom), the Sea of Sodom and Gomorrah (Arab., Buhayrat Sadum we-Amura), the Sea of Zoar (Arab., Bahr Zuar), the Sea of Lot (Arab., Bahr Lut), the Devil's Sea (coined by European pilgrims), the Stinking Sea (Arab., al-Buhayra al-Muntina), the Sea of the Aravah and the East Sea. Josephus described the 'Lake Asphaltitis', as it was then known, in the following way:

Its waters, as I have said, are bitter and sterile, but due to their buoyancy bring up to the surface even the heaviest objects thrown into them. It is difficult, even by deliberate effort, for a body to sink to the bottom. Thus when Vespasian came to explore the lake, he ordered some people who could not swim to be cast with their hands tied behind them into the deep water, and found that they all came to the surface as if blown upward by a current of air.

Remarkable as well is its change of colour: thrice daily it alters its appearance and reflects the sun's rays with different tints. Again, in many places it throws up black masses of asphalt resembling in their shape and size headless bulls. The labourers on the lake row to these lumps, seize them and haul them into their boats. When these are full, it is not easy to unload the asphalt which, because of its tenacious and glutinous quality, sticks to the boat until loosened by a woman's menstrual secretions, to which alone it yields.

It is useful not only for caulking ships, but also for curing bodily ailments, as it forms an ingredient of many medicines.

Next to it lies the land of Sodom which in olden days was a land rich in crops and in the affluence of its various cities, but is now entirely incinerated. It is said that it was burnt up by thunderbolts due to the impiety of its inhabitants. Indeed there are still marks of the fire from heaven and faint outlines of five cities to be seen. The fruits which grow there still contain ashes; they have all the appearance of edible fruit, but when plucked with the hand, break up into smoke and ashes. To this extent the legends about the land of Sodom are confirmed by visual evidence.

FLAVIUS JOSEPHUS: *JEWISH WAR* IV

It is assumed that this last reference is to the famous apple of Sodom (Arab. Osher). The fact that its fruit is 'fleshless, puffy and full of hairs' and its juice poisonous (it has been used to poison arrows and wells) is meant to symbolize the evil of Sodom and Gomorrah. It is a common plant in the Dead Sea area, growing to a height of 3–5 m. with corky stems, peeling bark and branches covered in a milky latex that is an aggressive irritant.

Superficially attractive it is a major let down, just like the sea itself.

The Nabateans used to extract the asphalt and sell it to Egypt where it was used to embalm mummies.

Geographical exploration of the area began in the 19th century with the arrival of the German Ulrich Jesper Seetzen, who travelled disguised as a Greek monk. An Irishman, Christopher Costigan, attempted, in 1837, to sail to the Dead Sea from the Sea of Galilee but he was forced to give up at Beth Shean and have his boat transported overland. Upon reaching the Dead Sea he put out to sail despite the August heat. After running out of water he 'drank the waters of the Sea, boiling it and brewing coffee to avoid its bitter taste. He began to hallucinate, and claimed that he saw the ruins of Gomorrah in the depths of the sea.' (Yadin Roman: *Old Salts*) Not surprisingly he died soon after reaching Jerusalem having been carried there by some kind-hearted bedouin. His tomb on Mt Zion bears the following inscription: 'Because of his wish to describe the holy places, he was attacked with fever on the Asphalt Sea, and was transported to Jerusalem by a good Samaritan.'

A British naval officer, T. Molyneux, followed in Costigan's footsteps in 1847 and was similarly unfortunate, dying of malaria in Beirut a few days after completing his journey. His boat was taken back to England by Captain Symonds where it remained on his Devonshire estate until sought out by Dr Zev Vilnay. It now sits proudly in the Dead Sea works museum at Neve Zohar on the Dead Sea's south-western shore.

W. F. Lynch, who led an American expedition in 1848 was far more successful with his specially constructed boats the *Fanny Skinner* and the *Fanny Mason*. It took them eight days to negotiate the River Jordan and they then spent 27 days exploring the Dead Sea. In his official report he wrote, 'We have carefully sounded its depth, determined its geographical position, taken topographical sketches of its shores, ascertained the temperature, width, depth, and velocity of its tributaries, collected specimens of every kind of mineral, plant, and flower, and noted the winds, currents, changes of weather, and all atmospheric phenomena. (Yadin Roman: *Old Salts*)

Nearly a hundred years passed before extraction of the sea's minerals began in earnest and only since 1967 has tourism flourished in the area. It no longer requires a major expedition to explore its shores though modern international borders make it impossible to consider sailing from one side to the other.

We rejoined the main road at the Qumran junction without stopping to visit the ruins of the (possibly Essene) community so closely associated with the Dead Sea scrolls. We had seen an audio visual presentation at Kibbutz Almog which gave an outline of the story of the discoveries and we had passed some of the caves where the scrolls had been found but, unfortunately, we had no time for further exploration. The scrolls themselves seem to have been the cause of more speculation, adventure, scholarly intrigue, legal writs and justified acclaim than anything else I can think of. This is not surprising considering their age and the potential impact of their contents on the religious convictions of millions. Our understanding of 'pre-normative' (that is pre-rabbinic) Judaism has changed beyond all recognition and provocative questions concerning the relationships of Jesus and John the Baptist to the Essenes are impossible to ignore. There are certainly many parallels in their teachings and lifestyles. John the Baptist is thought to have baptized his followers in the Jordan not far from the Qumran community so it is quite possible that he had some contact with them.

To our north we could see the tall water-slide of a relatively new resort while directly ahead lay the lush vegetation created by the pools of 'Ein Feshkha ('Einot Zukim). We were regularly surprised by outbreaks of green upon the shore, each signifying the presence of a spring. 'Those very same mountains that envelop the Dead Sea Valley in a haze of heat also release generous amounts of sweet water in numerous springs.' (Ya'acov Shkolnik and Yadin Roman: *Desert Waterways*)

'Einot Zukim is an oasis of 1,150 acres that consists of three groups of springs which between them produce 4,280 cu. m. of water per hour. Two species of tamarisk, the river tamarisk and the square tamarisk, dominate the area though 14 other species of plant life are also to be seen including ditch reed, shrubby sea blite, shrubby orache, the golden samphire and swamp lavender. (See Ya'acov Shkolnik and Yadin Roman: *Desert Waterways*) Four species of fish are also to be found in the shallow ponds close to the Dead Sea and even in the sea itself where it is sufficiently diluted by the spring waters. Perhaps this was the real secret of our Dead Sea fisherman.

Just beyond the entrance to 'Ein Feshkha at the headland of Rosh Zuqim the cliffs of the Judean mountains that drop so dramatically into this Great Rift Valley meet with the water's edge. There is a mark on a rock against the cliff, a little before the headland, that gives the height of the water in 1900. It provides a clear reminder of how far it has dropped.

It was tempting to follow the path from 'Ein Feshkha up to the heights of Rosh Zuqim but we had, yet again, to be overruled by the need to cover the required 30 km. before the heat of the day was upon us. After following the road, close to the water's edge but separated by security fencing, for a few kilometres, we saw the return of this path near the entrance to Wadi Mazin, close to an archaeological site that I later discovered is thought to be Middin, one of the 'cities' listed in the book of Joshua as being a part of the inheritance of the tribe of Judah. Far from being true cities they were in fact a line of fortresses that were established in the eighth century BCE to guard the *wadis* that provided routes inland to the mountain settlements, including Jerusalem. They were abandoned at the time of the Babylonian destruction of Jerusalem in 586 BCE.

Wadi Mazin is very close to the better known Nahal Kidron (the Kidron Valley) that can be traced all the way up to Jerusalem. Today it is infamous for the sewerage it carries. Fortunately we were distracted from this odorous flow by our first sighting of the orange-winged blackbird popularly known as Tristram's grackle (*Amydrus tristrami*): 'It is considerably larger than our blackbird, with lustrous black plumage and rich chestnut-coloured wings. Its note is of wonderful compass, rich and sonorous – I think the most powerful and melodious whistle I ever heard – as it re-echoes from cliff to cliff.' (Henry Tristram: *Land of Israel*)

A narrow plain opened up to our left, on the eastern side of the road, towards the end of which were two more archaeological sites. It is speculated that the southernmost of these, 'Ein el-Turaba, is the city of salt mentioned in Joshua. Its importance is seen by its walls which are 2 m. thick; and it has been suggested, by the archaeologist Pesach Bar-Adon, that it was used to store salt.

The importance of salt in the ancient world is not to be underestimated. All offerings at the Jerusalem Temple had to be seasoned with salt and it was used on a daily basis as a preservative for fish and meat. According to Zvi Greenhut it was also 'used to pickle vegetables and fruit, and for medical purposes (newborn babies were rubbed with salt)'. Salt was also used in the tanning of leather. As the sea level dropped during the summer months a line of salt would be left along the coast which could be collected by hand and then stored prior to distribution.

Leaving the city of salt behind us we climbed with the road obtaining spectacular views in the process. We passed 'Einot Kaneh and 'Einot Samah, two lesser known springs two kilometres apart that together form a nature reserve, almost without noticing them. Together they produce 1.7 million cu. mm. of water a year which sustains heavy thickets of ditch reeds, clusters of tamarisk, bulrushes, Italian sugarcane and hemp agrimony. Apart from the tamarisk our untrained eyes saw only a swathe of green. Shortly after kilometre mark 259 a small road led up into the cliffs to the holiday village and desert travel centre, Metzoke Dragot. If you have the right sort of vehicle it is possible to follow this road all the way to Tekoa, southwest of Bethlehem, a journey not to be undertaken lightly.

Rounding a small headland we passed the entrance to Nahal Darga, also known as Wadi Murabba'at, a popular location for hikers leading as it does to caves that were used as dwellings during the Second Jewish Revolt against the Romans, 132–5. A number of manuscripts were found there including a letter autographed by the leader Simon bar Kokhba. Kibbutz Mitzpe Shalem sits just south of the *wadi* looking very bland and unappealing. Nearby a large Ahava Dead Sea products factory advertises its wares (mud, bath salts etc) in large bold type. Life-enhancing products from a dead sea. The brash presence of the successful enterprise seemed to sit uneasily between the sea and desert.

Our 30 kilometres were up at the 253 marker near the bottom of a long steep ascent that leads through to 'Ein Gedi. We returned to Jerusalem to change cars and then did an extra three kilometres late in the day in order to climb the hill and reach the 250 mark at Nahal Qedem — about half-way to Eilat. Altogether we walked 33 km. in seven hours, not the fastest of days. The new trainers gave a spring to my stride but the blisters on the balls of my feet were now being replaced by worse ones on my heels. George and Roy were attempting to ban me from talking about them! We drove on to the youth hostel at Masada which was to be our base for the next 48 hours. It was very comfortable but, surprisingly, not much cheaper than Almog.

10 October, Day 15

We were through 'Ein Gedi, (Hebr. 'Fount of the Kid') before the world was awake, passing silent campers on the beach behind the petrol station to our left and a still kibbutz and nature reserve on our right. The one time I camped here I discovered the dangers of dehydration the hard way, loosing nearly eight per cent of my body weight in the process. The public beach is uncomfortably stony and notorious as a haunt for thieves who prey on would-be bathers who always seem to leave their belongings in carefully arranged piles. It is always preferable to pay for the security of one of the private beaches.

The history of 'Ein Gedi can be traced back to the Chalcolithic era (4,000 – 3,150 BCE) with the distinctive remains of a 5,500 year old temple built between the two major springs on the top of the cliffs overlooking the sea. It is an evocative place that lends itself to speculation about the rituals of the Ghassulian culture that once occupied the site.

The cultivation of aromatic plants, which created so much wealth during Hasmonean, Herodian and Roman times, is said to have begun during the sixth century BCE. As in Jericho it was the balsam shrub (if this is the correct identification of the *aparsemon* of which Josephus speaks) that was so highly prized, the resin (extracted at the painfully slow rate of a cup a day) being used to treat headaches and eye disease as well as for making perfume. An inscription found in 'Ein Gedi's fourth century synagogue threatens a curse against 'whosoever shall reveal the secret of the town to the Gentiles'. It is possible that this refers to the secret of the *aparsemon*.

Prior to 1967 the Jordanian-controlled West Bank came to within three kilometres of 'Ein Gedi. Our day began at one of the sculptured rock formations that mark the old border and celebrate the completion of the road north. We had now left the West Bank behind and were back in Israel as defined by its 1948-67 borders.

Kibbutz 'Ein Gedi has succeeded in returning some of the famed fertility to the area, particularly by the cultivation of large date plantations. The nature reserves of Nahal David and Nahal Arugot offer some of the best, and easiest, winter walking in the region. Waterfalls and rock pools abound among the rushes, reeds, tamarisk, willows, fig trees, cattails, native moringas and Euphrates poplars. There are almost 50 tropical plant species to be found in 'Ein Gedi. It is equally a dream location for ornithologists who are almost certain to see the bulbul, the blackstart, the white-crowned black wheatear, sand partridges and of course Tristram's grackle to list but a few. According to Uzi Paz, 'Perhaps nowhere else in Israel can such a rich assortment of creatures, in such large numbers be seen so easily.' A small naval station sits close to the public beach though I have yet to see the Israeli navy afloat on the Dead Sea. I imagine that the waters viscosity is such that movement is comparatively sluggish.

At the time we failed to appreciate that 'Ein Gedi was the last significant oasis before Eilat, eight walking days away. 'Ein Gedi spa, built around the Mazor hot springs, with its hot sulphur pools and ample supplies of Dead Sea mud appeared in the distance. The beach looked crusty, hot and uninviting, and remained thus for the remainder of the day. The smell of hydrogen sulphide is hardly appealing but once the baths have been experienced it is hard not to return. An elderly, almost tame, male ibex was scratching himself against one of the decorative palms outside the spa, totally uninterested in our passing.

Sunrise was upon us soon after leaving 'Ein Gedi. Each morning it was much the same unless hidden by clouds though its arrival seemed more aggressive than anything we had experienced in the Jordan Valley. The shades of night would quite suddenly be replaced by a thrust of red that burnt the tops of the hills until shifted by a relentless sun. The further south we travelled the less shade there was which made the pre-dawn hours all the more valuable, and enjoyable. There was an abundance of footprints in the sandy tracks beside the road and we managed to convince ourselves that every second one was that of a desert leopard, stripped hyena or wolf but they were probably nothing more than foxes.

By half-past nine it was a matter of pulling the hat down over the eyes, avoiding the glare of the sun and counting the kilometres home. Nahal Hever, which is honeycombed with interesting caves, Nahal Mishmar and Nahal Tze'elim both of which have superb hiking trails and the latter in particular some refreshing springs, were passed in silence. We were two-thirds of the way down the Straits of Lynch, before stopping for the day. The tedious 'bad lands' setting of the last two hours made each kilometre seem longer than it was, the only distraction being the site of microlights playing in the sky just east of Masada.

After returning to the youth hostel for a shower we drove south to the resort at 'Ein Boqeq where we dined and swam at the Hod Hotel. Like many of the new hotels in the region most business comes from people in search of the therapeutic qualities of the Dead Sea. The sun shines here for at least 320 days a year and many of its more harmful rays are filtered out by the haze that sits over the lake. This, together with the fact that the sun's intensity is bound to decrease as it reaches down to the lowest place on the earth's surface, makes it an ideal place for psoriasis sufferers. The Hod had a large number of such visitors from France and Germany who, care of their health insurance, were able to stay for three to four weeks at a time. This enables the sun, water and mineral-rich mud to slow down the rapid growth of the diseased cells. Some are fortunate enough to find their symptoms completely removed. There is an increasing body of evidence to show that rheumatoid arthritis sufferers can also benefit from such treatment.

We met one of the assistant managers beside the hot indoor pools and made the mistake of enquiring about the cost of staying there. He promised to give us a special rate and we agreed to meet in the foyer. After being kept waiting for 45 minutes he appeared with a grand discount of 10% leaving us a mere $170 to find, not including breakfast! We were happy to return to the youth hostel.

We must be the only people ever to have spent two nights at Masada youth hostel without visiting the mountain top fortress. I must have explored the site a hundred times already so I was not over enthusiastic to return and Roy and George seemed content to opt for the spa! They weren't even particularly keen to hear the story from me. For those not directly affected by the powerful symbolism of the place its main attraction has to be its setting, and impressive as that is it has little to add to what we had already seen. However irresponsible it didn't keep us awake at night, nothing could have done that.

11 October, Day 16

The sight of the mountains cascading into the sea, aloof in their barrenness, made the upper half of the shallower southern reaches of the Dead Sea every bit as impressive as the better-known northern shores. Unfortunately it was not to stay this way and the Dead Sea works which dominated the latter two-thirds of our day's walking proved to be the most tedious section of the whole journey. It felt like the stillness before a storm when we first set out. Not a sound of life or wind anywhere. We passed a military checkpoint which seemed to be disturbingly awake and a foot patrol checking the security track but 20 m. east of us seemed unusually alert. A few moments later a jeep passed us at speed with an officer standing up in the front seat and the sound of falling rocks could be heard just behind us. We didn't hang around to see what was going on, it was probably no more than the sighting of an unusual animal. Having said that, the southern end of the tongue does make an ideal place to attempt a crossing of the border.

Reaching 'Ein Boqeq we joined the attractive promenade that leads from there to the regional centre, holiday resort and health spa Neve Zohar (oasis of brightness). A few joggers were out building up an appetite before breakfast, the first I had seen since arriving in the country, apart from George. The effects of the Dead Sea works are clearly visible from 'Ein Boqeq south, where large dykes, built by dredgers in order to create new salt pans, regularly change the landscape. There is concern about the way in which the Dead Sea works is able to operate without any restrictions on its activities. According to Bilhah Givon of the Society for the Protection of Nature in Israel it is able to do pretty much what it likes within an area of 62,775 hectares (3% of all Israel) which includes part of the lake, hotels, nature reserves and hiking trails. Processing plants are built without the need for 'permits, studies or business licenses', roads are cleared without environmental studies being made or permits being obtained. Its enormous economic importance to the state of Israel enables it to ignore the 'fundamental obligations of any citizen, institution or financial organization'.

It is a tough battle between the demands of industry and the increasingly loud voice of conservationists. In the early 1980s when presented with the option of widening an already busy road or having an 18 km. conveyor belt built across the entire width of a nature reserve, in order to allow the volume of potash being produced to increase from 600,000 to over a million tons, a compromise was negotiated. The conveyor belt was seen to be less of an ecological hazard than the road and it was built under the watchful eye of a landscape architect who was given almost full power to decide on environmental aspects of the project. We would not have seen it if we had not been looking for it. It is perhaps appropriate that the main plant of the Dead Sea works is located just south of Mount Sedom, a hill 11 km. long by 1.5-3 km. wide that rises 245 m. above the level of the sea. Circumnavigating this hill we had plenty of time to speculate as to which of the many weird and wonderful rock formations is truly Lot's wife. 'The sages of Israel, of the third century, recommend: "If one sees [the pillar of salt of] Lot's wife . . . one should give thanksgiving and praise to the Almighty." (From Zev Vilnay, *Israel Guide*) A 'thick, hard and pungent' salt has been dug from this mountain since ancient times and the sages spoke of the 'salt of Sedom which makes the eyes blind'. It was more the thought of Sodom than the salt of Sedom that worried me! There are no similar memories of Gomorrah.

We were pleased to climb back into the car upon reaching the southern perimeter of the works. We drove on to the Nature Society Field School at 'Ein Hazeva in the Aravah which was to be home for the next four nights. They were not particularly sure what to make of us, they can't have had too many guests foolish enough to be hiking the length of the Aravah, let alone the length of the country. The accommodation was simple but clean and more than adequate, the only problem being that the kitchens were closed the week we were there. We visited the nearby Moshav Hazeva in order to do some shopping and enquire about a swimming pool that we had been informed of. To our amazement the pool was closed as this was now thought to be winter! It was hotter than anything we get during the hottest of our summers. This provoked a rush of madness that led us to take an afternoon tour of the southern Negev.

Following the Dimona road we cut through Hamakhtesh Hagadol to Yeroham and then on to Ben Gurion's burial place near Sede Boqer. Passing the miles of fencing around Dimona's nuclear reactor, that for years was passed off as a textile factory, my mind turned to Mordechai Vanunu who is serving a life sentence in solitary confinement for selling the secrets of the reactor to the *Sunday Times*. I had the bizarre task of taking him communion on a few occasions though we were not allowed to talk to each other. Communication was via written notes that were passed across two guards and beneath a door. He became a Christian when in Australia and he really wanted to see an Australian priest so, after a while, I was asked not to return. The words of the service were mouthed through the glass window of the door that separated us. At the time it felt as though I was participating in a bizarre black comedy and I still don't understand Israel's refusal to soften his sentence.

I take every opportunity I can to visit Ben Gurion's tomb which, sited above the head of Nahal Zin, offers the most spectacular views of the Negev Desert. It is not only the beauty that draws me but also the thought that here, somehow, 'the inspired vision of a mortal man combines with the eternal spirit of the desert'.

There is, perhaps, a certain simplicity in the desire we have to visit the burying-places of great men. Century after century the earth has gathered them into her belly and it is possible, we imagine, to catch from these cradles of treasured dust moments of high meditation.

LLEWELYN POWYS: *PAGAN'S PILGRIMAGE*

The energy contained in nature – in the earth and its waters, in the atom, in sunshine – will not avail us if we fail to activate the most precious energy: the moral-spiritual energy inherent in man; in the inner recesses of his being; in his mysterious, uncompromising, unfathomable and divinely inspired soul.

DAVID BEN-GURION, QUOTED IN DANIEL HILLEL: *NEGEV*

From Sede Boqer we drove on to Mizpe Ramon where we watched the sun set from an observation point beyond the town on the rim of the crater. It was half an hour of disturbing beauty over boundless horizons, restorative enough to charge the batteries for another few years in London. A cold beer in the nearby Desert Inn wound the day up before the long drive back to Hazeva.

12 October, Day 17

For the first and only time George and I both slept through the alarm, but Roy was there to push us out into the chill morning air. It was a relief to leave the Sedom plain behind us as, surrounded by impressive Lissan marl hills, we climbed with the main road through Nahal Tamar to the Aravah junction where the Dead Sea – Eilat road meets with that from Beersheva. It was this section, through the Negev Desert between the Dead Sea and Eilat, that we were dreading. Unbroken barrenness through which we had to follow a hot tarmac road. There promised to be few distractions.

The Aravah (Arab. al-'Araba, arid steppe, desert), though once the name for the area to the north of the Dead Sea as well as to the south has now come to mean only the latter. It is a deep cleft in the earth's surface almost 180 km. long which is divided into two by a watershed 243 m. high. It is a long, sandy desert with an average rainfall of less than one inch. Oases are few and far between, the largest in the central region being Hazeva.

> The main features of the Aravah are the shallow stream runnels where grow the three species of acacia – the twisted acacia (*Acacia raddiana*), the umbrella acacia (*Acacia tortilis*) and the Negev acacia (*Acacia gerradii*). Botanists . . . all agree that the appearance of this region has not changed in the last several ten thousand years.
>
> GIORA ILANI: *SHEIZAF NATURE RESERVE*

These botanists obviously haven't noticed the constant stream of enormous MACK lorries with trailers (full of products from the Dead Sea works) that regularly travel the full length of the Aravah when they declare that nothing has changed. Whenever possible we would walk on the left side of the road in order to face the oncoming traffic but we soon realized that our greatest danger was overtaking juggernauts coming up behind us!

An hour south of the Beersheva junction we entered Nahal Zin, the wildest of the Negev riverbeds. Some years see as many as six to eight flash floods crashing through to the Dead Sea from the Negev highlands. Beginning at 920 m. above sea level near Sede Boqer, Nahal Zin is 110 km. long and is fed by a drainage basin of 1,200 sq. km. Little wonder that they were building a new, heavily reinforced bridge, over one section of it. This was followed by a ten kilometre stretch that hardly saw a bend or rise in the road. Acacias became our sole companions, apart from the traffic. In the semi-hypnotic state induced by these surroundings I found myself counting the seconds of total silence between vehicles: 35 seconds was the maximum duration of peace given. We were able to see them well before we could hear them as they arose with an ethereal quality out of the heat haze on the horizon. With the rise in temperature the haze slowly took on the form of a shimmering sheet of water across the road ahead. We were ever walking towards the mirage but were never able to attain it.

I pushed myself an extra four kilometres in order to reach the field school where we were staying. George, keen to get out of the sun, joined Roy in the car and returned later in the afternoon to jog this section. For the second day running we took lunch at the nearby petrol station café, there being no other option. The food was surprisingly good, particularly the meatballs. Having strangers return two days running must have been an unusual occurrence for the maître d'hôtel came out from behind the self-service counter to check that all was well with us. She beamed from ear to ear with pride when we praised her cooking!

We slept most of the afternoon. It was day four of our only five-day walking stretch and it was beginning to take its toll. We woke in time to participate in the sunset, enjoying the glow that lit up the hills at the end of the day and the yawning stillness of the desert preparing for sleep. With the cooling of the air the soil let out a gentle sigh and even the buildings around us seemed to relax from the stress of the day's heat. The harshness of the sunlight was replaced by the purple hues of dusk and compline was sung, as it has been from the beginning, by the birds and wind together. I was beginning to feel in touch with the rhythms of the world. It was therapeutic focusing our activities around the rising and setting of the sun. I only had one problem to face each day and that was a physical one, how to complete the 30 km. I wasn't having to deal with ten things at once, emotional stress was at an all time low.

13 October, Day 18

Perhaps it was last night's wine, or the fact that this was our 13th walking day, for my legs felt like lead from the moment we set out. It was not helped by a strain just above the ankle on my right foot. Bleary eyed we marched for 15 km. through the gravel plains that lie due west of the Sheizaf Hills. If we had but left our path to explore we might have recognized this area as being similar to an African savannah for according to Giora Ilani it is 'the northernmost savannah on the globe' inhabited by an exciting variety of wildlife including ibex, hyenas, Dorcas gazelles, Aravah gazelles, Egyptian dabb-lizards, wolves, leopards, hyenas, caracals, Blandford's foxes, Negev lappet-faced vultures, bearded vultures, golden eagles, Bonnelli's eagles, eagle owls, houbara bustards, Burton's carpet vipers, etc. (Sheizaf Nature Reserve) Driven by the need to obtain our daily quota of kilometres we were frequently blind to our immediate surroundings. The walk was becoming a two-edged sword as my reason for being there threatened to prevent my 'being' there. All that we noticed were some large black ravens. This 'natural asset of international significance' passed completely unnoticed.

It did, however, feel more like a desert than anything we had previously experienced. Were it not for the tarmac road we would have been very isolated. I passed the time by attempting to invent descriptions of the surrounding landscape but my efforts were too self-conscious and they came nowhere near to capturing the essence of the place. Medium sized plains with a thin covering of stones broken by irregularly shaped hills, some jagged in profile, others wearing tiaras of a harder rock upon an eroded face, none more than 45 m. high. Small umbrella acacias and shrub size salt bushes spaced themselves as closely as water sources would allow. A thin haze took the place of an early morning mist adding a romantic hue. Larger mountains hugged the horizon to our right and left, the definition of those to the east remaining blurred until illuminated by the rising sun.

There is a fascination in the desert that seems to defy logic. Like a vacuum that draws, so the desert's emptiness, its impenetrable vastness, its enigmatic silence, its awesome grandeur and loneliness have captivated man's imagination. There is mystery in the desert. . . . There is the lure of romantic adventure in the desert. . . . There is enchantment in the desert: the camel caravans silhouetted against the skyline; the crystal-clear nights and piercing sharp stars; . . . the unobstructed view of the luminescence of dawn, the sumptuous burst of splendour at sunrise; the infinite beauty and glory of sunset.

There is a spirit in the desert: the spirit sought by ascetic hermits who built lonely abodes there, away from the vain world of men and events, the spirit sought by the prophets of old who wandered into the vast stillness to escape the mindless conformity and humdrum trivial busy-ness of life in ordinary society, and to meditate and ponder the ultimate meaning of man's calling and God's purpose. Here in the desert spiritual man can be truly alone and one with nature's elements, free of conventions and unencumbered by imposed duties. Here he is reminded daily of the greatness of creation, and a realization of his own frailty gives him a sense of true humility.

And there is a challenge in the desert: a defiance of man's self-proclaimed mastery of the whole earth; a barrier to life, to progress, to economic development; a fortress holding out against colonization and civilization. It is a challenge compounded of the fascination, mystery, romance, enchantment, and the spirit of the desert. And of its promise . . .

Let us respect and love the desert, and seek to live with it, not rape or despoil it. Considering the special character of the Negev, and the profound meaning of its rich history, we must refrain from regarding it merely as a place for economic development. Man's spiritual needs are as great as his economic needs. The balance we seek between the two is always tentative and tenuous, and the environment within which we seek it is itself an ever-precarious one. Total appropriation of the desert for the one set of needs denies the other. In the Negev we can still find places where silence and solitude reign, where spiritual communion with primeval nature and with human history are possible, where the memory of God's revelation yet echoes in the still, small voice. May such places always remain, even as we proceed to develop the resources of this and other deserts, and to utilize them for the betterment of life upon earth.

DANIEL HILLEL: *NEGEV*

Before finishing for the day we climbed past sea level for the first time since our fourth day – if 115 m. over 130 km. can be called climbing. After leaving Giv'ot Sheizaf we passed the isolated moshav at 'Ein Yahav (which was thought important enough to warrant a guard post during the British mandate), the regional centre Sapir and Moshav Zofar. We called it a day just south of Nahal Omer which was made famous by the ancient Nabatean spice routes that ran from Arabia, through Petra and on to Gaza, crossing the Aravah at this point. It was strange to think that we were not that far from Petra.

There is still the occasional story of reckless young Israelis attempting to cross the Jordanian border in order to lay eyes upon the famous rose-red city. Invariably caught by the Jordanians they are handed back and then given a hefty fine. Political developments are soon likely to make it possible for tourists to travel legally from Israel to Petra. There are rumours of a shared international airport near the Gulf and highways connecting Egypt with Jordan via Eilat. It would certainly change the face of regional tourism and it might encourage the growth of peace but I dread to think what it will do to the desert.

14 October, Day 19

Another free day where we managed to sleep in until at least half-past five! After a lazy breakfast we set out to explore the ruined Nabatean city of Mamshit before spending the heat of the day back at the Dead Sea. The Nabateans succeeded in building communities that were able to live in harmony with the severe conditions of the desert. There was no natural water source at Mamshit but the development of three systems of dams enabled enough run-off water to be collected from the occasional rains to provide for the needs of visiting caravans as well as local inhabitants. An ancient Nabatean farm, near Sede Boqer, has been reconstructed to show how it was possible to eke survival from the desert. The residents of Mamshit kept pigs and even bred horses that later became known as Arabian horses.

Next door to the ancient city is a very modern camel farm offering a 'genuine' bedouin experience to the well-healed tourist. The educational input is probably first rate and the camel rides are fun but the scale is too large. I am told that they even organize Lawrence-of-Arabia-style attacks on a nearby railroad as company incentives! The Israelis are excellent at turning the desert into an adventure playground but hopefully sufficient areas of natural beauty will remain undisturbed for those of us wishing to be left in peace.

We stopped briefly in Dimona in order to spend 35 minutes inside a bank which was every bit as exciting as at Beth Shean.

It was very relaxing sitting, once more, by the pool back at the Hod Hotel in 'Ein Boqeq. Tristram's grackles amused us with their deep-throated croaking as they drank from the children's pool followed by high pitched shrills when they flew off. My head began to feel permanently hot as though I was failing to cool effectively, despite the regular dips in the pool. I was going to have to be careful over the next four days. The day provided a welcome space in which to reflect on all that had happened thus far. We had walked during 13 of the past 16 days, it was all so different from home and had been varying dramatically on an almost daily basis. Jerusalem, Mt Hermon, the Golan Heights, the Hula

Valley, the Sea of Galilee, the sudden transition from arable land to desert, the invasion of sub-tropical Jericho followed by the dense atmosphere of the Dead Sea and now further and further into the desert.

I felt as though I was beginning to get a glimpse of what the journey was about but as yet I could not put it into words. Some events were like clues that I wanted to gather in the hope of discerning a common thread: the warmth of welcome at Kibbutz Snir, at the Sisters of Nazareth and from the hospices, the feast of Sukkot, the spirituality of Aaron Gordon, and the physical immediacy of the desert; the lack of external restraints and the refreshing nature of physical as against emotional exhaustion; the daily sense of achievement in the gaining of relatively straightforward targets; the slow transition from being dominated by possessiveness, to one where it was enough just to be, even if we were distracted by the physical demands of each day. It was dark by the time we began the journey back to Hazeva. The Dead Sea dredgers were lit up and looking like Mississippi steamers and the Dead Sea works themselves appeared before us as something from outer space, a galactic Sodom or Gomorrah in the throes of destruction. As we passed, the strident tones of Respighi's *Roman Festivals*, broadcast by the BBC World Service, turned the works into the backdrop of a legendary epic.

I rashly gave in to an overwhelming desire to shave. Having worn a beard for over 12 years I was fascinated to see what I looked like beneath it all. Photos were taken once the right side of my face was clear. The beard was easy to remove but I wasn't sure about the stranger that greeted me in the mirror. 'The growing of a beard is a tactic of charlatans who wish to pose as honest, truthful people; it contains elements of pretence and exhibitionism.' (Joseph Drory: *Beard Of The Prophet*)

15 October, Day 20

George keeps referring to the walk as 'a jolly' which may well reflect his physical well being. For me it was anything but. Agonizing, provocative, adventurous, a pilgrimage, but not a jolly! Because he is finishing at Eilat we have little celebrations each time a significant stage is passed. Today we passed the 99 km. mark. I was tempted to forget that there was still another 165 km. to do after his departure, the half-way mark was not half way to Eilat and it slipped by unnoticed. If there was any friction between us this was it, and my snoring perhaps.

It was impossible, however, not to count down towards Eilat. With almost 400 km. already under our belts it felt as though we could reach out and touch it. Without realizing it at the time we spent most of the day walking parallel to the Nahal Ashosh Nature Reserve which lies between Zofar and Paran.

> What a lucky break: so far, there are no big attractions in the Ashosh Nature Reserve. Here and there you'll find a rock, or an acacia tree, or wolf tracks. But there aren't any snack bars, or parking lots, or even a large selection of marked trails. Miraculously, most of the nature reserve isn't in a firing zone. The reserve, situated between the Negev highlands and the Aravah, is a pure desert.
>
> YA'ACOV SHKOLNIK: *Last Desert*

Yet another place to return to at greater leisure on another occasion. Irrigation has turned the desert green in the fields of Paran but the image was soon lost again in the ever increasingly arid environment.

Towards the end of our statutory 30 km. it looked as though we were going to walk into a sand storm but it did not materialize until later in the day. We moved our accommodation south to the Ye'elim holiday village at 'Ein Yotvata where we managed to enjoy a few hours on a water slide before the storm blew up. Roy and George left to explore the ancient copper mines of Timna while I slept and prepared a fax to send back to Harrow.

A small amount of rain, which is always a wondrous sight in the desert, gave a heightened intensity to the colour of the sand, date palms, and acacias. The ominously dark clouds spitting out forks of lightning onto the summit of the deep ochre mountains of Moab competed for attention with a setting sun determined not to be completely hidden. I found it impossible to sit still with all this activity around me so I took a short walk beyond the boundaries of the camp onto a large empty plain. Here I could feel the wind whipping up the sand beneath me and the heavy but scattered drops of rain. The storm promised more than it delivered as is often the case in the desert.

16 October, Day 21

Continuing to follow devoutly the dull black road we finally crossed the Sheluhat Noza ridge which, at 243 m. above sea level forms the watershed between the Dead Sea and the Red Sea. Eilat had to be downhill from here. The map had promised little of interest today, not even any hidden nature reserves that we could blithely ignore. Undistracted by expectation we surprisingly found ourselves drawn into the sparse beauty of the desert and I experienced one of the most enjoyable days thus far.

Water flowing from the watershed to the Gulf invariably soaks into the subsoil well before reaching the sea. During the hot dry summers it is drawn back up to the surface, by means of capillary action, forming *playas* or salt flats which are frequently covered with vegetation.

Just beyond the Sheluhat Noza a small range of hills – Har Ya'alon, Har Sha'alav and Har Qetura – joined the western edge of the road. Growing steadily in size this range was to accompany us well into Sinai.

Back at Ye'elim we chatted with a young Israeli girl who was working there in order to make enough money to travel. She spoke candidly in her broken English about the need she felt to extirpate her recent experience of military service. With great heaviness she talked also of the recent brutal murder of two young Israeli hikers in the Wadi Qilt by, it was assumed, an extremist Palestinian Hamas group. We could sense the degree to which she shared in the pain that their families must have been experiencing. I had noticed this before in Israeli and Palestinian society, this sharing of grief. A close friend she had grown up with had been killed in a senseless training accident and the large number of suicides in the military gnawed away at her. Hoping for peace she was doubtful of it ever being realized. Despite having been forced to mature beyond her years she retained an engaging smile and youthful vitality.

The storm blew up once more even as we spoke, the uncertain weather reflecting our conversation.

17 October, Day 22

George initially intended to cover 50 km. today in order to reach the outskirts of Eilat but after 33 km. he was as ready to stop as I was. Cloud-cover helped to keep the temperature down throughout the morning and the greatest distraction was caused by Roy getting the car stuck in the sand. After a lot of work we managed to force some wood beneath the rear tyre which gave it something to grip on and he was out.

Walking was particularly enjoyable on the soft tracks around the Hai Bar Biblical Wildlife Reserve where the recent rain had given the sand a bubblepack feel. Apart from the ostrich, which seemed to follow us, and some onagers (Asiatic wild ass) standing sensibly in the shade of an acacia tree we saw none of the reserve's animals. I have always wanted to see the onager run for they are said to be able to move at 104 km. per hour. The reserve also boasts some white orynx – an extremely rare animal – which have two impressive long straight horns. When seen in profile they can appear to have only one horn, and as such they were depicted by the ancient Egyptians. This, in turn, gave birth to the legend of the unicorn.

We originally intended not to visit Eilat until we reached it on foot but the food at Ye'elim was so consistently uninviting that we changed our minds. We made a journey of it by approaching Eilat from the Egyptian border road which offers spectacular views across the Gulf to

Aqaba. We found a moderately priced restaurant where we were well looked after by a Palestinian waiter who had been born in the Jewish quarter of the Old City of Jerusalem. He seemed very much at home in Eilat and had obviously taken on board an Israeli way of life. On the table next to us an Israeli couple, having supper with some German friends, were speaking in English. It was impossible not to overhear them as they said: 'We have a proverb about the English. You don't smoke; you don't drink; you don't spit; you don't shoot; what do you do?'

18 October, Day 23

It began to feel like the end even before we set out today. Eilat marks the successful conclusion of most of the walking and the completion of the stretch through Israel from north to south. We set off at a quarter to five, again well before sunrise, and, as on previous occasions we were soon stopped by an inquisitive Israeli army patrol. We found an old road that for nearly 15 km. kept us away from the main highway but in so doing took us close to the Jordanian border. There we were stopped a second time but there was no concern once they realized who we were. It felt as though word was getting round. Time had begun to pass casually on these treks and we were now able to tell the number of kilometres travelled without the presence of the markers. My body was at last beginning to slide into a rhythm, one which my blisters had previously distracted me from recognizing.

We indulged in photographs beneath the large 'Welcome to Eilat' sign and then the city simply slipped by. Local housing on the hill to our right and a concentrated cluster of hotels, all squeezed around a tiny section of beach, to our left. Even Taba arrived quicker than I thought it should though custom formalities lived up to their traditionally messy nature, on the Egyptian side at least.

George generously treated Roy and myself to two nights at the Taba Hilton. For him the journey was now over and this was time for a celebration. Champagne and olives were the order of the day once we had taken a shower. The Hilton is in a spectacular location and our rooms looked south down the gulf, with Jordan and Saudi Arabia in view on its eastern shore. The mountains of Sinai lurk provocatively and invitingly behind the hotel dictating the ethereal quality of sunset across Taba bay.

George and Roy both rested after the party but I was too excited to sleep so I sat out on the balcony greedily savouring each moment. I felt more in control of myself than I had done at any point so far. Over the past week the desert had once again invaded me, and this, together with improving health and feet, had helped me begin to focus. It was as though the adventure was only just beginning, the past three weeks being but an acclimatization process, an earning of the right to re-enter the sacred space that Sinai has become for me.

Birds in abundance announced the days ending supported by the dull humming of a hotel generator. German bathers began to rid themselves of another day's hire of sunbeds and sand space jealously guarded through daylight hours. Waiters carefully pushed trolleys to the Oriental Restaurant, on the beach, that opens each evening. A father fought with his young son who had decided to eat from a nearby ash tray. Late swimmers made final laps of the pool which surrounds a 'Paradise Bar' which remained distinctly empty, though as I watched lights came on in an attempt to suggest that this particular portion of paradise was not yet totally lost.

I observed the first neck-tie I had seen since leaving England, and black at that (Israelis are famed for their casual wardrobes which rarely seem to include a tie), and an Egyptian chef with striped trousers, white apron and hat carrying a cardboard box on his shoulders across the sand through the palm trees. An elderly couple helped each other from the toil of resting to the hoped for revival of a shower and supper. A mattress on wheels sneaked up behind me in the hope of not being seen – one of the many thousands of activities that enable the hotel to tick but from which the client must be protected. German evening dresses began to appear. It was time to get changed.

19 October, Day 24

Today was largely spent repacking bags and writing to Sarah. Apart from a pre-dawn swim the water did not appeal and I was inside for most of the day. After yesterday's initial excitement at the hotel's opulence it became, for me, something of a no man's land, a 'Hilton-land', anywhere in the world. The food was great but inappropriate for one in the middle of a journey. I felt somewhat out of place and I was not quite sure what to do with myself.

Even though it was a free day I could not sleep-in, so after the quickest of swims in the pool I sat on the beach listening to the gentle lapping of water over the coral and watched the slowly ascending sun. Apart from flies (which would have driven George and Roy mad), and thoughts of Sarah, Polly and Phoebe, I was quite alone. Looking out across the Gulf, with a small Israeli patrol boat just 200 m. away, and the mountains of Saudi Arabia gently beginning to reveal themselves through the morning haze; and then thinking of Sarah asleep at home, the sheets held tightly to her chin; and Polly and Phoebe abandoned in the unnatural postures of sleep that only children seem to know: I felt quite torn in two. Part of me accused myself of being selfish for ever having considered making this journey. Another part of me indulged in the addiction that Sinai has become.

Late in the afternoon after having completed my major repack the shadows were sufficiently long for me to crawl out onto the balcony and finish a letter to Sarah. An Israeli pleasure boat was on its way back to Eilat from Pharaoh's Island looking very full of people. (Whatever turns you on.) Chocolate that I took from our room bar was old and inedible which served me right. I tried closing my eyes and clicking my fingers in the hope that Sarah would magically appear. Even if touch was banned it would have been soothing to see and hear her.

Sarah had asked me on the phone whether it was living up to my expectations, which made me wonder whether I came with any. I'm not sure that I did – not for the Israel portion at least. It is all going to take a while to absorb, so many new perspectives have been uncovered. I never before realized just how false the picture is from air-conditioned, high, and fast coaches! It was great having George along but I was really looking forward to being on my own, our walking paces are not quite the same and I frequently found myself moving faster than I might have wished. I did not particularly enjoy it at the Hilton. It is a place for holiday makers, lovers or those finishing a venture. It will be easier to rest at the Sallyland.

The weather continued to be quite stormy. It suddenly darkened over and it looked as though Sinai was getting its annual share of rain, which could mean flash floods, which would add an interesting dimension to the trek.

In the letter I found myself reflecting on my priorities at home. There was a nagging concern about the amount of time I was spending at work. Polly and Phoebe are only given to us once and their years will slip through our fingers even as ours did our parents. I got quite carried away as I thought of the girls, a gift from the gods to be cherished and never taken for granted. Ours to comfort and befriend, ours to laugh and cry with. It was hard getting in to the writing of the letter but slowly it made me feel closer to them all. My thoughts turned to tomorrow's return to Sinai, walking and alone. I suspected that it might turn out to be the most important day of the whole trip for me. I was really looking forward to it.

We all had supper with an old work colleague of Sarah's and her husband. Almost the only other English people there, it's a small world.

✦

CHAPTER EIGHT

Through the Sinai Desert: 1

'You know, mister, this here country is not man's country, its God's country. So if anything should happen, just sit down and don't worry.'. . . not man but God was in command here — in other words, not will and intention, but inscrutable design.

CARL JUNG, MEMORIES

The unique character of the Sinai Peninsula lies in its striking contrasts, in the fact that it unites within itself incompatible contradictions and, in consequence, displays a particular kind of 'earthly spirituality'. Sinai is the meeting point of two continents — this is reflected in particular in its flora and fauna — as well as of two disparate worlds: the land of revelation, the 'celestial Sinai' of great religions, of ascetics and pilgrims, of monasteries and hermitages, as well as the ancient battlefield between Asia and Africa, the 'earthly Sinai' of turquoise and copper mines, of shepherd-warriors, of trade caravans and of wretched settlements. The cradle of monotheism and the scene of decisive historical events — in what is at the same time a dispiriting wasteland and an exciting sandy and rocky desert.

BENO ROTHENBURG AND HELFRIED WEYER: SINAI

20 October, Day 25

L EAVING THE HILTON at just before a quarter to five this morning without George and without Roy in support felt like the first day of my journey. I was jealous of every step I took. The rapid growth in infrastructure at Taba meant that I hardly recognized the Egyptian border positions. There is now a police station, fire station (without, it would seem, any appliances) and a small shopping parade though this was unoccupied apart from the United Colours of Benetton. A laundry looked to be busy around the clock, no doubt supported by the Hilton's business. To the south a sparkling new garage offered, among other services, 'Lube Change' which I assume is something to do with oil. The attached pharmacy and general store were yet to be stacked and the car wash stood idle. I later heard that it could not be used because of a lack of fresh water, much to the amusement of the locals who explained this to me, though others suggested that a recyclable fixture meant that it was in use.

Until its recent fame as a disputed border area Taba was best known to nomads as a small oasis and to botanists as the northernmost example of Sudanese date palms which are recognized by their split stems and wide fronds. Boundary arguments date back to when this was an ill-defined section of the frontier between British-supported Egyptian Sinai and Turkish-controlled Palestine. More recently it was controlled by Israel until a prolonged international arbitration decided in favour of Egypt and the border had to move a mile north. It is hardly significant when compared to the length of the Egyptian-controlled Sinai coastline, but for Israel it was a major loss.

Within ten minutes of departing, after waking a distressed looking official to pay my border tax, I was through Taba and enjoying an unexpectedly fresh breeze coming off the sea. At the Hilton the air had been still and stagnant so I was expecting a close and clammy journey. It was as though the breeze had arisen with the sole purpose of removing the stigma of opulence, so alien to the simplicity of the desert, that hung on my being. I indulged in the wind, allowing it to fill each and every part of me. Being thus refreshed my pace quickened, as indeed it had to in order to keep up with my spirit which was already exploring the hills ahead. Never had a morning felt better. Every view became a feast for the senses. I was intoxicated. The small hills that fell to the roads edge radiated a dull yellow glow laced with streaks of cream. Crumbly limestone with rivulets cut out by many years of spasmodic rain. Beyond these hills, looking towards Jebel el-Biyar and Jebel Abu Rutaeh, the subtle colour changes of the sedentary deposits sloping at 40° testified to the complexity of this peninsula's geological history.

In contrast to these immediate neighbours the hills ahead of me were rich in the austerity for which Sinai is famed. To the fore lay a jagged ridge laden with precipitously loose screes whose complex tapestry of shaded browns and veined rust, divided by the breaking out of darker minerals, beckoned me to follow contours and attempt to create recognisable shapes from the hypnotic confusion. The movement of clouds and slowly breaking light highlighted a previously unnoticed crevice, peak or ridge. The whole, a motion picture of great subtlety and tranquillity. As though this were not enough a higher range, beyond, shrouded in the mists of morning and reflecting the deep blues of the gulf provided a shimmering framework for the scene. The hills overshadowed the dyke of carefully positioned boulders that lined the eastern side of the road in order to prevent erosion by the sea that lapped within metres of where I walked.

Apart from some partially completed hotels with no signs of building being continued, a jetty construction, an MFO (Multinational Force of Observers) base and occasional Egyptian police positions there was little to distract for the 35 km. from Taba to Beer Suweir and the Sallyland Hotel, half way to Nuweiba. Large container lorries and cars laden up to three times their height in packing cases would suddenly appear as from nowhere. Some of them would have originated in the Gulf States where many Egyptians work. Driving overland to Aqaba they take the ferry down the Gulf to Nuweiba from where it is only eight hours more to Cairo. These, together with a handful of tourist buses and private vehicles were the sole disturbance. I must have appeared a strange sight to them as walkers are few and far between. Invariably they waved or nodded, and just occasionally I was given a rendition on a tuneful horn. Fortunately, though, for most of the time nothing was to be heard apart from the rhythmic striking of my staff and the pounding of my feet and heart.

The terrain was hillier than anything encountered since Mt Hermon as the groan of underused muscles was to remind me later in the day. The mountains that were one minute hugging the road, at the next gave way to the wide fanlike opening of a *wadi* where I was assaulted by the rich smell of sweet bedouin tea being brewed. This must have been the early morning cuppa taken just prior to leaving for a day with the goats. It was a scene that I had seen many times before but usually in a flash, driving past, the senses being given no chance to absorb it all. The dwellings closest to the road looked particularly impoverished being made of odd pieces of hardboard and corrugated iron which leant against a rock face thus saving the need for a wall or, alternatively, were positioned beneath an acacia tree for the shade it offered. The outline of traditional bedouin tents made of sacking or goatskin could be discerned further up the *wadi* but there could be no doubting the use of these shanty dwellings as women and children stood around in some number. No men were to be seen anywhere, probably because they were away working.

Those who can afford to do so are able to have more than one wife. Divorce is easy to obtain and there appears to be little stigma attached to it. The man simply has to say, 'I divorce you, I divorce you, I divorce you.' And that's the end of it. The woman does not have the same rights. If during this process the husband should say '*Talag bit Talat*', then that really *is* the end and he is not allowed to remarry her until she has had another husband. There have been cases where this has been said in anger and the ex-husband has arranged for a close friend to marry his ex-wife and then immediately divorce her so that he can marry her again. Problems begin to multiply when the friend falls in love with her and refuses the divorce!

A girl clad from head to toe in black cloth crossed the road in front of me with about 30 goats and five sheep. She disappeared alongside one of the unfinished hotels. There was little vegetation and it was strange watching them descend towards the gulf's edge. Later I discovered that a small well, Beer Murahi, was to be found there which also explains the location of a hotel at the site. Desalination plants have yet to appear (apart from one in Nuweiba) and are in any case too expensive so all developments rely on natural resources which are scarce at the best of times. The small black goats that led the way are of a special type, well adapted to the desert. They loose little of their body fluids through sweat or urine and they are able to live off remarkably little food.

Young girls can be seen wearing extremely colourful clothing but when they begin to show signs of becoming a woman this changes. To begin with the head and upper part of the body is covered with a simple black *hirga* which is a type of veil. Later a black dress is also worn and eventually a *latma* is added, a piece of simple material covering the face so as to avoid attracting men by exposing the nose or lips. I have seen young mothers breastfeed in front of a group of foreigners without a second thought but they are always most careful to ensure that the *latma* never slips. As young as eight a bedouin girl will accompany others with the goats in order to learn the trails and places of shelter. The many hours of leisure are likely to be used embroidering.

There have been many arguments as to why black is worn. Common sense would seem to say that it is unbearably hot. Is it a sign of modesty or something which the goats can recognize? Another possibility concerns the girls' safety, for being recognizable from a distance there is no excuse for a strange man ever to approach her. Under bedouin law to do so is to risk punishment. The most likely reason is more straightforward. There was a time when black goats wool would have been the only material they had readily available and the colour has stuck despite the ready accessibility of alternatives. It is often the case that colourful dresses are worn beneath.

This particular plain, a quarter of a mile across at its widest, acts as the drainage area for two *wadis* – Wadi Murahi and Wadi Hulayfiyah – whose floods cannot be too aggressive because of the limited deposits which are to be found. By contrast, just a little further south, in Wadi Mukaybilah, the after effects of heavy and violent flooding can be seen in what appears as a protracted lava flow of boulders and rocks of all dimensions. I made the mistake of trying to cross this obstacle course in order to cut a corner in the road – a detour which ended up with my walking at least twice as far and taking three times as long!

Not far south of Taba I passed Jezirat Fara'un, an attractive island, lying but a few metres from shore, that is dominated by a clinical looking fortress which has recently been rebuilt by archaeology students from the University of Cairo. It is also known as 'pharaoh's island', a name chosen I suspect for the tourist as there is no evidence of a pharaoh ever having visited the site. Israelis call it Coral Island, their hedonistic interest focusing more on the sun and water than the ruins! There are many good stories attached to the island and Sinai's most famous explorers have each attempted to recreate its history.

Among the first of the modern explorers to visit the site was the German, Rupell, who in 1829 called it 'Emrag' after the 'Emradi' a tribe whom he believed had once occupied it. He also thought that they were of Jewish origin. The painter David Roberts used it as a backdrop for a self-portrait in the early 1830s. In 1836 the French explorer Leon de Labord planted a flag on the island and took possession of it in the name of France. In 1838 Lt. J. B. Wellstead of the Royal Indian Navy sailed to the island and commented on the protection offered to ships in the small strait between the island and the shore. Dr E. Robinson (1841) believed the fortress to be Arabian, 'without doubt the former citadel of Ailah' which was unsuccessfully besieged in 1182 by that Crusader rogue Reynald of Chatillon. (He was wrong.) In 1906 one of Flinders Petrie's assistants, Currelly, described the fortress as Turkish. Burckhardt named the island 'Koreye'. Between 1914 and 1915 Woolley and T. E. Lawrence made a more thorough examination of the site, despite the fact that their primary intention seems to have been that of spying. They found little to support an early date for the fortress though they did suggest that it had been 'strongly fortified at various periods'. They associated it with the Crusader 'Graye' and not Ailah which was positioned in Aqaba. Nelson Glueck made a brief visit in 1926 when he found a few Byzantine pottery shards but nothing to associate it with the Crusades. In 1956 Beno Rothenburg discovered the remains of foundations of a solid casemate wall that seemed to encircle the island, a well-built inland harbour that had previously been mistaken for a pool, and further Byzantine remains. He also came across some ancient Egyptian pottery from the time of the Rameses pharaohs. This led him to wonder whether the island was originally a mining harbour used to support the activities at Timna, less than 30 km. north.

The underwater archaeologist Alexander Flinders takes this a step further and suggests that it is none other than the site of Etzion Geber, port to the ancient city of Eloth, mentioned in the Bible: 'King Solomon built a fleet of ships at Etzion-Geber, near Eloth on the shore of the Red Sea, in Edom. Hiram [King of Tyre] sent men of his own to serve with the fleet, experienced seamen, to work with Solomon's men; and they went to Ophir and brought back 420 talents of gold, which they delivered to King Solomon.' (1 Kings 9:26–8) It does not over exercise the imagination to visualize the queen of Sheba passing through with her camels, gold, spices and 'hard questions' on her way to Jerusalem in order to test the famed wisdom of King Solomon. Every three years Solomon's fleet of merchantmen would return bringing 'gold and silver, ivory, apes and monkeys'. Today's trade is limited to tourists.

It is also said that the French King Louis IX was incarcerated here after his capture during the Seventh Crusade while negotiations for his ransom were taking place.

It is a good example of how improved archaeological methods can increase our knowledge of an ancient site. It also provides a salutary warning not to believe everything the experts tell you for sooner or later another expert arrives on the scene with a revised version of the story!

The next landmark after the island is the appropriately locally-named fiord, an inlet of water enclosed on three sides by imposing cliffs. An entrepreneur from Cairo has opened up a café and campsite above the alluring sandy beach. He described himself as an artist escaping from the pressures of city life and attempting to encourage indigenous art in Sinai. I was shown some naïve rock carvings of animals claimed to be by a local elderly bedouin. I really didn't know whether to believe him or not and this uncertainty made me begin to feel uncomfortable. This was heightened when I returned later with some locals and he hardly spoke to us. They claimed that the carvings are to be found all over Cairo! Perhaps he really worked for the police as he went on about the problems caused by drug smugglers who bring drugs ashore under cover of darkness. He said that the drugs enter Sinai from Israel. Israelis say that the drugs entering Israel come from Sinai. I do know that they grow extensive crops of hashish in the high mountains behind St Catherine's Monastery; I have seen it myself. Perhaps he is one of the smugglers.

I was in danger of spending too long at the café. I did not have the discipline of George's presence and to saunter seemed fast enough. Realizing that there was not that long to go before I was due to be met by Egyptian friends who were organizing our passage through Sinai, I attempted to increase my pace. Just beyond the fiord the road turns inland and a range of hills cuts it off from the sea. For the first and only time I felt totally isolated. The impact of this unexpected solitude was at the same time electric and slightly frightening.

I immediately recognized the old Toyota jeep when it appeared on the horizon, bright red with a bouncy white soft top. Upon seeing me the lights began to flash and after pulling over, Muhammad, the liveliest of all the driver-cooks that I have travelled with, raced Rabia to be the first to greet me. Hugs and kisses followed as though, by British standards at least, we were long lost brothers being reunited. It is hard to describe the depth of feeling I have for Rabia and Muhammad, created perhaps by a common love of Sinai and the many nights spent together beneath the stars. Though from totally different worlds there exists a bond that I have rarely found at home.

Rabia is a man of few words but totally reliable actions, gentle but never lacking in the ability to make a decision. He is one of Egypt's 11 million Coptic Christians.

When I first met him he was providing jeep transport for Israeli companies wanting to operate in Sinai who would bring all their own equipment with them. As soon as he obtained some cooking utensils I arranged for St George's College to begin working with him and together we introduced hundreds of people to Sinai.

After marking the spot where they met me, in order to complete the walk the next day, we returned to Taba to collect Roy and the luggage. Just a few minutes from where they picked me up we came across a bus that had crashed off the road after its brakes had failed. It must have happened less than an hour after I had walked past. Fortunately no one was hurt though a very shaken and bruised driver's companion stood on the edge of the road opposite a severely crumpled front end. Some years ago a coach with German tourists suffered the same fate on the far steeper hill that drops down into Nuweiba. There were a number of fatalities on that occasion and today there are signposts every few yards warning drivers to stay in low gear and test their brakes. We collected our bags from our room and upon exiting the lift in the hotel foyer found ourselves surrounded by photographers and television camera crews. Suddenly the value of our walk had been recognized! The reality was that they were there because talks were taking place between Israeli and Palestinian delegations concerning the proposed boundaries of Jericho.

21 October, Day 26

There was only ten kilometres left to complete this morning and Roy joined me for the stroll. We attempted to walk along the beach but had to give up after three kilometres because it was such heavy going. We covered the distance in a little over two hours and I was then able to say that the 'walking only' section of the journey was complete. It was a great feeling and breakfast tasted particularly good. It also enabled a day of ease without itchy feet to be moving on.

There is no comparison between the Taba Hilton and the Sallyland tourist village. The opulence and anonymity of the former is magnified by the stylish simplicity and friendliness of the latter. The Sallyland is owned and operated by an Egyptian—American partnership that first came together operating a liquor store in the USA. After being made an offer that they could not refuse they hunted around for another venture in which to invest their money. Sinai was just beginning to open up for development at this time and beachfront was being sold at a vastly subsidized rate. It was too good an offer to refuse. The major obstacle to development on a far larger scale in the area is the lack of fresh water but here this was not to prove a problem. Not that John or Zac did much by the way of tests before purchasing, theirs was an informed guess.

Fresh water moving below ground is forced to the surface when it comes into contact with salt water and thus you find palm trees (which require fresh water) growing right up to the edge of the sea. Beer Suweir had a healthy collection of palm trees and thus there was bound to be fresh water just beneath the surface. The gamble was in guessing whether or not there would be enough for the wasteful habits of holidaying westerners. It was a gamble that paid off and by using local style architecture a little piece of paradise has been created. With the Gulf of Aqaba and the mountains of Saudi Arabia directly east, the hills of Sinai to the west, and no human settlements for 30 km. either north or south, this is the ideal escape from the stresses of daily life. It did not surprise me to discover that they now have a number of clients who stay for a few months at a time. It is no place for those who need constant amusement and raucous parties but for the self-contained it's a tonic.

Because I know that time is always time
And place is always and only place
And what is actual is actual only for one time
And only for one place
I rejoice that things are as they are.

T. S. ELIOT: *ASH WEDNESDAY*

Late in the afternoon eight participants for this final section of the journey arrived from England. To begin with I had mixed feelings about their presence as a part of me wanted to continue alone and I felt that my personal space was being invaded. However, their obvious enthusiasm for the venture helped to dispel lingering doubts, this and their carrying a letter from home. London felt further away than ever and the pace of life there a disease that I was pleased to be temporarily rid of. I wanted to reach up and lift the family out of it all. This desert could not offer, however, permanent escape; it would not satisfy. It provides an opportunity to re-evaluate and recharge so that one might return sensitized and more aware of our surroundings perhaps, but it could never replace them, for all their shortcomings.

22 October, Day 27

A rest day and an opportunity for us to begin to get know each other. We were a diverse group thrown together by the briefest of adventures.

Eric, at 67, was our patriarch. He was ever full of encouragement and a good story was always to hand whatever the degree of his personal discomfort. Once an insurance underwriter in Kenya and then in Japan, he was ordained later in life and assisted in the founding of St Catherine's Hospice in Crawley. 'A wise man climbs Mt Fuji once; a foolish man returns again', he was heard to mumble upon mounting the camel for a second time! Though enjoying himself it was soon clear that this was not a journey that he would wish to repeat.

Anabelle, ever vivacious and cheerful, even when ill, managed to find time to paint during the briefest of stops. She didn't really know why she had come, it 'just sounded wonderful and if I hadn't done it it would have haunted me as something that I might have done.' She left her three children with the Rector, her husband.

Tim Blewitt was the youngest of the party and never one to miss such an opportunity. He was using the journey to raise money for the Anglican Centre in Rome. We first met in Jerusalem when he was helping out in the cathedral. It was not a great success. Sarah threw him out of our flat because of his chauvinistic views about women and narrow perceptions of the role of a clergy wife! He insists that he was only being provocative.

Len Lunn, chaplain of St Christopher's Hospice, came with a greater sense of purpose than anyone else. He desperately wanted to experience the desert and this seemed the ideal way of doing so. The spiritual impact of the journey was particularly important to him.

Completely out of the blue, Geoff Burdett phoned me up at work one day. Explained that he had heard about the journey and wished to know whether he and Betty, his wife, could participate. This was simply the type of trip that they enjoy. He was a good amateur ornithologist who opened our eyes to see birds that we would not otherwise have noticed. He also brought a telescope with him that came into its own when pointing to the moon at night, which was a sight that particularly captivated the bedouin.

Theresa Wallis and Charles Buddenal Bruce were the two unknowns who heard about the venture through a mutual friend. Theresa, once an olympic skier, was the sort of person who could immediately fit into any group. Similarly Charles, though he was quiet and he never succeeded in befriending the flies that faithfully accompanied us during daylight hours.

At supper Eric asked me to say grace on behalf of the whole group which I refused to do. I had made it clear to everyone before they signed up that this was not going to be a formal pilgrimage and I was not going to take a 'religious' lead in any way. I had to refuse three times before Eric let it go and did it himself though in future he chose the silent option. I have no particularly strong feelings about saying grace but I didn't want to have myself put into a role. Everyone quickly learnt to follow their own leanings. Before supper finished I introduced three Arabic words which I hoped would help everyone adjust to the way of the desert: *Inshallah* (God willing), *Bukrah* (lit., tomorrow, though in reality an undefined period of time), *Mahlesh* (roughly translated as 'so what; does it really matter?').

I warned them that in the desert the emphasis has to be on being rather than doing. If asked, 'are we ever going to reach camp?' the answer can only be *inshallah*; if asked 'when are we going to arrive?' the answer will always be *bukrah* (with the added proviso that a day can be a thousand years); if anyone begins to get annoyed because we are not keeping to a proposed timetable or because a bedouin 45 minutes drags into three hours then the response will always be *mahlesh*. So what if this is the only chance you ever get to come to the Sinai Desert and for some reason we are prevented from reaching Mt Sinai. If you are still alive be happy. Learn how to be and don't worry about doing. It may sound a little extreme but to take this simple philosophy on board always makes for an easier journey. Every day has to be taken as it comes with no expectations. These words − *inshallah*, *bukrah*, *mahlesh* − are not a fanciful excuse for gross irresponsibility on my behalf. To date I have never failed to reach Mt Sinai, and usually to a pre-determined schedule. It is rather a statement about attitude, about unwinding, relaxing, letting go of the life of the city and pulling on the skin of the desert. (It has been suggested that these words make up the computer of the desert: IBM.)

I have learnt that an individual's external behaviour in the desert is not always a true reflection of their internal experience. I was once asked whether I had ever had any particularly difficult individuals with me and I started to tell the story of the only occasion in which I was driven to distraction and finally lost my temper. I refrained from mentioning any names and the person asking proceeded to tell me that her spiritual director had travelled with me the previous year and spoke of it as the most profound experience of his life to date. Needless to say he was one and the same person who gave me such grief.

23 October, Day 28

The camels had arrived at our meeting point, just beyond the hotel's western boundary, before we were up. Seeing them hobbled and feeding, against the backdrop of hills made golden by the morning sun, I had to pinch myself to check that I was awake. It was as though a scene from a childhood dream was materializing before me. These near miraculous creatures together with their colourful bedouin owners wearing the traditional *gebaliyah* blended naturally in to their desert home. Even the Sallyland seemed intrusive by comparison.

It is said that 'the camel is a horse invented by a committee'. This, surely, can only be spoken by those who have never acquainted themselves with this veritable miracle of evolutionary diversity. The committee may well be an animal invented by a horse; but the camel, the camel stands in a league of its own. Surprisingly, the camel began life 50 million years ago, no bigger than a rabbit, in North America. Known as *Protylopus* it was to take millions of years for today's camel to evolve and spread throughout the world. Flourishing in desert areas they roamed in wild herds until about 4,000 years ago when the process of domestication began in the Arabian peninsula. Apart from a small number of wild Mongolian camels all of today's camels are descendants of domesticated stock.

Today the camel's role as the economic cornerstone of nomadic pastoral communities has been replaced by goats, sheep, cash crops and, among the more affluent, the pickup truck. Though being used less for transportation – so perhaps no longer accurately the ship of the desert – its value as a rich source of protein through its milk (up to ten litres per day) and meat, as well as of shelter and warmth from its hair (approximately three kilograms per animal) and skin, is being re-evaluated and a number of countries have set up camel research centres. The breeding of racing camels is also a growth industry.

To me a camel is a camel is a camel though I can distinguish a two-humped bactrian from a one-humped dromedary. Those in the know say that there are, within the dromedary family, dozens of different types, each clearly recognizable. It has been suggested that the major classifications might conveniently be beef, dairy, dual-purpose and racing, to which may soon be added the tourist camel – bred to be both docile and comfortable!

Most remarkable of all is the camel's ability to go for up to 17 days without needing to replenish its water supply. Ora Lipschitz has listed the following traits which together qualify the camel as 'the beast best adapted to the desert'.

1   Its ability to withstand fluctuations of body temperature exceeding six degrees which means that it needs less water for cooling purposes. (Humans can't cope with more than a half a degree variation.)
2   Its large body mass means a slower rise in body temperature.
3   Its ability to loose up to 27% of its body weight in water without any ill effects because it is able at the same time to keep its plasma volume constant. (Humans cannot tolerate more than an eight to ten per cent loss.)
4   When water is available it is able to replace its entire loss in a few minutes.
5   Owing to a special kidney mechanism its urine is very concentrated and its faeces dry. The latter is used by the bedouin as fuel.
6   Its hair serves as an effective barrier against heat flow from the environment.
7   Its long legs keep it well away from the heat of the ground and you will rarely see it lying down in the sun during the heat of the day.

Katherine Sim notes that 'To the Egyptian Arab even the worst possible desert journey was preferable to a sea voyage, however brief. Louis records a typical saying that robustly expresses this feeling: "Rather the flatulencies of camels than the prayers of fishes." ' (*Desert Traveller*)

By eight o'clock we had loaded the night luggage onto the jeep – nicknamed the 'ambulance' as it could evacuate us if emergency demanded – imbibed our dose of caffeine, each selected our camel and departed. What other way could there be to travel, and not just in a three-day circle as do the tourists – but with a goal and a purpose. We slipped into the desert as though beamed down to another world. Quietly and without mishap we set off south, along the beach for the first 20 km., accompanied by a slim, long-legged, sandy coloured saluki bedouin dog. The saluki is said to have been among the first dogs to be domesticated in the ancient Near East. A welcome breeze accompanied us as we synchronized our movements to the swaying undulations of the ship of the desert.

Everyone managed to get into the stride of things remarkably quickly, apart that is from Eric who took almost two hours before succeeding in finding a position of 'masculine comfort'. The saddles were pitiless contraptions with 'handles' to the front and rear that constantly squashed or rubbed if you sat out of place. There were long stretches when I could only find comfort by sticking both legs straight out in front of me but then it was not long before my muscles died. The ideal position is to swing one leg up in front of you and across the camel's neck and then hook the other leg over your foot. Easy if you are in to yoga and double-jointed in half a dozen places! I wasn't helped by the large quantity of goods stored beneath my camel blanket which had the effect of giving my creature a particularly wide berth and making any repositioning of my legs nearly impossible.

When once started, I cannot speak too highly of the camel: he is the right beast in the right place; in colour, in outline, in movement he fits his environment; his spongy paws pass in perfect silence through the sand of the wilderness, his gentle ambling gait is a perpetual joy to the beholder, while the fascination of his supercilious expression never palls. . . . 'Though appearances are against me,' he seems to say, 'I am doing this journey for my own purposes, and at my own pace: I am stronger and wiser than you are. There are, indeed, ninety-and-nine attributes of Allah which man has collected from the Qur'àn, but there is a hundredth, and that the most beautiful, which I alone know, and which I shall never reveal.' These last words embody an Arab tradition of the camel, which sums up his whole character. . . . If asked, 'How do you ride a camel?' I reply, 'invent as many attitudes as you can, and employ them all in turn. . . . Ride how you will, and when you will; but above all, walk.'

M. RENDALL: *SINAI IN SPRING*

Just before stopping for lunch Betty began to feel faint which was more the result of the length of time since last eating than the swaying of the camel. The problem with lunch was always that we had to find shade from the sun, which meant a large enough tree and these are not all that plentiful. We had just turned from the coast, east into the mountains along the northernmost of two identically named Wadi Malha, when we stopped. The southern Wadi Malha is said to be the greener of the two; that is to say it has one or two acacia trees in it!

Part of a tent folded over a heavy stick was hanging in the tree that offered us shade during this first lunch break. If it had been left lying on the ground then anyone could help themselves to it, but it's hanging from a tree informed passers-by that it was owned by someone and should therefore be left alone. The amusing story is told of hikers who took everything of value from their car before leaving it parked in an isolated desert location. Bedouin, stumbling upon it, concluded that it must have been abandoned because none of the tell tale signs of owner-ship remained. They therefore thought it to be perfectly in order to help themselves and when the owners finally returned they found nothing more than the shell of a car! No doubt the story is apocryphal but it illustrates well the tension between the desert-dweller's respect for another's belongings and the city-dweller's needs to protect items by hiding them.

We continued as far up Wadi Malha as the jeep could reach before stopping for the night. After unpacking the luggage everyone set out to choose the potentially most comfortable location for their bed. Any number of factors might affect the final decision. For example where would offer the most shade from the morning sun or the greatest protection from the wind? The need for maximum potential comfort was usually at the top of the list. Sand, with a small hollow carved out for the bottom, could work if you are not prone to moving too much in your sleep. I had brought a thin mattress that automatically filled with air as you unrolled it and this seemed to offer greatest comfort on hard, flat, surfaces.

It was wonderful being under the stars again. Nothing that I have experienced elsewhere comes even close. The space, the wind, the fire-light, the companionship, the sky, even the rocks that always seem to lodge themselves uncomfortably beneath you however well you prepare your bed. Rabia explained that he had been a practicing doctor for only a year because he fell in love with the desert, with Sinai, and it was only a move into tourism that enabled him to return.

Conversation over supper focused on the state of the Church of England which felt strangely irrelevant to me. I was more detached from the structures of the Church than I had hitherto acknowledged. Tim and I sat and listened to Rabia, Muhammad and the bedouin gossiping away in Arabic around the embers of the fire long after the rest of the group had retired. Ghostly shadows were cast against the disturbed hills of loose gneiss (a coarse-grained metamorphic rock) that surrounded us. It felt like a homecoming. 'We were fond together, because of the sweep of the open places, the taste of wide winds, the sunlight . . .' (T. E. Lawrence: *Seven Pillars*)

24 October, Day 29

It was not difficult to rise with first light. Late evenings and early mornings are particularly savoured, free as they are from the activities and heat of the day. The hottest part of the day was between ten and two o'clock and it was almost dark by half past five. In the height of summer the heat shifts to between one and four o'clock though it is likely to be uncomfortably hot very soon after sunrise.

We ascended a pass that connected the two Wadi Malhas pulling our camels behind us. It was only on the level or on mild gradients that we would stay in the saddle. Sure footed as they appear they are not at there best on rugged climbs and the soft padded feet react against the sharp stones of Sinai's mountains. Half-way up, I disturbed a small snake that was bathing in the sun. It had chevron-shaped markings in a deep orange colour, almost brown. It moved far quicker than I and was into the rocks before the bedouin could arrive to identify it. Later discussions led to the conclusion that it was one of the most poisonous in Sinai (though I suspect that that would have been the conclusion whatever the snake).

It was an invigorating climb, in the shade most of the way, and the setting became more impressive with each step taken. From sea to mountains in a matter of minutes. There followed a strenuous three hours as we traversed the second Wadi Malha in order to reach the Colour Canyon. The one break in the journey came with the unexpected sighting of a Nabatean inscription which seemed even to surprise our guides. It was a welcome reminder that we were following an ancient route and it was easy to allow the mind to create images of what it might have been like to have travelled here 2000 years ago.

We could tell when the Colour Canyon was near because of the signs of so-called 'civilization' that began to afflict us. One small valley that we crossed was littered with empty plastic water bottles, the tourists' flotsam and jetsam lazily left behind. There seemed no excuse for it, since they are light enough to carry and burn easily. It made me angry and ashamed. I have always worked on the philosophy that a place should be left exactly as it is found, apart perhaps from a few footprints which the wind, in time, will take care of. We found an acacia and stopped for lunch just before walking through the canyon. A young Spanish couple with a wrinkled bedouin guide were camping there, spending a lazy morning overcoming stomach upsets. If they were distressed at having their shade invaded by 16 strangers they didn't show it and their guide seemed to be glad of the company. Survival in the desert is only possible by sharing carefully the meagre resources that exist, be they food, water or even shade. This is no place for the rush to the sunbed. It was natural to share whatever we had – tea, lunch – with them. However, I could foresee this desert hospitality breaking down as the number of tourists grows.

Our lunches were nothing to write home about though Muhammad always managed to surprise us at night with his pastas, chicken, kebabs and salads. Our daytime menu was dictated by what was available and what could be carried. There were occasional variations but it usually consisted of the following: tinned peas or beans, pilchards or spam, tuna, feta cheese, tomatoes, cucumbers, halva and locally made pitta bread. Tea would always come first, made by bringing a blackened kettle full of water to the boil and then adding fistfuls of tea and sugar. Its sweetness came as a shock first time around but its energy content was quickly appreciated and we fast became as dependent upon it as our hosts seemed to be. The bedouin made the pitta by kneading a simple mixture of flour, salt and water, spreading it out as you would a large pizza, in the manner of the most extrovert Italian chef playing to a full house of appreciative diners, and then laying it on the hot coals of the fire and covering it with hot ash. Some minutes later it would be snatched from the fire and, with the assistance of a nearby stone, the charcoal would be scrapped away and we would all partake. It tasted divine, though I am not sure that I would order it out of the context of the shade of an acacia tree in the middle of the desert on a hot day when we were all famished.

It is not only the colours that make the Colour Canyon impressive but the shapes that they come in: swirls, concentric circles and waves to describe but a few. Geologists fail to agree on how the colours entered the sandstone in such a manner. It is better to enjoy than speculate. In places the canyon becomes very narrow and a number of obstacles have to be negotiated which adds to the fun. We walked up the canyon whereas the majority come down and we were fortunate enough to have the place to ourselves until we reached the end (that is, normally the beginning) where we bumped into a small United Nations group. Whichever way you go you have to start with a descent and end with a climb. We were well pleased to see the camels waiting for us as we crawled up the final few steps of the cliff face. It was a strange day, one minute we were totally alone with little chance of meeting another tourist and the next we were in a location where they come by the jeep full. I should be grateful that the canyon exists as it seems to satisfy the need of many to experience the desert thus leaving the remainder of this vast wilderness to those of us who would venture further.

We travelled on through Wadi Nahayl, a large stony plain ringed by layers of hills each of an individual and unique beauty, until we found a suitable spot to camp for the night. To the west, dykes of varying colour competed to push their wares into view. As we travelled these last few miles Len asked whether it might be possible to request total silence from everyone in our convoy in order to absorb the stillness of our surroundings. I could well relate to the desire but was not convinced that such stillness could be created at will. There were to be occasions when a silence fell upon the group as a whole, perhaps caused partly by weariness but also I suspect by the subduing effect of the desert which seems to penetrate even the thickest of skins. The chatter and joking of the bedouin never disturbed me and even those occasions when their radio was working and Arabic melodies could be heard seemed not to matter as they were almost a continuum with the environment.

After making camp everyone apart from Charles and myself climbed a nearby rock and celebrated a Eucharist. There was something constructive and purposeful about this ritualistic way of drawing together the various diverse thoughts and experiences of the day. It is the complete lack of structure in the desert that has convinced me, more than anything else, of the need for ritual in our lives. Signposts that mark significant experiences and stages of life. Form and structure in what can otherwise be a frightening and boundary-less space. There is nothing that says that these rituals need to be religious but we seem to have lost the ability of creating our own and we have nothing else to fall back on.

On one journey across a large plain in western Sinai the jeep in which I was travelling suddenly stopped and the driver climbed out, washed his hands and feet with a minimal amount of water, knelt in the direction of Mecca and began to say his prayers. There was something about the use of the body in harmony with the words in that dramatic setting, as the sun sat low on the horizon, that caused a welling up from some hidden source deep within myself of a desire to walk over and join him. My traditions gave me no tools with which to respond and I felt bereft.

Rituals that may work in the city were found to be barren and inadequate in the desert.

It is fascinating to watch the different ways in which Christian pilgrim groups respond to the desert. For some an unadorned liturgy or saying of compline last thing at night is enough. Others though need to build some form of sanctuary within which to pray. I remember going to a site, at which I had frequently camped, and finding four crosses on hills surrounding the area and an altar built of broken sandstone fragments. I was surprised by the extent of my anger. Why this need to convert the environment? To make it safe perhaps? It seemed to me to be far holier in its pristine state and these structures appeared as an unsightly scar, a blasphemy even. I wonder how the Muslim bedouin drivers felt seeing this take place on their land. I doubt whether there sensitivities were considered, not that the bedouin of Sinai have a reputation for being particularly devout.

Just to spend time in the desert is to be confronted sooner or later by the presence of God. Perhaps the building of 'religious' artifacts acts to protect us from the disturbing nakedness of this encounter. We create recognizable forms in order to ensure the presence of a recognizable god. There is something about the aridity and lack of pretension of the untouched desert that invades the spirit and challenges the props of organized religion .

The bedouin could not look for God within him: he was too sure that he was within God. He could not conceive anything which was or was not God, who alone was great; yet there was a homeliness, and every-day-ness of this climatic Arab God, who was their eating and their fighting and their lusting, the commonest of their thoughts, their familiar resource and companion, in a way impossible to those whose God is so wistfully veiled from them by despair of their carnal unworthiness of him and by the decorum of formal worship. Arabs felt no incongruity in bringing God into the weaknesses and appetites of their least creditable causes. He was the most familiar of their words; and indeed we lost much eloquence when making him the shortest and ugliest of our mono-syllables.

This creed of the desert seemed inexpressible in words, and indeed in thought. It was easily felt as an influence, and those who went into the desert long enough to forget its open spaces and its emptiness were inevitably thrust upon God as the only refuge and rhythm of being.

T.E. LAWRENCE: *SEVEN PILLARS*

The Church came *en masse* to the desert with the arrival of the desert fathers and mothers, those strange shadowy individuals who succeeded in building a number of religious cities in the wilderness. There sayings, which were at first passed on orally and only later collected and written down, are said to provide the most authentic picture of what they believed and the way in which they lived. The problem is that the sayings are very diverse and every commentator seems to reach a different conclusion concerning the central elements of their thought. I doubt whether such even existed.

It was a variety of reasons that provoked individuals to join these communities. For some it was as matter of fact as the desire to avoid conscription or the payment of taxes and for others it was an escape from the increasingly unbearable pressures of village life. Abba Matoes said, 'If you cannot contain yourself, flee into solitude. For this is a sickness. He who dwells with brethren must not be square, but round, so as to turn himself towards all. . . . It is not through virtue that I live in solitude, but through weakness; those who live in the midst of men are the strong ones.' (Benedicta Ward: *Sayings*) Peter Brown suggests that it was this act of withdrawal, (*anachoresis*), in itself and not any supernatural powers that brought them popularity. They were 'acting out, heroically, before a society enmeshed in oppressive obligations and abrasive relationships, the role of the utterly self-dependent, autarkic man.' (*Late Antiquity*)

After the conversion of the Emperor Constantine, monasticism, in some instances, became spoken of as a type of bloodless 'white' martyrdom. Overnight the Church found itself occupying a position of influence in high society which invariably led it to lose something of the moral power and independence it had known throughout the Era of the Martyrs, the age of the great persecutions. The monks attempted to keep this alive and their numbers were increased by many who were concerned to oppose this creeping conformity. As Fr Louis Bouyer comments, 'it was not so much the monastic life which was a novelty . . . but rather the life of adaption to the world led by the mass of Christians at the time when the persecution ceased. The monks actually did nothing but preserve intact, in the midst of altered circumstances, the idea of the Christian life of the early days.' The direct call of God was also an extremely important factor. 'The Gospel alone, heard and taken literally by simple souls in Egypt and in quite different places as well – caused the rise of anchoritism.' (Bouyer)

Fr Tom Brown SSM who has accompanied me to Sinai on a number of occasions liked to focus attention on the following elements of the desert tradition that seemed particularly relevant today.

Simplicity: the detachment from dependence on other people and things, in order to stand empty-handed before God. The desert is a place of stripping and purifying, a place where there are no luxuries, spiritual or otherwise.

Waiting: A desert spirituality is a spirituality of waiting upon God. There is an element of timelessness, of eternity, about the desert. The characteristic prayer of the desert is a prayer of simple waiting.

Struggle: Desert spirituality is a spirituality of struggle, which is inevitable as we seek to know and to journey into ourselves, to face the demons in the depths of our personalities. It is a struggle with the apparent absence of God and a struggle in the darkness of our own emptiness and insufficiency.

CHAPTER NINE

Through the Sinai Desert: 2

He longed to taste the joy of the desert again; it is a strangely gripping joy that fires all who have known it to impassioned expressions of delight. In fact the stimulus of desert travel is quite unbelievable to those who have never experienced it — its ardours, its dangers and, transcendingly, the wonder of the ever-changing sky, the play of light and shade on vast expanses, tremendous horizons. Man is very small in the desert but he responds to the challenge in a way that acts as a tonic to the spirit, since as the Arabs say 'voyaging is victory', and to cross the desert is to voyage triumphantly.

KATHERINE SIM: *DESERT TRAVELLER*

At night, lying awake under the stars, the cities of the west seemed sad and alien — and the pretensions of the art world idiotic . . . Yet here I had a sense of homecoming.

BRUCE CHATWIN: *SONGLINES*

25 October, Day 30

L AST NIGHT I DREAMED that I had returned home and could not get in through the door because of all the tea-towels (or were they *keffiyehs?*) that were tied, spider web fashion, throughout the house. I am sure that Sarah will interpret this as my feeling trapped by domestic trivia but I am not convinced that it is so straightforward.

Continuing south through Wadi Nahayl we reached the tarmacked Wadi Watir at the oasis 'Ein el-Furtaga. Wadi Watir forms part of the main road from Nuweiba to Suez via the village of Nakhl in central Sinai. It is also a major drainage basin for east Sinai and when there are heavy rains the flood-waters build up when they reach the narrow section near 'Ein el-Furtaga. The power of these flash floods is seen by the ease with which the tarmac road is destroyed, large chunks being thrown against nearby rockfaces as though they were so much tissue paper. Less than 24 hours after we crossed Wadi Watir such a flood struck. It could have held us up for a day or more if it had come earlier.

Crossing Wadi Watir with care, to avoid the vehicles travelling at reckless speeds that seem to appear out of nowhere, we entered Wadi Gazella, the valley of the Gazelles. This is an important north-south artery which was used by the Ninth Brigade of the Israel Defense Forces on their epic push through to Sharm el-Sheikh during the 1956 Suez campaign. The vehicles that broke down *en route*, or became stuck in the sand, remain to this day as reminders of recent occasions in which the peninsula's silence was violently shattered.

At the bottom of Wadi Gazella we watered the camels from a square concrete trough positioned next to a small bedouin garden against the eastern wall of the valley. With their necks bent low they took in vast quantities of water remarkably quickly. Altogether a timeless scene, which I observed from a ledge some 20 m. above.

On previous visits when travelling by jeep Wadi Gazella had seemed to go on for ever. I was not therefore looking forward to this section of the journey and the thought of having to proceed uphill, with little in the way of shade, lowered my expectations even more. The northern section is very rocky and sharp bends appear at regular intervals which prevented us from seeing where we were going or how far we had come. The southern reaches are far more exciting with heavy sands and sculptured sandstone rock formations. In the middle of the last century Sir Richard Burton made the following comment during his visit to Sinai:

> we journeyed on till near sunset through the wilderness without *ennui*. It is strange how the mind can be amused by scenery that presents so few objects to occupy it. But in such a country, every slight modification of form or colour rivets observation; the senses are sharpened and the perceptive faculties, prone to sleep over a confused mass of natural objects, act vigorously when excited by the capability of embracing each detail.
>
> RINNA SAMUEL: *THE NEGEV AND SINAI*

To my surprise we passed through the valley without boredom or discomfort. It must have had something to do with being on camels instead of shut up in a jeep. Everything felt so much closer. It was impossible not to interact with our surroundings.

> All around us was nothing. . . . The environment both humbled and exalted. . . . At the same time the vast emptiness of the desert reduced our tiny, struggling world to absolute insignificance: a small nest of living creatures with no more permanence than a gust of wind playing across the face of the ocean. . . . I discovered that my surroundings were having a strange effect. My mind became unusually clear and lucid, and I found myself following logical trains of thought for several hours without losing the thread. I was able to think more profoundly about myself than I had been for many years, to examine my motivations, aims and objects in a new and surprisingly fresh light. This was totally unexpected, and I guessed that it was a result of the low sensory input which one experiences in the desert. In our normal environment, our thoughts are constantly

bombarded by information gathered from our surroundings which are in a state of perpetual change. In the desert, though, the surroundings are static and featureless, liberating the mind and allowing strings of ideas to run and develop in logical chains.

MICHAEL ASHER: *FORTY DAYS ROAD* .

I noticed Tim reading T. S. Eliot and Len a book on the desert fathers, while swaying back and forward on the camel's hump. Geoff was constantly on the look out for new birds and Anabelle was enjoying the company of Salah, who, at about 11 years of age (no one knew for certain) was the youngest of the bedouin. He was sharing her camel by sitting close up behind her. Betty was just beginning to discover comfortable ways of surviving in the saddle and Charles and Theresa were walking hard to keep up. Eric had taken a day out because of saddle sores. We later discovered that he spent much of the time resting in a bedouin tent, pitched for the entertaining of tourists, at the southern end of Wadi Gazella.

After lunch, about two-thirds of the way through the valley, we turned south west into Wadi Hudra (the green valley) so named because it leads to 'Ein Hudra, the largest oasis in this part of Sinai. By this time sand had replaced the stones beneath us and Nubian sandstone formed the rock formations around us. We passed a few gardens (by desert standards that is, not English) marked off by barbed wire in order to keep out ravaging goats, but otherwise only the white broom (*retama roetam*) bushes that littered the *wadi* floor broke up the sand.

The broom survives the heat by shedding a large part of its body which would otherwise lose precious water by transpiration. It is also helped by an extensive network of roots, the main one descending very deep and other, lateral roots, spreading along the ground over a wide area. These roots make excellent charcoal and are ideal for camp fires: 'For all other coals are extinguished inside (when they are extinguished on the outside), but coals of broom still burn within when they are extinguished without. . . . It once happened that a broom tree was set on fire and it burned for eighteen months: winter, summer and winter.'

(Midrash Genesis Rabbah XCIII:19) The charcoal is made by placing the broom bush into a hole and then covering it with sand. A small opening is kept through which the bush is kindled. This ensures that the burning is slow and the bush is therefore carbonized rather than destroyed. The white broom grows to a good size and Elijah is recorded as laying beneath one during his flight from Ahab and Jezebel (*1 Kings*, 19). I have not seen one large enough to provide shade to cover a human but there is plenty of room for the head and throughout the early morning and late afternoon they cast a refreshing shadow.

It is a haunting experience to sit, towards the end of the day, seemingly alone, in the middle of nowhere, listening to the desert wind whistling through the spidery branches of the white broom. It is often the case that wind can be seen coming from afar, disturbing the surface of the sand, carrying dust in its train, before it can be heard, and then it is heard before it is felt. In London wind has only ever been something instinctively to cover up from, here it becomes a force to be exulted in.

> At last Dahoum drew me, 'Come and smell the very sweetest scent of all', and we went into the main lodging, to the gaping window sockets of its eastern face, and there drank with open mouths of the effortless, empty, eddyless wind of the desert, throbbing past. That slow breath had been born somewhere beyond the distant Euphrates and had dragged its way across many days and nights of dead grass, to its first obstacle, the man-made walls of our broken palace. About them it seemed to fret and linger, murmuring in baby-speech. 'This', they told me, 'is the best: it has no taste.' My Arabs were turning their backs on perfumes and luxuries to choose the things in which mankind had had no share or part.

> T. E. LAWRENCE: *SEVEN PILLARS*

It was clear, by the way in which his pace began to quicken, that Farraj, owner of the camel I was riding, came from this area. He was not one to rush at the best of times and his beasts, faithfully imitating their master, were always to be found at the rear of the convoy. Together with his brothers he owns one of the largest gardens at 'Ein Hudra. All of our bedouin guides – Farraj, Salah, Selim, Suleiman, Alian and Sheikh Hamad ('Sheikh of the camels', responsible for the hiring out of camels within his tribal territory) – seemed to be in good spirits.

Salah was described as 'pure bedouin' by the others for he was born and brought up in Wadi Saal, inside Sinai, away from the outside influences found around the coast. His accent was different from the others and he knew many specialist bedouin words unknown even to the rest. This was all a constant source of animated discussion and amusement. His speech was always rapid yet it had a melodic purity about it. When asked why he wasn't at school he raised his arms into the air and asked how he could stay within four walls and a low ceiling when presented with the option of wandering in the desert. There is a famous bedouin legend which runs:

From the heavy cloud which brings blessings to the land, the Lord took a piece and created the camel – heavy and beneficial. He shot an arrow, caught it again, and thereof he created the horse – swift as an arrow and true to its target. From the wind which spins around the earth he created the bedouin – roaming like the wind and just as free. He took a handful of dust from the earth and created the donkey – humble and low and close to the earth. As he stood up and dropped his excrements, he created from them the *fellah* [farmer]. . . . And up to this day the bedouin feels himself as light as the wind, wandering forever, not knowing where he will spend the night.

DAPHNE DEKEL: *BEDOUIN FOLKLORE*

We asked Rabia about the transition from boyhood to manhood within bedouin society and whether there are any rites of passage. He told us that 20 plus years ago, when the Gebeliyah bedouin around St Catherine's Monastery were very poor, they depended on the monastery for bread. Two loaves would be given to the women and boys and three to the men which led to the question, when does a boy become a man? The answer was very practical, namely that you become a man when you are able to walk from St Catherine's Monastery to the town of et-Tur on the Gulf of Suez between the ringing of the monastery's three o'clock mid-night bell and that for the evening service at et-Tur. There does not seem to be clearly defined rites of passage but there must come a time when they are included in the councils that are frequently called to discuss all manner of issues that affect the life of the tribe. It struck us that Salah was treated as an equal by the others even though he was less than half the age of the next youngest. There seemed to be no condescension in their attitude to him. Most boys in western society are removed from their fathers place of work, not so here where a pre-industrial lifestyle still allows room for a son's progressive involvement in all aspects of a father's life. Muslims and Coptic Christians in Egypt are circumcised sometime between ages one and four. The Copts claim to have inherited the practice as an ancient pharonic tradition.

On this third night under the stars we camped in a sandy promontory just a few hundred yards from 'Ein Hudra. Laying back against my rolled sleeping bag I was able to look down Wadi Hudra along the track we had earlier traversed. It presented a beautiful vista of undulating sand surrounded by honeycombed sandstone hillocks of deep yellow and gruff red. It was another of those timeless moments that I wouldn't have swopped for the world. 'The deeper we penetrated into the Sahara, the more time slowed down for me; it even threatened to move backwards . . . and when we reached the first palms and dwelling of the oasis, it seemed to me that everything here was exactly the way it should be and the way it had always been.' (Carl Jung: *Memories*)

26 October, Day 31

It was only a few yards from where we camped to the lush oasis, 'Ein Hudra, which was a hive of activity. Burckhardt was the first European scholar to visit this area and he identified it with the biblical Hazeroth (*Numbers*, 12). Later, Palmer and Wilson went so far as to claim that they could identify traces of the Israelite camp though it is now generally accepted that no incontrovertible archaeological evidence of the Israelite Exodus has yet been found anywhere in the Sinai peninsula.

Hazeroth was the stopping place of the Exodus where 'Miriam and Aaron began to speak against Moses . . . who was in fact a man of great humility, the most humble man on earth.' (I wonder who wrote that?) The result of these grumbles was that Moses received approval from the Lord and Miriam suffered a seven day skin disease for her grumbling. Aaron seemed to get off scot free. 'Hear my words: If there is a prophet among you, I the Lord make myself known to him in a vision, I speak with him in a dream. Not so with my servant Moses; he is entrusted with all my house. With him I speak mouth to mouth, clearly, and not in dark speech; and he beholds the form of the Lord. Why then were you not afraid to speak against my servant Moses?' (*Numbers*, 12:6–8) Given these events it is hardly surprising that they were quick to move on.

Reaching Hazeroth was our first direct encounter with the memory of Moses. His presence haunts the wilderness, such are the stories told of him, and however much they may be distorted by the ravages of time the kernel remains remarkable. The escape of a persecuted minority into an unknown future through an unfriendly wasteland. We may not wish to take all the details literally (if you take some of the numbers at face value – hoards marching four abreast and one metre apart – then it has been calculated that the first would have entered the promised land before the last left Egypt) but there is no doubting the heroic nature of this trek that has since become a paradigm for oppressed individuals and liberation movements throughout the world, 20th century Palestinians excepted of course.

The Exodus may have been of hundreds rather than thousands but it remained a sufficiently powerful experience to become the unifying creed of a new nation. I don't envy Moses his title role. It's bad enough when the group has paid to come, had plenty of time to prepare and carries the latest in portable camping comforts such as self-inflating air mats and gas fired curling tongs! Would Miriam have moaned if Moses had provided these I wonder. I once had an American Episcopal priest with me who compared being in Sinai to his experience in Vietnam. He added that if he had to choose one to return to it would be Vietnam! But he was an exception: it had been the hottest May temperature on record and he did insist on drinking beer as we drove into the desert. Dehydration was a foregone conclusion and I had little sympathy for him as I observed the increasingly frequent visits to the nearest broom bush.

Toilet procedures and body hygiene are invariably the greatest psychological problems that the desert initiate has to face. There is usually only enough water for cleaning teeth and drinking, and toilet paper is never used apart from a box of matches. If it doesn't burn, and won't decompose, then into a rubbish bag it has to go. Some people prefer to remain uncomfortably constipated over a five-day trip. You can usually tell who they might be by measuring their level of grumpiness against their normal disposition! We are out of touch with the more basic activities of our bodies in the city, unless sickness forces us to be otherwise. In the desert, keeping an eye on urine output is a simple litmus test of health. If you are passing water too often and it is extremely weak then you need to replenish body salts. If on the other hand it is both infrequent and highly concentrated then it is time to drink more. Unfortunately if you only drink when thirsty you will never take aboard enough liquid and you run the risk of dehydrating. The desert is a very physical place and can also be a very sensuous one.

'Ein Hudra is the largest oasis in east Sinai but to an outsider it appears dwarfed by its barren surroundings. It is divided into a number of plots of date palms (*Phoenix dactilifera*) each tended by different family groups from the same tribe. The garden cared for by Farraj and his brothers has a good-sized sunken reservoir that collects water from the spring prior to its being used for irrigation. If you are lucky enough to arrive when it is full then it is possible to enjoy a dip, that is if you don't mind the algae and oversized hornets whose 'sting' hangs beneath them like a bomb carriage.

Whenever obtaining drinking water from a spring it is important to go as close to the source as possible. In this instance the thin hose that filled the pool came directly from the mouth of the spring so we were safe in filling our water carriers from it. I have always drunk Sinai's water, from spring and well, without precautions and to date I am none the worse for it. That is not to say that all sources are fit to drink from. Many, though good for camels, are too salty for humans.

We arrived at 'Ein Hudra at the end of the harvesting season when the bedouin families were all in residence. For the remainder of the year the place stands strangely deserted. The woman unfurled blankets for us to sit on, beckoned us to drink tea and tried, with a refined technique, to sell us trinkets, shells, unusual rocks, locally-made mascara, *keffiyeh's* (unashamedly stamped with 'made in China'), items of pottery, and even embroidered dresses and ornately woven camel blankets. Young children barely walking and in nothing but rags tottered among the wares with months of cold showing from eyes and nose. Finding a patch of shade with somewhere to rest my back I drank in this feast of the senses which was ruined all too quickly by the arrival of another (a tourist) group.

According to legend the date palm has its head in fire and its feet in water, which is a way of expressing its need for plenty of groundwater as well as heat. Once it takes root it is almost immovable and though a flood may destroy a tarmac road with relative ease the palm trees, invariably survive. After planting they don't require a great deal of tending. Each spring a delegated member of the tribe, who has to be a good climber, transfers pollen from the male to the female trees, and then they are left until the harvest. The bedouin make good use of every part of the date palm by 'eating the fruit and drying the rest into pulp; feeding the kernels to camels and goats; and employing the trunk for construction and fuel, the branches for roofing, the fibre for rope and basket making.' (Ora Lipschitz: *Sinai*)

As the new group slowly succeeded in occupying the garden we decided to retreat to a nearby *magaad*, that is a traditional bedouin guest house. Normally, a portion of tea, sugar and perhaps even flour would be left here so that passing travellers can cater for themselves. Even entertainment was provided for by way of a board cut into the ground for the popular bedouin game *seega*. After talking for a while about the history and customs of the oasis, Rabia led us on to the 'rocks of inscriptions' via the White Canyon.

The rock of the White Canyon is powdery and it covered us when we rubbed against it. The final ascent out of the canyon is steep and involves climbing a ladder that is fixed only at the bottom and swinging precariously at the top. It triggered a memory that I couldn't quite place; it made me wonder whether I had been this way before. Two eagles hovering above saw us safely through to Hadabat Hejaj, the wide flat plain of the pilgrims that leads south towards a 'café' and the main road from the Gulf of Aqaba to St Catherine's Monastery. We briefly turned aside in order to enjoy the view back towards 'Ein Hudra:

> Through a steep and rugged gorge with almost perpendicular sides, we looked down upon a *wadi* bed that winds between fantastic sandstone rocks, now rising in the semblance of mighty walls or terraced palaces, now jutting out in pointed ridges – rocky promontories in a sandy sea. Beyond this lies a perfect forest of mountain peaks and chains. . . . But the great charm of the landscape lies in its rich and varied colouring;
>
> E. H. PALMER: *DESERT OF THE EXODUS*

With the intense greens of the oasis being made to excel by its surroundings and all this framed by the clearest of skies this has to be one of the great sights of Sinai.

Close by stood the first of a series of rocks upon which pilgrims from another age have left their mark. At the time it may have been condemned as graffiti but for us it was a comforting reminder of others who had felt equally compelled to make this journey. In a survey undertaken by Abraham Negev in 1971, 128 Greek, 17 Nabatean, five Hebrew, one each of Arabic and Armenian, one unidentified and two modern inscriptions on this rock were recorded. The rock is now surrounded by a low wall but sadly this has not prevented modern tourists from scraping their offerings over these ancient biddings (taken from Abraham Negev: *Inscriptions*) most of which appear to be simple prayers for help: (after A. Negev) 'O Lord Jesus Christ remember and help you servant Sammasas son of Abraham, and Peter son of Anastasia.' 'Saint Stephen, protect your servant Theophilus.' It seems that we were not the first to find the going tough. 'Christ conquers! O Christ, help Marcellus.' Some brought their families along with them: 'O Lord, guard under your protection your servant Stephen son of Antison, and his wife and children.' Some were travelling in fulfilment of a vow and others were in search of forgiveness. 'O Lord, grant me forgiveness for my sins. *Kyriakos*. Amen.' As well as these Christian pilgrim inscriptions there is also a large rock carving of a *menorah* surrounded by Hebrew–Nabatean script. Traditional Nabatean pottery has been found at a number of sites in the area which would suggest that they once lived here, organizing perhaps the growing, drying and shipping of dates to Europe.

For a long time it was assumed that the majority of pilgrims travelling between Jerusalem and Mt Sinai went via the Mediterranean (Ashqelon and Gaza) and the Gulf of Suez. More recently a growing body of opinion has suggested that a shorter route was taken through the Nabatean (and latterly Byzantine) cities of the Negev to Aila (Eilat) and then via Wadi el-Heri, Wadi Watir, Wadi Gazella and Wadi Haggag to St Catherine's. This would have included 'Ein Hudra as a major source of water. We were on the right track. 'There was once a party of 800 Armenian pilgrims who passed this way and while they were on the holy summit in order to see from a distance the holy stone where Moses received the Law . . . the holy summit and all of them were enveloped in flame.' (Philip Mayerson: *Pilgrim Routes*) It would appear that the best was yet to come.

'Ein Hudra café, a scruffy wooden shack with a barred serving window, on the edge of the tarmac road, 200 m. from this the largest of the rocks of inscriptions rudely returned us to the 20th century. The choice of goods was minimal, consisting of a few tins of concentrated guava juice, individually wrapped wafer biscuits, some bottled water and the ever present Cleopatra cigarettes. Young smiling faces beamed out from the darkness as we did our bit towards boosting sales. The shack was divided into two and a noisy bedouin conference was taking place in the side room. We weren't there long enough to find out the details.

We took lunch in the nearby Wadi Gibi, far enough away to forget the existence of the road. A wizened elderly bedouin lady and two young girls appeared and sat silently while we ate. We offered them food but they would not participate until we had finished. Not long afterwards, Atwa, an elderly gentleman, arrived and immediately everyone was on their feet showing formal signs of respect. Whether it was just his age or because of who he was I don't know, but it was a tonic to see the universal deference offered him. He did partake of some food with us; more, I suspect, in order to fulfil the obligations of hospitality than from hunger.

> The elders of a family have a special status. They are the only ones who do not work. Their main duty is to preserve the peace of the family and care for the women when the young men leave the encampment to work outside. The members of the family honour their elders deeply for their past exploits. From the elders the young ones get their lessons in tribal lore. They hear about how leopards were once hunted in Sinai, about past intertribal warfare, and of course romantic stories of love, hate and blood feud.
>
> DAPHNA DEKEL: *BEDOUIN FOLKLORE*

Five minutes after lunch we arrived at 'The Nawamis', one of the most exciting archaeological sites in Sinai. It consists of a cluster of small beehive-shaped buildings made of slate-like sections of the local Nubian sandstone. This sandstone has a high iron oxide content that has helped to preserve the buildings; elsewhere they have collapsed as a result of weathering. Each structure has one opening in a westerly direction and they are built with two walls, the internal one arching into the middle to form a curved roof. There is a bedouin story which says that these structures were used by the children of Israel to protect themselves from a plague of mosquitoes, hence the name *nawamis* meaning mosquito. There has been much argument as to their true purpose but it seems to be generally accepted that they are secondary burial sites which possibly date back 5–5,500 years. If this is correct then they must be among the oldest man-made roofed buildings that still stand unaided.

The most important discovery in Sinai, not from finds but in their absence, was the *noa'mis (nawamis)* culture – the nomads. It represents a tremendous philosophical revolution in the approach to human history. . . . 'Because of isolation,' Goren explains, 'southern Sinai can serve as a very good model of the relationship between man and the environment. . . . The important thing was to understand what we had found. It was clear to us in the beginning that each *noa'mis* belonged to an individual family. Groups of *noa'mis* belonged to an extended family, and every burial field to a tribe, so that the structure of the *noa'mis* society resembled that of the present-day bedouin societies. It is impressive and incredible that in 6,000 years, nothing has changed.

'If we return to prehistory the most important period was the Neolithic revolution, in which humans began to produce food, rather than being dependent upon hunting and gathering. What was revealed in post-Neolithic Sinai was that during that period, the subtropical regions began to dry up, and the deserts of the Levant came into being. The hunters and gatheres had nothing left to hunt or gather.

'The people of the desert were at an impasse. They had to begin raising goats for milk, meat and wool. This, in fact, is the first appearance of a pastoral society – a society of nomadic shepherds

. . . We believe that the people of the *noa'mis* culture comprised the first society, which was followed by the appearance of similar nomadic societies.'

AVNER GOREN IN CONVERSATION WITH TSUR SHEZAF:
LEAVING NO TRACKS

The best time to visit is towards the end of the day when you gain the impression that the openings were positioned in order to face the setting sun. The slight variation in alignment could be explained by the fact that they were built at different times of the year. This makes sense if they are associated with death and burial. It is easy to get carried away imagining the rituals that may once have taken place in the area as nomadic groups brought the previously interned remains of their kin to a final resting place. The need to acknowledge death is a timeless one that acts as a point of connection between ourselves and these unknown ancestors.

Today the bedouin frequently bury their dead in the vicinity of a sheikh's tomb. A sheikh is an outstanding personality in the tribe who becomes a saint in his lifetime and then, after his death, an object of veneration. Two unadorned stones are used to mark the body's location, one at the head and one at the feet. The head is positioned in such a way as to face Mecca. Upon asking why it is that no name is inscribed on a headstone I received the following reply: 'Those who knew and cared for me in life will remember where I lie. For the others, what does it matter?' This is a good example of an understated simplicity that remains with the bedouin from life through death. The bedouin do not hide from death, it is accepted as a part of life. Buried upon the day of death the bones will be gathered together 40 days later and moved to their final resting place. 'To die in the open, under the sky, far from the insolent interference of leech and priest, before this desert vastness opening like a window onto eternity – that surely was an overwhelming stroke of rare good luck.' (Edward Abbey: *Desert Solitaire*) I like the idea of my grave being marked by two blank stones, though I would want the pretension of their having being brought from Sinai (that is, if I wasn't already there).

In sombre mood we set off towards our camping site. A long trek lay ahead of us as I had insisted on our travelling via Jebel Muhroom, a mountain with a hole bored through it by the wind. It is a site that has many powerful associations for me. From the Nawamis we passed through Wadi Kiri to Jebel Baracha which I was informed is the tourist name for Jebel Barga, a term used to describe a rock that has a little sand on its summit. The area surrounding this rock, which is more a small mountain, is known as Farsh el-Barga. Farsh simply means wide *wadi* so we have a very descriptive term for the large open space surrounding the mountain that wears sand on its head! This was the sandiest section of our trek and, as I discovered to my confusion, the bedouin have a number of expressions for differing sand formations. Jebel Mahroom is one of the many smaller hills on the Farsh el-Barga. It may well be that I got the wrong end of the stick with these explanations, but it seemed to make sense at the time. It has been suggested to me since that the word *muhroom* might be associated to that meaning forbidden or sacred.

Upon entering the Farsh el-Barga I decided to walk, despite the soft sand. Most of my blisters had healed by now and I felt as fit and healthy as ever I could remember. In order to keep abreast of the camels I began to jog, and the next thing I knew was that there was a full-scale race going on. It was late in the afternoon and a cool breeze accompanied us. The three participating bedouin were cheering their mounts on against this lone overweight Englishman. As I upped my pace I expected to tire quickly but to my amazement I found a spring in my step and a degree of stamina previously unknown. It was an exhilarating few moments that seemed to go on for ever. Concerned to make the most of being out in front I declared the race over, a decision totally ignored by the bedouin.

We were temporarily travelling due east, and we had managed to spread ourselves out over quite a distance. Everybody was tired and the sun was now low in the sky. It was an electrifying sunset as the dying rays bounced off clouds behind us creating fan like patterns across the sky ahead onto a distant chain of mountains. Three such radiating beams of light stayed with us for a good 20 minutes, changing colour and intensity as the clouds moved and night approached. I was mesmerized by the beauty of the event and a corporate sense of awe spread through the group. No one had seen anything quite like it and the bedouin began to ask what it might mean. We kept walking as the jeep had not yet arrived and we were not too clear about where we should be camping. A saker falcon, attacking in large swooping dives two trespassing ravens, added to the sense of the dramatic. I bemoaned my rationalist disposition that prevented me from asking what it meant. It did not, however, prevent me feeling slightly overwhelmed by this juxtaposition of events. To me this place was already the nearest thing to holy ground that I knew and the phenomena simply confirmed it.

As I lay inert, while the water boiled for tea, the sun slid down between my outstretched legs out of a paling sky, its edges trembling for a moment, as though liquid, before it disappeared. The camels, browsing among a bit of scrub, were outlined against its glow, darkening into mere shapes as they rapidly lost all hint of substance. We had set up camp beside the only tree for miles, and a cricket was singing somewhere deep within its thorny branches. Apart from that noise and the sputtering of the flames, the world was soundless, without even a wisp of wind; it seethed with silence. Apart from the slow, ponderous shuffle of the hobbled beasts, it was entirely still. In this stillness, I could see, lay the fruitfulness of the desert that mystics had found across many ages. It calmed the soul and made it possible to fix the attention at any point one chose without distraction. I wished, that evening, I could remain in that spot, motionless, until I had so absorbed the desert's balm that something unknown to me dawned upon my understanding. Lying there at peace, one felt so close to a brink of revelation that it seemed almost within willpower.

GEOFFREY MOORHOUSE: *FEARFUL VOID*

Jebel Muhroom has always been a place of such encounter for me and my thoughts were quick to wander back to previous visits.

25 June 1990

To think, Sarah, that you have never been here to Jebel Muhroom. Yes the same old place. Already I am in need of ritual and though there is no group with me the same journey is made to this vast open space ringed by mountains of ghostly form. There is no debris of history here. No interference of man. I can pick up stones that have never been moved before – I can be the first to marvel over their form and diversity. I can leave my prints in the sand and feel by so doing that in some small way I am creating the world.

Here you don't need to dig to find the past for it lies on the surface, together with the present and the future. Here I become a part of this world and it becomes a part of me. My own past, present and future also become jumbled and my deepest thoughts and secrets sit lightly to my skin.

26 June 1990

Sarah, you would have been proud of me last night. After supper the three of us sat with our backs to the rock waiting for the stars to appear. It was like that moment in the cinema after the lights have gone down and before the film has started. After about ten minutes I rose and strode off, bare foot still, into the darkening silence. It was not long before the jeep became indiscernible against the cliff and then with not a little hesitation I undressed. The shirt was easy, my pants and watch less so. I stepped out of my clothes and into the wind and felt as though I was stepping into a cool pool of water. I did not feel like skipping or dancing but slowly I placed one step in front of the other as though for the first time.

The wind was cool but not cold. No tingling on the spine but a return to native simplicity. . . . I looked down and seeing the marks left by the sun I saw my body for the first time. Then I looked up and saw the nights first star awakened by my discovery. I felt no shame and I was very content to own this shape that protruded down from my neck.

I had not been alone in this freedom.

My companions and I had the good fortune to taste the world of Africa, with its incredible beauty and its equally incredible suffering, before the end came. Our camp life proved to be one of the loveliest interludes in my life. I enjoyed the 'divine peace' of a still primeval country. Never had I seen so clearly 'man and other animals' (Herodotus). Thousands of miles lay between me and Europe, mother of all demons. The demons could not reach me here. There were no telegrams, no telephone calls, no letters, no visitors. My liberated psychic forces poured blissfully back to the primeval expanses.

CARL JUNG: *MEMORIES*

27 October, Day 32

Young Salah may not be too clear about his age but he has a fair understanding of bedouin law. He argued that because the punishment for the killing of a woman or a sheikh is the same, that is the taking of four lives in return, a sheikh must be the equivalent of a woman! This caused endless mirth and fortunately Sheikh Hamed failed to take offence.

It was a gentle day of wide sandy *wadis* and rapid, melodic, humorous conversation among the bedouin that we didn't understand but nevertheless participated in. No one was in a hurry and the day slowly slipped by. Anabelle had returned to Nuweiba with Muhammed because of some sickness in the night and had the exciting experience of seeing a bus caught in a flash flood. After tearing ourselves away from Jebel Muhroom we travelled via Wadi Hamam to Beer Safra where we watered the camels and cooled the backs of our necks, the water being too salty for us to drink. We enjoyed a lengthy lunch break in Wadi Saal before continuing through Wadi Hamatameer to Wadi Matura where we set up camp once more. As the shadows lengthened nearby rocks began to take on mysterious forms. As with clouds it was possible to discern changing shapes and patterns. A crocodile wearing a large back-pack hung upside down beside my sleeping bag. Suleiman gave Anabelle a local herb, *baitheran*, for her stomach and to everyone's surprise it had the desired effect.

28 October, Day 33

Within minutes of setting out we left the wide sandy *wadis* for narrow mountain paths. Apart from an occasional set of camel prints there were no signs of other travellers on these tracks. Instead of being protected by valley walls we found ourselves climbing over hill tops and across high plains. It was very similar to the high mountains beyond St Catherine's Monastery. We felt more alone than at any point so far. The terrain was pristine, no litter, no water, no gardens, nothing but us, the rocks and the sky above. Even trees were few and far between and it was only after travelling non-stop for six hours that we found somewhere with suffi-cient shade for lunch. After a two-hour break it was difficult getting back into the saddle for yet more punishment. They insisted that we only had half an hour left to go but it managed to stretch to three hours! At times they were arguing about the route and I couldn't help wondering whether we had inadvertently taken a few unnecessary detours.

We all agreed that eight days was too short for this section of the journey. Ten would have taken the pressure off and given more time to explore *en route*. My ability to focus on the journey was directly propor-tional to my physical state of well being. When I was over-tired and uncomfortably trapped by the camel saddle, reaching the end of the day was all that I could think about. My desire for Sarah changed from a physical one to a personal one. It made me realize afresh how important her friendship is. I began to dream of a spinach salad, by candlelight, with a bottle of wine. My body was too exhausted to contemplate much else. With only a week remaining my thoughts were turning increasingly to home.

From Wadi Matura we passed through Wadi Nagbein, Wadi Hmeera which gave us our first views of the twin peaked Jebel Katarina and Jebel Musa (Mt Sinai), Wadi Alphara where we stopped for lunch, and Wadi Gieg where we called it a day. We were able to lie in our sleeping bags looking at Mt Sinai ahead of us, the end was now firmly in sight.

I finally managed to get Muhammed to sing to us as we sat round the embers of the fire. He is of large build and has a voice to match. Slowly he placed his hubbly-bubbly to one side, climbed into a more comfortable position and quietly began. The guttural sounds and intonation of Arabic song was perfectly suited to this setting. We could not understand the words but the yearning and agony clearly came across. The story was of a young Muslim man who fell in love with a Christian girl. The problems of such a liaison are legion and seeking comfort she took herself off to a convent in the desert. He followed at a distance and then circled the convent telling of his dilemma to the moon. Finally, after some days, he built up enough courage to knock on the door and ask to see her. The mother superior, upon hearing his tale of love and devotion said that should he have arrived a day earlier she may have been able to help but it was now too late as final vows had just been taken.

29 October, Day 34

From Wadi Gieg we continued through Wadi Hamata and Wadi Rmeithe before crossing the wide Wadi Zaghra with its famous blue mountain.

The first sight of these markings occasionally causes travellers to smile with disbelief. This blue joke on a monumental scale is not well done, and one is surprised, like Dr Samuel Johnson on another occasion, to see it done at all. But astonishment turns to anger when one realizes that the gorgeous, muted colours of the granite, ranging from deep purple through every subtle shade of red and rosy pink to pure white, are not hidden under blue cloth. They have been sprayed with paint; the desecration of the Wadi Zaghra is permanent.

HANS EBSTEIN: *BLASPHEMY IN BLUE*

Jill Kamil suggests that it was carried out in 1980 by the Belgian 'artist' Jean Verame who called it his 'Sinai Peace Junction'. She also mentioned his attempt to have the area denoted a holy place!

Man has imposed his will on nature in other lands. But the prehistoric representations of men and horses on English hillsides do not offend us; they were cut into the turf with humility, for tribal or religious purposes. The Precolumbian lines and drawings that stretch mysteriously across Chile's Atacama Desert and the Nazca Plain in Peru are an integral part of the ground; they were created not to shock but to be viewed by the gods.
In the Wadi Zaghra, God and man weep. The Sinai Peninsula is too precious to be treated like a New York subway car on which graffiti is tolerated.

HANS EBSTEIN

We crossed over in silence spreading out as we did so. It was a long climb out of the valley, over Nagb Thouwa, which was rewarded by our first sighting of the Sinai rosefinch which is indigenous to the high mountains of Sinai. At the top of this pass, at a height of 1,524 m., we entered Wadi Faroush where we found an overhanging rock with enough shade for us to take lunch. Suddenly overcome by tiredness I lay down and slept for almost an hour before we moved on again. I was beginning to feel hunted by an enormous fatigue that had been building up over the past four weeks and I was fearful of it catching me before Mt Sinai had been climbed.

The journey through Wadi Faroush to our campsite in Wadi Sbaiyah was both arduous and exciting. There was plenty of climbing and we had to lead the camels most of the way. We passed carefully cultivated walled gardens with a surprising collection of fruits including figs, pomegranates, almonds, apricots, quinces, apples, peaches, plums and grapes. It was our last night under the stars and I fought to hold on to every minute. Long after most of the group had retired I sat by the campfire, writing with the aid of light from a full moon. The bedouin crouched silently to either side observing my scribbling in an alien hand across the empty white page.

What has it all been about? A small dream being fulfilled, money raised for charity, and more even than the external adventure a sense of inner fulfilment. An exercising of my spirit in this environment that first gave it life. It is said that the desert fathers sought to know themselves and we have often interpreted this as an internal knowledge. The desert, by also putting us in touch with our physical self and terra firma, provokes far more than mere introspection. The whole self is explored within this unavoidable framework of earth, wind, stars, mountains, relentless sun and cold nights.

The eyes of our bedouin leaders showed no guile. They sparkled with the joys of living and nearly all conversations were liberally sprinkled with humour. Sheikh Hamad singed my legs as he stoked up the fire and Farraj observed my scrawl with an intense fascination. 'We laughed together in the desert, we who shared neither language nor country, race nor creed; only our humanity did we share and that was enough.' (Ted Edwards: *Last Oasis*)

It will be strange within the monastery guest house tomorrow. My body is ready for a shower and a good night's sleep, and my heart yearns for home, yet the desert floor and stars are always painful to leave. I haven't learnt any secrets about how to bring the desert back with me into the city but I sense some small doors opening within myself. I appreciate now that my movement away from the structures of the Church was largely a result of the need to create space for myself spiritually. It was only reluctantly that I allowed myself to fall asleep, the silent communion round a dying fire echoing in my dreams.

✧

CHAPTER TEN

Mt Sinai — Jebel Musa

On the mountain of Sinai there live monks, whose life is a diligent concern with death, since in the solitude which is dear to them they find an undisturbed delight.

PROCOPIUS

It seems to me that a mountain is an image of the soul as it lifts itself up in contemplation. For in the same manner as the mountain towers above the valleys and lowlands at its foot, so does the soul of him who prays mount into the higher regions up to God.

THEODORE OF STUDIUM

30 October, Day 35

W E ALL FELT A LITTLE heavy of heart as we set out this morning knowing that we would soon be saying farewell to our bedouin guides. We were also a little nervous at the thought of re-entering society and having to start mixing again with other people. We had become self-contained and comfortable with the space and silence offered us by the desert.

It was a short journey across Wadi Sbaiyah, the main 'road' to Jebel Katarina, followed by a brief climb over the saddle between Jebel ed-Deir and Jebel M'neiga that brought us within sight of the monastery. Jebel ed-Deir (2,065 m.; Arab., Mount of the convent) provides the north-eastern wall of Wadi ed-Deir where St Catherine's Monastery is sited and Jebel M'neiga (1864 m.; Arab., Mount of conference: that is, the conference that took place between Moses and the Lord) marks the south eastern end of the valley. Making our way around the flank of Jebel M'neiga we descended into Wadi ed-Deir and approached the monastery from the south.

Positioned as it is at the bottom of the valley close to the impressive cliffs of Jebel Safsafa (2168 m.) and Jebel Musa (2285 m.) it seemed very vulnerable. Its impressive walls – begun by the Emperor Justinian around 550 and subsequently strengthened over the years, the buttress towers being built by Napoleon's General Kleber in the 19th century – would do nothing to prevent attack from above. This seems to have been a concern shared by Justinian himself to the misfortune of the commissioner responsible for siting the building. Eutychius left us the following account in his *Annals*:

The monks of Mt Sinai, having heard of the goodwill of the emperor Justinian, and how he took pleasure in the foundation of churches and monasteries, went to him and complained that the Ishmaelitish Arabs were doing them injury, in that they consumed their stock of provisions, and destroyed their settlements. . . . The emperor therefore at once dispatched a commissioner to go back with them . . . to Mt Sinai, where he found, in a narrow space between the mountains, the 'Burning' Bush, and also a tower erected nearby, and springs bubbling out. The monks were living dispersed in the valleys. He intended to abandon the place . . . and build the monastery high up on the mountain. This plan, however, he gave up . . . for there was no water on the top of the mountain. He therefore built the monastery beside the Bush. . . . The monastery thus stood on a narrow site between two mountains, with the result that if anyone climbed the northern summit and threw a stone, it would fall right into the monastery and harm the monks.

On the commissioner's return to the Emperor Justinian, he described to him the manner in which he had built the monastery on Mt Sinai. The emperor answered: 'You have acted wrongly and have done grievous harm to the monks, because you have given them into the hand of their enemies. You must reduce the mountain, which dominates the monastery to the north, to ground level.' The commissioner answered him, 'If we applied to that task all the resources of Rome, Egypt, and Syria, we still could not level that mountain to the ground.' At this the emperor was enraged, and had him beheaded.

After this the emperor sent another commissioner with some Roman domestic slaves and their families totalling 100 persons. To these were added a 100 Egyptians and together they were placed at the monastery in order to protect it and its monks. From these two groups came the Gebeliyah tribe. They later became Muslims and, though the outsider would find it hard to distinguish them, they have never been accepted as true bedouin by the other tribes of the peninsula. An official guide was on one occasion heard to say that blood tests have proven them to be of Norwegian stock: that takes a bit of believing! To this day some of the Gebeliyah still work directly for the monastery though many have discovered that more money is to be made from the tourist trade. They only have a small tribal area consisting totally of mountains, but within these they have developed fertile gardens and flocks of goats are ever to be seen roaming the heights.

In many ways it felt as though I was arriving for the first time. Previously I had always been transported here by coach or jeep. It is certainly something of a novelty to approach the monastery by camel and the well-groomed tourists waiting outside the main entrance were highly amused by the site of our motley crew descending upon them. When arriving by road you come from the north, swinging south into Wadi ed-Deir from the Plain of er-Raha (Arab., the waiting), named such because it is thought that the Israelites camped there while Moses ascended the mountain. Coming from the south we succeeded in totally missing the day's tourist trade until we reached the monastery itself.

The camels passed through into the courtyard of the hostel where our luggage was quickly unloaded and before we knew it they were gone. There was barely time even for a farewell photograph. They felt uncomfortable there, perhaps because it was out of their tribal area, and they were keen to be on their way home. They left at a pace that made our journeying seem like a crawl. The traditional haggling over the amount of their *baksheesh* (tip) made me realise that at the end of the day we were just another group to them however much we had liked to think otherwise.

I had mixed feelings about being back at the monastery. It was good to see old friends among the bedouin, particularly Gebaly who is responsible for the hostel and his son Salah who runs the bookstore and new coffee shop. The monks seem to be different every time I come and my hopes of seeing the young librarian, who had once shared a night in the desert with me, were dashed when I was told in whispered tones that he had returned to Greece and got married. And Brother Michael who had introduced me to the various monastic ruins on the surrounding hills and once described me as the monasteries 'favourite schismatic' had long ago left for Mt Athos though it was rumoured that he would be returning.

Unless you are Greek Orthodox it is difficult to feel a part of the monastery however hard you try. It helps a little to stay in their hostel because that distinguishes you slightly from the other tourists but at the end of the day unless you carry an impressive letter of introduction, are a diplomat or other such VIP or have a personal friend among the monks you are treated no differently from the myriad of other visitors. We managed to obtain permission for some of the group to join the early service in the chapel but when it came to it the monastery door refused to open to them. The monks don't find themselves in an easy situation; they did not come here to be tour guides or keepers of treasures, but that is in effect what they have become. They do not have the power to limit visitors, as do the monks on Mt Athos, even if they so desired, for the Egyptian Government would not hear of it. Thousands of visitors can pass through in a single day and solitude can be hard to find.

It is important to arrive expecting nothing, then anything that happens is appreciated. Doors might unexpectedly open to parts of the monastery normally closed to the public; but nothing is certain. I would always try to arrange for a visit to the Chapel of the Burning Bush, but only if I thought it really important would I request a tour of the library because I know how inconvenient it is. I have no desire to make the monks lives any harder. To come and be is enough and whatever happens will suffice. I am quickly irritated when I hear tourists arguing to be allowed beyond the carefully roped-off sections of the church as though everything should revolve around their desires.

Many people come to the fathers in the desert for their life giving words. There were plenty of opportunities for theological discussion in the towns; it was for another kind of wisdom that they came to the desert.

The fathers, for their part, were shrewd enough to know that some of those who came to them were moved by curiosity rather than devotion, and they distinguished the genuine 'hearers' of the word, whom they called 'visitors from Jerusalem', from the superficial and curious, whom they called 'visitors from Babylon'. The latter were given a bowl of soup and sent away. The former were welcome to stay all night in conversation.

Len made time to visit the hermit at Magafa on the side of Jebel ed-Deir where he was made to feel welcome as a 'visitor from Jerusalem' even though he spoke no Greek and could not be understood. The volume of traffic at St Catherine's Monastery is now such that it is no longer possible to make time to discern the visitor's intention.

There are some disturbing rumours of government plans for tourist developments around the monastery that will make it possible for over 500,000 people to visit each year. The present total is 30,000. A signboard but a few kilometres from the monastery reads as follows:

MISR SINAI TOURIST CO.
TOURISTIC PROJECT
DELFALAND

500 Villas different capacities
Touristic Village 250 rooms
2 Hotels 400 rooms
1 Shopping Centre
1 School
1 Hospital
All these projects supplied by all facilities

A report by Lance Morrow in *Time* magazine 19 March 1990 commented that: 'The "great and terrible wilderness" described by Deuteronomy is on its way to becoming a tourist trap.' There is even talk of a cable car to 'whisk the pilgrim up the volcanic rock. At the upper terminus, according to one plan, he will find a restaurant, a casino (which in Egypt is not a gambling house but a non-alcoholic nightclub) and probably an asphalt walkway lighted at night to take the visitor to where Moses and God met.' The monks only heard of the plans after they had been leaked to them and their protests have since been ignored. A Swiss engineer commissioned by the Ministry of Tourism has confirmed that the project is soon to go out to tender. A newspaper report quotes Paul Glassey, a project engineer, as saying: 'As the plan stands, the car will not be visible from the monastery, but the monastery will be visible from the top of the car.' It is hard to see how *that* is possible.

The effects of such an invasion do not bear thinking about. I am sure that the monks would finally give up in despair and there are also fears about the effects on the environment. The plant life of the vicinity is particularly rich, and vulnerable: 812 species are to be found in Sinai, half of them in the mountains around the monastery, of these 27 are not to be found anywhere else in the world. What will happen to the already threatened animal species that inhabit Sinai such as the Nubian ibex, the slender-horned gazelle, the Sinai leopard, the houbara bustard and the Arabian rock pigeon? Equally worrying is the thought of what would happen to the sanctity of the site.

No one would propose to raze the city of Jerusalem, which contains some of the holiest sites of Christianity, Judaism and Islam, in order to make way for parking lots and discotheques. But because Mount Sinai is mere raw nature, somehow it is more vulnerable to the idea of 'development' — a business word suggesting (ridiculously in this case) improvement.

Somewhere this bulldozing desanctification for money must end. If the attraction of Mt Sinai is its holy wilderness, and even the physical effort required to approach it, tourist development threatens to destroy the uniqueness and transcendence of the pilgrimage. The Egyptians are often haphazard about protecting their dead treasures. Now they seem ready to sacrifice a powerful, living mountain that is in their care. Perhaps they will make the cable cars in the shape of calves and gild them. The golden calves can slide up and down Mt Sinai and show God who won.

LANCE MORROW: *TRASHING*

We settled ourselves into our rooms, fought over the showers which were mostly cold, had lunch and then visited al-Milga, St Catherine's village. There are no more than half a dozen shops yet we managed to spend three hours there! We must have been suffering from withdrawal symptoms, not having had the opportunity to spend money for over a week. I tried phoning Sarah and thought that I had managed to leave a message on the answerphone until I discovered 24 hours later that I had not operated the payphone correctly. We retired early in order to be refreshed for the day on Mt Sinai, the culmination of the journey. It was hard to believe that the end was suddenly upon us.

31 October, Day 36

> Here then, impelled by Christ our God and assisted by the prayers
> of the holy men who accompanied us, we made the great effort of
> the climb. It was quite impossible to ride up, but though I had to go
> on foot I was not conscious of the effort – in fact I hardly noticed it
> because, by God's will, I was seeing my hopes coming true.
>
> JOHN WILKINSON: *EGERIA'S TRAVELS*

We decided to ascend via Sikket al-Basha, the path that zigzags its way up to the south-eastern face of Jebel Musa. It was begun in 1853 by 'Abbas Pasha who intended to build a villa for himself on the summit. Though longer than Sikket Saidna Musa (Arab., the Path of our Lord Moses) that consists entirely of steps, it is easier to follow and is the only way to go with a mixed-ability group. Most tourists leave in time to see sunrise from the summit so we arranged to go after breakfast hoping thereby to have the mountain to ourselves. It had also been carefully planned that we should be here on a Sunday as the monastery is closed and this greatly reduces the number of visitors. It was to pay off as we hardly met anyone all day: a rare treat.

I have climbed Mt Sinai more than 20 times and yet no two occasions have ever been quite the same. When leading pilgrim groups I use a 'Stations of the Mountain' that I developed (See Appendix 1). It helps to give a framework to the climb. It doesn't matter to me that this mountain probably isn't the real Mt Sinai or that the events may never even have occurred as described. It has been a focal point for pilgrims, enquirers, those searching for a meaning, Christians, Jews, Muslims, agnostics and atheists for as long as we have records of the site.

In the world of myths, and the infancy of nations especially, mountains often play a notable part. With their peaks rising to the heavens and their roots reaching down to the obscure depths of the earth, they visibly unite heaven, earth and underworld. Mountains are thus forms of the manifestation of the divine, and indeed come to be regarded as themselves divine beings. . . . The mountain-tops are often looked upon as dwelling places of the gods, and they are also, because of the nearness of God which is experienced there, holy places for ritual, prayer, and pilgrimage. . . .
The concept 'mountain' had been understood not merely as a physical and geographical entity, but as a place of divine nearness, divine operation, and divine dwelling. This significance of the holy mountain was a matter of feeling rather than conscious thought, and thus the feeling of holiness was linked with the mountain independently of all intellectual explanations. Sinai in particular is an outstanding example of the fact that the holiness of a place survives the change of cults and religions: after the moon and daystar, worshipped on Sinai by pagan peoples, comes the revelation on this spot of the One God.

L. EIKENSTEIN: *HISTORY OF SINAI*

On this occasion I had forgotten to bring a copy of the stations with me so formal prayers were omitted until we reached the summit. It was the first experience of this group without a guide and now I enjoyed taking the lead. We set off at a slow pace to ensure that everyone would keep up and we stopped three times between the monastery and the summit. We had the whole day ahead of us and there was no need to hurry. For the first 40 minutes we were plagued by a young bedouin on a camel touting for trade. Seeing the age-span of the group he was convinced that someone would succumb and his whining began to grate on our nerves. We almost had to scream at him before he would leave us alone. It was the first time that I had had any such trouble with the locals. Rabia had warned me that the hassling was becoming more aggressive and I was forced to admit that he was right.

There was a time when this track was little more than a narrow and isolated path, but today it is almost a shopping parade. Small bedouin huts built of local stone have appeared at every possible juncture. Painted white on the outside, presumably to help keep them cool within, they are visible from a distance. All are well stocked with water, cola, juices of various flavours, biscuits, wafers, chocolate, unusual varieties of stones, herbs and a selection of bedouin bric-a-brac. Tea, coffee and hot chocolate are also available. We would have stopped at least once but because it was Sunday and potential customers were few they were all closed, apart, that is, from the four on the summit! We made it to the top in two and a half hours which was fairly good going. Eric did particularly well. Almost without realizing it I was there.

No one could have wiped the grin off my face! This was it, I had made it! It is hard to describe exactly how I felt at that moment — a mixture of euphoria and sadness — looking out across the wasteland that surrounds Jebel Musa on all sides and realizing that we had arrived here without mechanical aid, I was thrilled: I felt as if I had arrived for the first time. At the same time I was overwhelmed by a sense of the walk being over, of it now being in the past. It suddenly felt as irretrievable as if it had taken place 50 years ago. Never before had the past moment felt so far away. The satisfaction of attainment was heavily mingled with a grief which took me quite by surprise.

A favourite Charlie Brown cartoon sprung to mind. The psychiatrist is in; Charlie Brown is in the chair asking questions:

Charlie: Do you think it fair to compare life to a series of mountain top experiences?

Psychiatrist: I suppose so.

Charlie: Would it be right to say that one of those mountains has to be higher than all the others?

Psychiatrist: Well I suppose it must be.

Charlie: What do you do if you have already been there?!

Before consuming the picnic lunch which we had carried up with us we all joined in celebrating a Eucharist which had been organized by Eric and Len. During the sermon slot I ruminated on the walk and what I had been hoping to find *en route*. I heard myself explaining that much religious language had become meaningless to me and how silence spoke far more clearly of the mystery of God. It was a relief to be able to talk freely of my journey which seemed, temporarily at least, to be taking me away from traditional religious forms and structures. I talked of finding God in unexpected places and the importance of ever being open to change. I tried simply to share something of my story and my search. It may not have been orthodox but it was honest. We took time to soak up the atmosphere and we made the most of having the summit to ourselves.

The view from the summit does not embrace so comprehensive a prospect of the peninsula as that from the more commanding peaks of Katarina, or Serbal; but the wild desolation of those majestic crags, solitary ravines, and winding valleys, added to the solemn and sacred associations of the scene, cannot fail to impress the beholder with wonder and awe. Yet the desolation of Horeb does not oppress the soul, for in the clear sky, the pure air, and the unbroken stillness of the ancient rocks and labyrinthine valleys, there lurks the 'still small voice' that tells us of a present God.

E. H. PALMER: *DESERT OF THE EXODUS*

Jebel Katarina (2,642 m.) dominates the view to the south-west. It is the highest peak in Sinai and on a clear day up to three-quarters of the peninsula can be seen from its summit.

St Catherine upbraided Maxentius, the Roman emperor, for his cruelities and demanded from him to give up the worship of the idols. The emperor, unable to defend himself, sent for pagan philosophers to argue with her, but St Catherine refuted their arguments. Maxentius ordered her to be broken on the wheel, but the wheel was shattered by her touch. Thereupon, the emperor ordered her to be beheaded. The martyr's relics were borne by angels to Jebel Katarina, where, four centuries later, monks of the monastery discovered them and translated them to the monastery.

There is both a chapel and a mosque, standing within a few feet of each other, on the summit of Jebel Musa, both built with red granite blocks. The chapel, dedicated to the Holy Trinity, is partly built on the foundations of Justinian's original basilica. It is always locked unless you are lucky enough to be there on the one day of the year that the monks celebrate the liturgy. The bedouin sacrifice sheep next to the mosque once a year after celebrations at the tomb of Nebi Saleh. There is a cave beneath the mosque where Moses rested during his 40-day sojourn on the mountain. It is now used as a store.

Such matter of fact descriptions were all that I could cope with emotionally. That and the silence and the views, the wind and the sun. I really needed to be alone with my jumbled collection of thoughts. I had suddenly reached the end too quickly and it caught me by surprise. It was only later that I was able to rationalize that, though this may have been the end of the sponsored walk, it was but another stage in the overall scheme of things.

Those of us taking the 3,400 steps back to the monastery cut down into Elijah's plateau from the junction with Sikket al-Basha. This mountain belongs every bit as much to Elijah as it does to Moses though Elijah's cave is some way from the summit. His plateau is dominated by a tall cypress tree standing in majestic isolation. Two chapels (also locked), a well and a recently-built dam complete the scene. It is a popular place in which to spend the night for those who wish to see the sunrise from the summit. Beyond the dam a path leads over a small saddle to Ras Safsafa, an adjoining peak which, from geographical considerations, is thought by many to be better suited as Mt Sinai than Jebel Musa. I always attempt to visit the area, not in a vain search for the correct location, but because of the quiet and beauty of the area. It is only a few metres from the main path, yet to all intents and purposes it is another world.

Ras Safsafa is named after the willow tree that grows beside the Chapel of the Sacred Girdle of the Holy Virgin. The 'venerable willow's' trunk has twisted itself into a complex cork-screw formation which endows it with an air of agonized tranquillity. There is a tradition that says Moses cut his miraculous staff from this tree. A nearby cistern still provides water for the hot and thirsty. Just north of the path leading to this chapel is the valley and chapel of St John, close to which there is a large cross that marks the ancient (and now unusable) stepped path, Sikket Armezia, that leads down to the monastery. The view to the monastery from the cross is truly spectacular.

After exploring the area briefly we returned to Elijah's plateau and rejoined Moses' path that leads from behind the dam. A small hermitage, long deserted, is to be found in the cliffs some ten metres above the path as it leaves the plateau. On the way down we passed through a number of small arches that were once used to control access onto the summit. The uppermost of these is known as the Gate of St Stephen the porter.

Monks, of whom St Stephen the Porter was the most famous, used to be stationed here for the purpose of receiving from the pilgrims who wished to receive the Holy Sacrament on Mt Moses a certificate that they had made their confession in the monastery. At the first gate they were handed a receipt, which they presented at the second gate. St Stephen still sits at the entrance to the charnel house [immediately outside the gate of the monastic enclosure], his skeleton dressed with a purple robe.

At the bottom of a long line of steps immediately after the second of these gates we passed another chapel, painted white, dedicated to the Virgin of the œconomos of which the following story is told:

Once upon a time the supplies from Egypt failed, and our monks had nothing to eat. But famine was nothing to the plague of fleas which infested the convent; these made it quite uninhabitable, from their numbers and size; and the brethren at last determined to forsake the place, and seek their fortunes elsewhere. Before leaving, however, they marched in solemn procession up these very steps to perform a last pilgrimage to the summit of Mt Sinai. The œconomos [of the monastery], or bursar, remained behind to lock the doors, and, as he was hastening up to rejoin his companions, he beheld the Virgin Mary, with her child, seated upon a rock. She bade them return, and promised to help them out of their difficulties. On coming back to the convent, they found a hundred camels laden with provisions, and not one of their tiny persecutors left. Since that time, said my informant, such a thing as a flea has never been seen within the convent walls. But they have been felt, as I can testify.

E. H. PALMER: *DESERT OF THE EXODUS*

The one remaining site of interest on our climb down was Mayet Musa, Moses' spring, which the bedouin claim is the identical fountain at which Moses watered the flocks of Jethro but the monks regard as the spring of a cobbler saint, Sargarius, who lived there.

Immediately after a quick shower I press-ganged Rabia into driving me back to the village in order to phone Sarah. Our conversation proved to be a painful clash between my excessive exuberance and Sarah's sense of isolation. Sarah, Polly and Phoebe had all been hit by a nasty gastric bug at the same time and life hadn't been much fun. A crackly telephone line doesn't make for the easiest form of communication. Remarkably, despite the illness and understandable sense of isolation that comes with that, Sarah still didn't begrudge me this venture. Without any doubt she was the invaluable silent partner who enabled me to realize my dream.

CHAPTER ELEVEN

St Catherine's Monastery, and the Journey Home

Two roads diverged in a wood and I
I took the one less travelled by
And that has made all the difference

ROBERT FROST: *THE ROAD NOT TAKEN*

You need but look at one who has scaled the highest pinnacle, tearing his knees on the crags and straining his wrists to breaking point, to perceive that this man's joy is far above the mean joy of the sedentary who, after having dragged his flabby self there on a day of rest, lies sprawling in the grass on the comfortable dome of an easy foothill. . . . Therefore hearken not to those who seek to help you by bidding you renounce one or another of your aspirations. You are conscious of a driving force within you, the thrust of your vocation. If you play false to it you are mutilating yourself; yet bear in mind that your truth will take form slowly, for it is the coming to birth of a tree and not the finding of a definition, and therein time plays an essential part. The task before you is to rise above yourself and to scale a difficult mountain.

M. MIGEO : *ST-EXUPERY: A LIFE*

1 November, Day 37

WE WERE FIRST THROUGH the heavy, studded iron doors of the monastery when they opened at half past nine. Fahan, a wrinkled, stooping bedouin who has for many years been the proud keeper of the keys to the monastery, shuffled to one side (with his box of rags for the immodestly dressed) as we surged past. I like to think that there was the briefest sign of recognition as our eyes momentarily met. It was not that long ago that I persuaded him to let me unlock the door, much to the surprise of the crowds waiting outside. He reckoned that I was the first Englishman to do this since the Mandate. Slipping past the tourist police Rabia and I ascended the stairs beside the chapel and found our way to the monastery office. The monk in charge, whom I had never met before, was more than happy to give us the slip of paper that would provide the access we desired to the Chapel of the Burning Bush, which to me is the most evocative space within the monastery. Gathering up the group we waited outside an unmarked door near the chapel in the eastern apse of the conventual church ready to dash inside when it opened. The aim was to create as little unrest as possible among those not offered access. The door leads into the Chapel of St James the Less which adjoins that of the Burning Bush. Here we removed our shoes and passing through the icon screen of St James we entered into the dimly-lit, inner-sanctum of the Burning Bush whose walls are covered with blue and white Damascene tiles, and which sees a solitary ray of sunlight once a year. Careful not to lean against the icons which hang from all the walls, we formed a semicircle around the altar which tradition claims marks the spot where the bush originally stood before it was moved to its present location.

The story of Moses' encounter with God at the Burning Bush is so full of mystery and has become such a powerful image that it is impossible not to sense the sanctity of the site. It doesn't matter if this particular location is a fraud, if Moses never came near here, if the event never even happened exactly as it is described, for the story is in itself powerful enough. The young Irish monk who had let us in spoke briefly and softly of the history of the site and the decor of the chapel. He finished by commenting on the icon that portrays the Virgin Mary within a flame: God was present within the bush and yet it was not destroyed, which surely is miraculous. Similarly, God was present within Mary and yet she was not consumed by his presence. Thus Mary is seen as a 'type' of the Burning Bush. And so with Jesus in the Transfiguration (to which the church is dedicated): filled with the fire of God and not consumed. Finally, we were reminded, God resides in us and we are not consumed either. We were then left in silence to ponder these mysteries.

It is always something of a wrench leaving the stillness of this space. It has an almost seductive quality which evokes idealized pictures of the monastic life. At home genuine stillness seems extremely hard to find; here stillness resides and you are absorbed by it. I have often told Sarah that should I ever go missing this is where I would be found! Why *do* we choose to live in London?

As soon as our shoes were back on we were taken into a small vestibule to the side of the main sanctuary of the sixth-century church behind the 17th-century gilded icon screen. This hid us from the other visitors who were held back behind a rope midway down the nave. A majestic marble altar, inlaid with mother of pearl, stands alone in the centre of the sanctuary. Behind it lies a marble sarcophagus that houses the relics of St Catherine that are still retained by the monastery – her skull and left hand – the remainder having been sold off at various times during the monastery's history when funds were low. Rouen Cathedral boasts more than its fair share.

I once drove all the way to the monastery from Jerusalem in order to be present during the feast of St Catherine. It was late in the year and the church was freezing. We had to participate in an all night vigil in order to earn the right to kiss the skull and receive in turn a ring made of tin and a small round loaf of monastery bread stamped with an impression of the saint. Not understanding any Greek, and being total strangers to their liturgy, we had no idea of what was going on around us. At one point we were led into the Chapel of the Burning Bush where two young novices took the equivalent of their final vows. Not long afterwards I was afflicted by a call of nature and not knowing where within the monastery the toilets are I returned briefly to our room. To my horror I discovered, upon my return, that I had been locked out and no amount of banging brought me any help. A ritual that has faithfully been carried out for centuries reached its climax in my absence. I only know of the skull secondhand, and it was only the quick thinking of Br Gilbert SSM that obtained for me a ring and loaf.

In the 11th century it was the oil that flowed from St Catherine's reliquary that drew the pilgrims. One of the monks of the monastery, Simeon, was collecting it when three fingers 'became detached from the body and fell' into the flask. It sounds just a little too accidental and convenient to me. The oil and fingers were later delivered to the newly-founded Abbey of the Trinity in Rouen which subsequently became famous for numerous miracles of healing. Thus the fame of the miraculous powers of the relics of St Catherine began to spread and many churches and chapels throughout Europe were founded under her patronage.

Charles Martel, in thanksgiving for his victory over the Arabs at Poitiers, founded the Chapel of Sainte-Catherine de Fierbois where St Joan of Arc later found her miraculous sword. St Joan developed a special fondness for St Catherine who frequently appeared to her and counselled her during the wars against the English. St Joan claimed that on one occasion St Catherine healed her within 14 days of being wounded. The thought of St Catherine being such a francophile is a little disturbing for an Englishman but it makes me wonder what might have happened if those fingers had found their way to an English abbey. The extent of the cult that grew up around this Alexandrian virgin martyr is measured by the fact that the monastery, originally known as the Monastery of St Mary, after the mother of Jesus, became known as the Monastery of St Catherine from the 14th century onwards. Legend has it that Jesus took Catherine as his bride, hence the ring. This mystical wedding later became the subject of numerous works of art.

Above the altar and sarcophagus the vault of the apse is covered with a remarkable sixth-century mosaic depicting the Transfiguration of

Christ. Described by Kurt Weitzmann as the most outstanding mosaic left to us from the early Christian period, it would have dominated the church before the erection of the Icon screen largely blocked it from view. Moses and Elijah stand either side of a sombre Christ whose eyes are by ancient iconographic practice focused far into the distance. Peter, James and John lie at his feet, and the whole is enclosed by 30 portraits of apostles and prophets together with John the Baptist and the Virgin Mary. In Orthodox iconography this latter group, focused on Christ at the centre, is known as a *deisis*, or intercesion. Above this apsidal layout, on the flat of the wall either side of a small double window are scenes of Moses, on the left removing his shoes before the Burning Bush and to the right receiving the Law in the form of a scroll. It is a work of art that deserved more time than we were able to give.

All too quickly we were ushered back out through the side door and left to our own devices. To our right on the outside of the chapel dedicated to it the Burning Bush itself stood contained behind a high stone wall enclosure to prevent it being destroyed by over zealous pilgrims in search of cuttings! It is rather a miserable looking specimen of the bramble family which neither blooms nor bears fruit. It is claimed that this species is not to be found anywhere else in Sinai and I was happy to believe it until a local bedouin showed me a *wadi* full of it only a day's walk away in the mountains. 'Shh! Don't tell the monks.'

The Hebrew word used for the bush is *sneh* and there is an ancient tradition passed on by the sages which says that this is a kind of blackberry bush.

A pagan asked Rabbi Joshua ben Jonah, 'Why did the Lord God speak to Moses from the *sneh*?' He answered him, 'And if he had spoken from the heart of a carob or a sycamore you would still have asked me the same thing! Obviously it will not be possible to let you go without a concrete answer. Why from the *sneh*? To teach you that there is not a single place where the Holy Spirit is not present, even in the *sneh*.

NOGAH HAREUVENI: *BIBLICAL HERITAGE*

Turning our backs on the bush we walked down the outside of the north wall towards the main entrance of the church which was by this time thronging with visitors. Beer Musa (Arab., Moses' well), the monastery's largest water source, sits in front of the main entrance, beneath the 19th-century bell-tower and beside the 11th-century mosque which was probably built in order to stave off a possible attack by our old friend, the mad Egyptian Fatimid Caliph al-Hakim. The well, by tradition, is where Moses met Jethro's daughters, one of whom he later married. It is very convenient for the pilgrim to have so many significant sites so close to one another.

After a brief drink at the well we entered the gloom of the church's narthex, which houses a small but unbelievably impressive array of icons including three of the world's oldest, and then passed through into the nave of the church. I positioned myself in one of the tall wooden stalls and listened to Rabia introduce the nave interior to us: the original sixth-century (Justinian) cypress-wood doors with its 28 carved panels, the 12 monolithic granite columns each bearing an enormous and uniquely carved capital, the side chapels that house among other things the skull of St. John Chrysostom, the arm of St Basil and the lower jawbone of St Gregory of Nyssa, the 18th-century green roof that hides the original rafters (one of which clearly states that the church was roofed during the lifetime of Justinian but after the death of the Empress Theodora; so between 548 and 565), the pulpit and thrones, the lamps and chandeliers, the huge candlesticks and glitzy icon screen, the many pictures and icons. Altogether a jumbled blaze of colour and form which can appear so confusing that the wealth of individual detail ends up being ignored. It is the perfect place to sit back and observe as visitors from all over the world pass through, most staying for no more than a few minutes. Days of travel for such a cursory inspection. To see it at its evocative, candlelit best you have to attend a night vigil.

The narthex is too small to explore effectively other than on one's own, so we all went our own way. I have a strange personal ritual that I invariably follow in the narthex among the icons. First I go to see the famous late-12th-century icon of the Heavenly Ladder. It is a narrative icon, portraying the *Ladder to Paradise* of St John Climacus (Gr. lit., of the ladder; *c.* 570 – *c.* 649): small demonic figures pulling monks from the 30-step ladder which leads them direct to Christ. St John Climacus's spiritual text-book, outlining the steps in its 30 chapters, is still the primary ascetical teaching of the monastery. Then I move to the early-sixth-century icon of Christ Pantoctrator. Christ's eyes in this icon are, famously, differently focused: one on the middle distance, one on infinity, so (according to some commentators) as to portray the human and divine natures. (I change my mind as to which conveys which sense. Is the cold, distant gaze that of the divine or the human? and what of the warm intimate look? It seems that God and man are truly interchangeable here.) Finally, I stand before the sixth-century Virgin and Child between the two soldier saints St Theodore and St George. There is something about this composition that totally captivates me: the way the two angels behind the Virgin look heavenwards, her white face and rosy cheeks, the youthful innocent George, and the infant Christ on her lap that bears an expression reminisent of old age. Having paid my due respects I ever so lightly touch the ancient cypress doors and, thus, connected to the ancientness of the place, I leave.

The novelty of the charnel house where the fully-dressed skeleton of St Stephen the Porter sits in splendid attire within a glass box surrounded by hundreds of skulls and jumbled limbs has long since worn off. The rest of the day was free to explore, walk, climb, write, read, visit the village. I slept.

2 November, Day 38

We had nothing more left to do than pack our belongings into the jeeps, enjoy a leisurely breakfast and say our farewells. We were on our way home. What had taken eight days by camel took no more than a couple of hours by diesel. It was strange watching the desert rush by and without realizing it we quickly returned to a former mode of life as we focused only on our goal and not on our journey. We crossed our path

near the rocks of inscriptions, by the café, and we all waved enthusiastically to no one in particular – to our footprints perhaps and the
memory they triggered that was all too quickly escaping us.

It was a quiet journey broken only by the noise of the engine and
occasional snippets of conversation between Rabia and Muhammed. We
decided to break our journey in Nuweiba as we were not expected at
the Sallyland before lunch. It was a mistake. The village is exactly what
you would expect from a community that is just beginning to deal with
the advent of visitors. Clichéd cafés in dusty squares overflowing with
tourist patter from imported waiters at which we felt obliged to laugh.
We stumbled in and out of trinket shops hunting out presents to take
home wondering why it was that we felt so ill at ease. We were not
ready so casually to re-enter society.

It was a relief to arrive at the Sallyland knowing that we had 36 hours
in which to unwind, acclimatize and prepare ourselves for the long trek
home. Inordinately competative games of volley ball helped this process
of inculturation! Locally brewed beer, donkey beer as it is affectionately
known, provided another point of contact. It acquired this name after a
team of American health officials visited the brewery to see whether it
was safe to allow their soldiers (serving in the multinational force of
observers) to drink it. Untethered donkeys urinating on the barley prior
to its being processed ensured the continued importation of American
beer!

3 November, Day 39

After carefully looking after ourselves for ten days in the desert we
threw caution to the wind and sat around on the beach in nought but
our swimming costumes. A strong wind blowing in off the sea disguised
the heat of the sun and for the first time some of us succeeded in getting
ourselves burnt. Roy reckoned that it was a force three, good sailing
weather, with the white horses forming from the deep blue of the
central gulf. Nearer to shore the coral created a tapestry of turquoise

and pale green with breakers turning golden brown as they churned up the sand. I moved my chair into the water and enjoyed the sensual caress of foam bloated with sand washing between my feet. My world moved as the waters ate slowly at my foundations threatening to pull me out with the tide. I felt giddy writing with the constant swirl of motion beneath me.

A bedouin boat bobed near the shore 228 m. to the north and just beyond lay the dozen palms of Beer Suweir. A margin of golden land topped with a lighter sand broken up by bushes sat above the sea — separating it from the dirty creams, dull russet reds and rich greys of the hills which descended to the water's edge. Surely this has to be one of the world's most beautiful places. I wanted to try and draw together all that had happened over the previous six weeks but the intense and demanding beauty of the site made it hard to concentrate. I could remember other such moments there when I had been similarly overwhelmed by a sense of oneness with the environment.

The constant sound of the breakers blocked all other noise from my ears and memory. The heartbeat from the earth's core synchronized by the heavens. I closed my eyes and became entranced, hypnotised by the constant, melodic salty invasion of all my senses. It was a day for sitting in the waves and allowing the spirit to find its equilibrium. Tomorrow could be the day of reflection when, assailed by the caccophonies of urban noise, I would need to find solace in my memories of Sinai. Every breaker broke over me, I moved out with the tide. The previous night's moon that rose so seductively slowly, just past its prime, burning gold, striped by a ghostly darkness of whispy clouds, now in its hiddeness continued to haunt me by its control of the seas. There was nothing else but wind and sun and shadow and sand and sea and hills and breath. Flickers of another life whence I laboured and toiled and loved and lost and fought and died sought vainly to surface.

I ran through the waves, as far as the bedouin boat, my feet pounding, my heart rejoicing, my legs floating. I exploded with an exhilaration of life that made me sing and dance and cry and splash and lie in the water — happier and more complete than humans generally know how to be. Ever alone and yet so totally a part of a greater whole. It is this passion that Sinai awakened in me. It cannot be bought or discovered or obtained — only accepted. It is also invaribly the first victim of my return to civilization, numbed by the necessities of our vast, impersonal, communal lives.

Jesus is reported as having said that he came to give life and give life more abundantly. But that was the last thing that I was discovering in the Church and thus, if my liberating passion and vitality at the end of my endeavour was not to be totally neutralized, I had to take at least a temporary leave of absence. The essence has become lost for me: in the ritualized droning of familiar words long devoid of mystery; in the increasingly tight boundaries drawn by beleaugered theologies; in the intoxicating emotion of repeated choruses and waving hands. The pounding of one of those waves held within it more of s/he who created than all our attempts at expression within formalized structures. The worship by the earth within the boundaries of the heavens. To lose myself within this was to find myself suffused with a passion and zest for life to such a degree that it hurts when I turn away, when I allow pettinesses to eat away at this restored humanity.

Wind of the earth return with me to
the stagnant breath of the city;
Breakers from the depths sing to me
above the noises of our making;
Intensity of the stars break through the
cloud-cover of my blindness;
Stillness of Sinai invade my being
with your life
Mountains of Horeb guard my spirit
within your fastnesses.

4 November, Day 40

It was a long journey back. First by jeep to Taba, then bus to Eilat and another to Tel Aviv, where we had to wait six hours for our night flight to London. I was fortunate in finding Elie Wiesel's book *Forgetting* in an Eilat bookshop which helped to pass the time. The Aravah appeared as empty as I remembered it prior to the walk, my perceptions becoming once again that of the 90 km. an hour blur. Already the desert and the walk felt as though on another planet.

We stopped briefly at the bus station in Dimona for toilets and felafal. Everything smelt and sounded very Israeli, I felt strangely at home again. The slight traffic jam in the outskirts of Beersheva was something of a novelty and a sharp reminder of the days ahead and my journeying to work. Shanty accommodation stood on either side of the road just south of the city and I clearly remember thinking that if we broke down and I was never able to leave that place I would not be sad, were it not for the family.

Tel Aviv's new bus station has to be experienced to be believed. Built to over six storeys it doubles up as a shopping mall and focal point for cafés and live musical entertainment. It was about as appropriate a place to finish our journey as Ben Gurion Airport was to start it. After choosing a café where we deposited all our luggage, taking it in turns to watch over it, we wandered through the metropolis. Eric and Len took to watching *Top Gun* on an oversized video screen, others just wandered in a daze killing time before we had to leave for the airport.

Two floors up from the café I stumbled upon a lingerie store. Even though I had a number of bits and pieces from Sinai for Sarah and the girls I thought that it would be fun to take some beautiful underwear home, never before having bought any. I stood for a while outside the shop trying to build up the courage to enter. In the end my embarrassment won over and I left empty handed. Bumping into Tim on the stairs I talked him in to returning with me to the shop. We were standing there considering the options when the owner stuck her head out and shouted at me. 'I saw you here earlier staring into the window. Clear off, I don't want peeping men around my shop!' It took me a while to regain my composure and explain to her that it was only nerves that prevented me entering in the first instance. It may have been the English accent, but she instantly believed me, invited us in and couldn't have been more helpful. What it was to be back in the city.

CHAPTER TWELVE

✧

Afterthought

In my town, long ago, there was an old man who told stories; I loved to listen to him. He would tell me what he liked and what he knew, and I would remember what I needed.

ELIE WIESEL: *SOULS ON FIRE*

God made man because he loves stories.

ANONYMOUS

It is now almost a year since the journey took place and I am still trying to assimilate it. Practically speaking it is straightforward: more than £30,000 was raised for various charities, mainly hospices for which an enormous debt of thanks is owed to all who went out of their way to complete the sponsorship forms. At another level the journey still goes on and it will continue to do so for as long as I live.

The challenge of the journey has changed and in many ways has become harder. How, in the city, do I retain a belief in life as adventure? or find space for the continual struggle of self-understanding? or discover a spiritual essence – a sense of the sacred – within structured religion? or experience awe at the mystery of life in a London traffic jam? or resist the acquisitive drive of our secular materialist culture? or be content with just being? or retain that sense of trust needed to build friendships and camaraderie for which I would happily give my life? or interact with the earth? or bathe in silence? or be restored by the rising and setting of the sun, the expanse of open sky and the majestic splendour of a clear sky at night?

I could go on. I do not wish to idealize the desert but it has become necessary for me to escape occasionally into wilderness so as to remind myself forcibly that the norms of so-called civilization are not the complete picture, that there is another way of being. If there is, for me, a connection between these two disparate worlds it is that they have both become a part of my story and I cannot imagine life with just one or the other. I am certainly no ascetic; but neither can I find spiritual ease solely in the schooling of the city. There is perhaps hope if the tension can be held creatively in my heart.

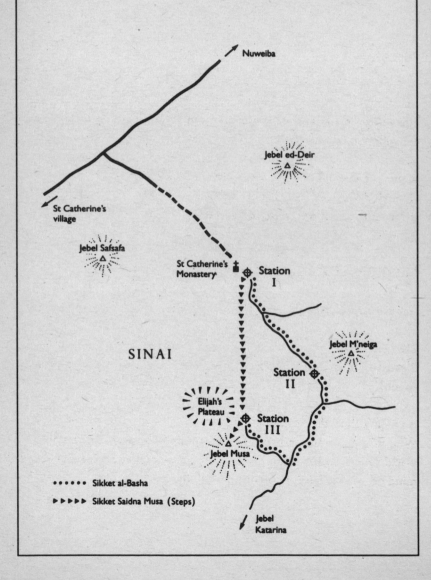

STATIONS
OF
MT SINAI

Nuweiba

Jebel ed-Deir

St Catherine's
village

Jebel Safsafa

St Catherine's
Monastery

Station
I

SINAI

Jebel M'neiga

Station
II

Elijah's
Plateau

Station
III

Jebel Musa

•••••• Sikket al-Basha

▶ ▶ ▶ ▶ ▶ Sikket Saidna Musa (Steps)

Jebel
Katarina

✦

Stations of Mt Sinai

This series of 'stations' or stages on a journey, deliberately analogous to the widely-used Stations of the Cross, has been compiled from a variety of sources for use by Christian pilgrim groups. Given the setting, the source of the form of confession and absolution from the eastern Orthodox liturgies seems appropriate. Quotations here from the Bible are from the *Revised English Bible* (1989).

FIRST STATION: *Holy is the true Light*

Location: south of the monastery enclosure, where the path up the mountain begins.
The Leader says:
Blessed be our God, both now and for ever and to the ages of ages. Amen.

A reading from the Psalms:
Who may go up the mountain of the Lord? Who may stand in his holy place? One who has clean hands and a pure heart, who has not set his mind on what is false, or sworn deceitfully.

(Psalm 24:3–4)

The Leader gives a short explanation of the Jesus prayer ('Lord Jesus Christ, Son of the living God, have mercy upon me, a sinner.') *and suggests the possible use of the prayer in rhythm with the pace of the climb. In this way the mind is focused on the sacred and spiritual aspects of the ascent. There is no reason why the words may not be adjusted to suit the occasion or the person, so long as the direction and basic content of the prayer are not altered. There is a tradition that this prayer, which is prevalent throughout the communities of Orthodoxy, attained its classic form in Sinai. Certainly one of its greatest teachers, St Gregory of Sinai, was a monk of the peninsula.*

All **Lord Jesus Christ, Son of the living God, have mercy on me, a sinner.** *(three times in all)*

Leader In the beginning of creation, when God made heaven and earth, the earth was without form and void, with darkness over the face of the abyss.

All **God said, 'Let there be light', and there was light. God is light and in him is no darkness at all.**

Leader God has brought us out of darkness to the light of the morning. The world is visible and lies open before us. So does the day, and time itself.

All **God is light and in him is no darkness at all.**

Leader Let us thank him that he has brought us safely to this point and pray to him that by his Holy Spirit the darkness of sin and ignorance may be dispelled.

Silence follows for the examination of conscience.

All **I confess to you, O Lord, my God and Creator, glorified and worshipped, One in Holy Trinity, the Father, the Son and the Holy Spirit, all my sins; which I have committed every day of my life and every hour, and at this present time, in deed, word, thought, sight,** hearing, smell, taste, touch, and all my feelings of soul and body alike, in which I have offended you, my God and Creator, and done wrong to my neighbour. In sorrow for these I present my guilty self to thee, my God, and desire to repent: but I pray, O Lord my God, help me humbly ask you with tears, out of your mercy forgive me my past transgressions, and absolve me from them all. For you are gracious and love all humankind.

Leader   May God who pardoned David through Nathan the Prophet when he confessed his sins, and Peter weeping bitterly for his denial, and the sinful woman weeping at his feet, and the publican and the prodigal son, may the same God forgive us all things, both in this world and in the world to come; and set us uncondemned before his terrible judgement seat.

Let us have no further case for the sins which we have confessed. Let us depart in peace.

Making the sign of the cross over the penitent(s) the leader says:

May Christ our true God through the prayers of his most holy Mother and of all the saints have mercy upon us and save us, for he is gracious and loves all humankind.

Silence follows.

All   Our Father in heaven,
hallowed be thy name,
your kingdom come,
your will be done,
on earth as it is in heaven.
Give us today our daily bread.
Forgive us our sins as we forgive

those who sin against us.
Lead us not into temptation,
but deliver us from evil.
For the kingdom, the power, and the glory
are yours now and for ever. Amen.

All   *Lord Jesus Christ, Son of the living God, have mercy on me, a sinner. (Three times in all; and thereon up the mountain as individuals so wish.)*

SECOND STATION: Moses' encounter with God.

Location: at the top of the valley south from the monastery, just below the saddle between Jebel M'neiga and Jebel Musa. This gives the first views of the summit of Jebel Musa; the monastery and the Plain of Waiting (ar-Raha) can also be seen.

All   *Lord Jesus Christ, Son of the Living God, have mercy on me, a sinner. (three times in all)*

Readings read by members of the group as appropriate:
        Exodus 24:15–18 *Moses on this mountain*
        Exodus 32:1–6 *The golden calf*

Leader   When God saw this rebellion and is tempted to destroy this 'stiffnecked people', Moses intercedes for them.

Readings: Exodus 32:11–14 *The Prayer of Moses*
        Exodus 32:30–32 *Moses prays again*

Leader   They are forgiven and Moses is commanded to lead on to 'the land flowing with milk and honey'; but before they depart Moses asks that he may see the glory of God.

Reading: Exodus 33:19–23 *Moses on the mountain*

Leader   Moses is told to cut two new tablets of stone and return in the morning alone to the mountain.

Reading: Exodus 34:28–32 *Moses returns from the mountain summit*

The Leader says:
God spoke all these words: I am the Lord your God: . . . you must have no other gods besides me.

All respond   **Amen. Lord have mercy.**

You must not make a carved image for yourself, nor the likeness of anything in the heavens above, or in the earth below, or in the waters under the earth. Thou shalt not bow down to them to worship. **Amen. Lord have mercy.**

You must not make wrong use of the name of the Lord your God. **Amen. Lord have mercy.**

Remember to keep the sabbath day holy. You have six days to labour, and do all your work; but the seventh day is a sabbath of the Lord your God. **Amen. Lord have mercy.**

Honour your father and mother. **Amen. Lord have mercy.**

Do not commit murder. **Amen. Lord have mercy.**

Do not commit adultery. **Amen. Lord have mercy.**

Do not steal. **Amen. Lord have mercy.**

Do not give false evidence against your neighbour. **Amen. Lord have mercy.**

Do not covet . . . anything that belongs to your neighbour. **Amen. Lord have mercy.**

All   **Lord Jesus Christ, Son of the living God, have mercy on me, a sinner.** *(Three times in all; and thereon up the mountain as individuals so wish.)*

THIRD STATION: Elijah's encounter with God.

Location: at the foot of the 700 steps to the summit.

All   **Lord Jesus Christ, Son of the living God, have mercy on me, a sinner.** *(three times in all)*

Readings: 1 Kings 19:4–14 *Elijah's journey to Mt Horeb and his encounter with God*
Psalm 107:1–9, 33–43 *God is a refuge in every danger*

Prayers are offered in an extempore fashion, by the leader or members of the group as appropriate.

FOURTH STATION: Our encounter with God.

Location: On the summit of Jebel Musa, wherever room can be found, possibly overlooking Jebel Katarina, or in the shade of the Chapel of the Holy Trinity.

The Leader says:

> The fruit of the Spirit is love, joy, peace. If we live in
> the Spirit, let us walk in the Spirit.
> The peace of the Lord be always with you.

All **And also with you.**

Minister Let us offer one another a sign of peace.

Prayers are offered, again as appropriate. The group, having provided for this before they depart, may according to the disciplines of their church, celebrate the Holy Eucharist, continuing from this point with the Eucharistic Prayer, Lord's Prayer and other traditional texts.

✧

Birds seen in Sinai

The following birds were positively identified during the walk: Booted eagle, Saker falcon, Lichtenstein's sandgrouse, rock dove, turtle dove, short-toed lark, desert lark, crag martin, pale crag martin, sand martin, house martin, pied wagtail, yellow wagtail, common bulbul, great grey shrike, graceful warbler, scrub warbler, willow warbler, chiffchaff, wood warbler, whinchat, wheatear, pied wheatear, white-crowned black wheatear, redstart, bluethroat, linnet, Sinai rosefinch, house sparrow, Tristram's grackle, brown-necked raven.

GEOFF BURDETT, FROM A PERSONAL NOTEBOOK

❖
Book List

The following list, incorporating all the journal articles and monographs cited in the course of the text with additional material, is offered for the reader's interest and use. It is arranged in alphabetical order of author surname.

Edward Abbey: *Desert Solitaire* (New York, 1968)

Michael Asher: *In Search of the Forty Days' Road* (London, 1984)

——: *A Desert Dies* (London, 1986)

——: *An Impossible Journey* (London, 1988)

Naïm Stefan Ateek: *Justice and Only Justice* (New York, 1989)

Joseph Baratz: *A Village by the Jordan* (London, 1954)

J. R. Bartlett: *Jericho* (London)

Verne Becker: *The Real Man Inside* (Michigan, 1992)

Gertrude Bell: *The Desert and the Sown* (London, 1907)

Meron Benvenisti: *Conflicts and Contradictions* (New York, 1989)

Carol Bode, ed., *The Portable* [H.D.] *Thoreau* (New York, 1947)

Louis Bouyer: *A History of Christian Spirituality* in 3 vols.

British Union of Liberal and Progressive Synagogues: *Service of the Heart: weekday, sabbath, and festival services and prayers for home and synagogue* (London, 1967)

Peter Brown: *The World of Late Antiquity* (London, 1971)

Carta's Official Guide to Israel, 2nd edn (Jerusalem, 1986)

Owen Chadwick: *Western Asceticism* (Philadelphia, 1958)

Bruce Chatwin: *What am I doing Here?* (London, 1989)

—: *The Songlines* (London, 1987)

Thomas Chetwynd: *A Dictionary of Symbols* (London, 1982)

Edward de Bono: *Future Positive* (London, 1979)

Daphna Dekel: *Bedouin of the Sinai: folklore and traditions*

Joseph Drory: 'By the beard of the Prophet: the Muslim debate about shaving', *Eretz*, 2/3 (1987), pp.43-47

Hans Ebstein: 'Blasphemy in Blue', *Archeology*

Edward Echlin: 'Of Wilderness, Fields and Archbishops' Gardens'

Edward Edwards: *Beyond the Last Oasis* (London, 1985)

L. Eikenstein: *A History of the Sinai* (New York, 1921)

T. S. Eliot: *Collected Poems 1909–1962* (London, 1936)

Michael Evenari, Leslie Shanan and Naphtali Tadmor: *The Negev: the challenge of a desert* (Harvard, 1982)

David Field (ed.): *The Future for Palliative Care* (Oxford, 1993)

Henry M. Field: *On the Desert* (New York, 1883)

Alexander Flinder: *Secrets of the Bible seas* (London, 1985)

Erich Fromm: *To have or To be* (London, 1978)

Robert Frost: *Selected Poems* (London, 1955)

Jogn Galey: *Sinai and the monastery of St Catherine* (Jerusalem, 1979)

Bilhah Givon: 'A law unto itself', *Eretz*, 8/4 (1993), pp.70ff

Mordechai Glaser: *Sinai and the Red Sea* (Tel Aviv, 1978)

Nelson Glueck: *The River Jordan* (Philadelphia, 1946)

Stephen Graham: *With the Russian Pilgrims to Jerusalem* (London, 1914)

Zvi Greenhut:, 'The City of Salt', *Biblical Archeological Review*, 19/4 (1993) pp.32–43

Hassadah Bat Haim: *Galilee and Golan* (Jerusalem, 1973)

Nogah Hareuveni: *Tree and Shrub in our Biblical Heritage* (Kiryat Ono, Israel, 1984)

—:*Nature in our Biblical Heritage* (Kiryat Ono, Israel, 1980)

Marianne Heilberg and Gier Øvensen: *Palestinian Society in Gaza, West Bank and Arab Jerusalem* (Oslo, 1993) ['FALCOT 1992']

Chaim Herzog: *The Arab–Israeli Wars* (London, 1982)

Daniel Hillel: *Negev: land, water, and life in a desert environment* (New York, 1982)

Yizhar Hirschfeld: *The Judean Monasteries in the Byzantine period* (Yale, 1992)

Eugene Hoade: *Guide to the Holy Land* (Jerusalem, 1981)

Joseph J. Hobbs: *Bedouin Life in the Egyptian Wilderness* (Texas, 1989; Cairo, 1990)

Giora Ilani: 'The Sheizaf Nature Reserve in the Northern Aravah, Israel', *Land and Nature*, 9/3 (1994), pp.106–117

C. S. Jarvis: *Yesterday and Today in Sinai* (London, 1931)

Flavius Josephus, ed. G. Cornfield: *The Jewish War* (Michigan, 1982)

Ann Jousiffe: 'Camel economy', *Geographical Magazine* (May 1991), pp.22–4

Carl J. Jung: *Man and his symbols* (London, 1964)
   —:*Memories, Dreams, Reflections* (London, 1961)

Jill Kamil: *The Monastery of St Catherine in Sinai* (Cairo, 1991)

Kathleen Kenyon: *Archeology in the Holy Land* (London, 1960)
   —:*The Bible and Recent Archeology*, revd. edn. by P. R. S. Moorey (Atlanta, 1987)

Sheldon Kopp: *If you meet the Buddha on the road kill him!* (London, 1974)

Arthur Kutcher: *The new Jerusalem: planning and politics* (London, 1973)

Thomas Edward Lawrence: *Seven Pillars of Wisdom* (for private circulation only, London, 1926)

Ora Lipschitz: *Sinai* (Jerusalem, 1978)

Konstantinos Manafis, ed.: *Sinai: the treasures of the Monastery of St Catherine* (Athens, 1990)

Philip Mayerson: 'The Pilgrim Routes to Mount Sinai and the Armenians', *Israel Exploration Journal*, 32/1 (1982), pp.44–57

Thomas [Fr Louis] Merton: *The Wisdom of the Desert* (Kentucky, 1960; London, 1961)

James. M. Monson: *The Land Between* (Jerusalem, 1983)

Geoffrey Moorhouse: *The Fearful Void* (London, 1974)

Lance Morrow: 'Trashing of Mt Sinai', *Time*, (19 March 1990), p.26

Jerome Murphy O'Connor OP: *The Holy Land: an archeological guide from earliest times to 1700* (Oxford, 1980; revd and expanded 3/1992)

Avraham Negev: *The Inscriptions of Wadi Haggag, Sinai* (Jerusalem, 1977)

Henri Nouwen: *The Way of the Heart: desert spirituality and contemporary ministry* (London, 1981)

Conor Cruise O'Brien: *The Siege* (New York, 1986)

Efraim Orni and Elisha Efrat: *Geography of Israel* (Jerusalem, 1964, 4/1980)

Linda Osband: *Famous Travellers to the Holy Land* (London, 1989)

E. H. Palmer: *The Desert of the Exodus* (New York, 1872)

Uzi Paz: 'Down among the sheltering maringa trees', *Eretz*, 2/3 (1987), pp.6–14

Carol Pearson: *The Hero Within* (San Francisco, 1986)

Daniel Perry: 'Back to Spring', *Eretz*, 2/4 (1987), pp.6–12

Diane K. Pike: *Search* (New York, 1970)

Laurens van der Post: *A Far Off Place* (London, 1974)
—: *A walk with a White Bushman* (London, 1986)
—: *A Story like the Wind* (London, 1972)

Llewelyn Powys: *A Pagan's Pilgrimage* (London, 1933)

H. F. M. Prescott: *Once in Sinai: the further pilgramage of Friar Felix Fabri* (London, 1957)

A. Whigham Price: *The Ladies of Castlebrae* (London, 1985)

M. J. Rendall: *Sinai in Spring: the best desert in the world* (London, 1911)

Yadin Roman: 'Old Salts – sailors, scholars and the Dead Sea', *Eretz*, 1/2 (1986), pp.17–27

Beno Rothenburg and Helfired Weyer, trans. E. Osers and B. Charleston: *Sinai* (Washington and New York, 1980)

Beno Rothenburg: *God's Wilderness: discoveries in Sinai* (London, 1961)

Steven Runciman: *The History of the Crusades*, in 3 vols (London, 1951)

Antione de Saint-Exupery: *Wind, Sand and Stars* (London, 1939)

Rinna Samuel: *The Negev and Sinai* (Jerusalem)

Tsur Shezaf: 'Leaving No Traces', *Eretz*, 9/4 (1994), pp.54–8

Ya'acov Shkolnik and Yadin Roman: 'Desert Waterways: *Eretz* guide to the nature reserves of the Dead Sea Valley', *Eretz*, 6/4 (1991), pp.11–42

Ya'acov Shkolnik: 'The Last Desert', *Eretz*, 9/1 (1994), pp.51–8

Katherine Sim: *Desert Traveller: the life of Jean Louis Burkhardt* (London, 1969)

George Adam Smith: *The Historical Geography of the Holy Land* (London, 1894)

Arthur P. Stanley: *Sinai and Palestine in connection with their History* (London, 1910)

Columba Stewart OSB: *The World of the Desert Fathers* (Oxford, 1986)

Wilfred Patrick Thesiger: *Arabian Sands* (London, 1959)

Richard Trench: *Arabian Travellers* (London, 1986)

Henry Baker Tristram: *The Land of Israel: a journal of travels in Palestine* (London, 1865)

Alan Unterman: *A Dictionary of Jewish Lore and Legend* (London, 1991)

John C. van Dyke: *The Desert* (New York, 1901)

Zev Vilnay: *Legends of Galilee, Jordan and Sinai* (Philadelphia, 1978)

—: *Israel Guide* (Jerusalem, 1982)

Helen Waddell: *The Desert Fathers* (London, 1936)

Benedicta Ward SLG and Norman Russell: *The Lives of the Desert Fathers* (Oxford, 1980)

Benedicta Ward SLG: *Harlots of the Desert* (Oxford, 1987)

—: *The Sayings of the Desert Fathers: the alphabetical collection* (Oxford, 1975)

—: *The Wisdom of the Desert Fathers: the anonymous series* (Oxford, 1975)

James Wellard: *Desert Pilgramage* (London, 1970)

Elie Wiesel: *The Forgotten* (New York, 1992)

—: *Souls on Fire and Somewhere a Master* (London, 1984)

John Wilkinson, revd edn: *Egeria's Travels to the Holy Land* (Jerusalem, 1981)

Roy Willis (ed.): *World Mythology* (London, 1993)

C. W. Wilson: *Sinai* (Jerusalem, 1976): repr. from *Picturesque Palestine, Sinai and Egypt*, vol. 4 (1880)

Ofer bar-Yosef, Anna Belfer, Avner Goren, and Patricia Smith: 'The Nawamis near 'Ein Huderah', *Israel Exploration Journal*, 27/2–3 (1977), pp.65–88

Yehuda Ziv: 'The Green Ones', *Eretz*, 2/4 (1987), pp.36–44

Michael Zohary: *Plants of the Bible* (Cambridge, 1982)

Index